THE BAB BALLADS

MACMILLAN AND CO., Limited
LONDON · BOMBAY · CALCUTTA · MADRAS
MELBOURNE

THE MACMILLAN COMPANY
NEW YORK · BOSTON · CHICAGO
DALLAS · SAN FRANCISCO

THE MACMILLAN CO. OF CANADA Ltd.
TORONTO

THE BAB BALLADS

WITH WHICH ARE INCLUDED

SONGS OF A SAVOYARD

BY

W. S. GILBERT

WITH 350 ILLUSTRATIONS BY THE AUTHOR

MACMILLAN AND CO., LIMITED
ST. MARTIN'S STREET, LONDON
1927

PRINTED IN GREAT BRITAIN
BY R. & R. CLARK, LIMITED, EDINBURGH

AUTHOR'S NOTE

ABOUT thirty years since, several of "The Bab Ballads" (most of which had appeared, from time to time, in the pages of *Fun*) were collected by me, and published by Messrs. George Routledge and Sons. This volume passed through several editions, and, in due course, was followed by a second series under the title of "More Bab Ballads," which achieved a popularity equal to that of its predecessor. Subsequently, excerpts were made from these two volumes, and, under the title of "Fifty Bab Ballads," had a very considerable sale; but I soon discovered that in making the selection for this volume I had discarded certain Ballads that were greater favourites with my readers than with me. Nevertheless this issue was followed by many editions, English and American, of "Bab Ballads," "More Bab Ballads," and "Fifty Bab Ballads," to the no little bewilderment of such of the public as had been good enough to concern themselves with my verses. So it became desirable (for our own private ends) that this confusion should be definitely cleared up; and thus it came to pass that a reissue of the two earlier collections, in one volume, was decided upon.

Author's Note

Some seven years since, I collected the most popular of the songs and ballads which I had written for the series of light operas with which my name is associated, and published them under the title of " Songs of a Savoyard." It recently occurred to me that these songs had so much in common with " The Bab Ballads " that it might be advisable to weld the two books into one.   This is, briefly, the history of the present volume.

I have always felt that many of the original illustrations to " The Bab Ballads " erred gravely in the direction of unnecessary extravagance.   This defect I have endeavoured to correct through the medium of the two hundred new drawings which I have designed for this volume.   I am afraid I cannot claim for them any other recommendation.

W. S. GILBERT.

GRIM'S DYKE, HARROW WEALD,
    4th December 1897.

CONTENTS

Contents

Contents

Contents

Contents

Contents

THE BAB BALLADS

CAPTAIN REECE

OF all the ships upon the blue
No ship contained a better crew
Than that of worthy CAPTAIN REECE,
Commanding of *The Mantelpiece*.

He was adored by all his men,
For worthy CAPTAIN REECE, R.N.,
Did all that lay within him to
Promote the comfort of his crew.

I

Captain Reece

If ever they were dull or sad,
Their captain danced to them like mad,
Or told, to make the time pass by,
Droll legends of his infancy.

A feather bed had every man,
Warm slippers and hot-water can,
Brown windsor from the captain's store,
A valet, too, to every four.

Did they with thirst in summer burn?
Lo, seltzogenes at every turn,
And on all very sultry days
Cream ices handed round on trays.

Then currant wine and ginger pops
Stood handily on all the "tops";
And, also, with amusement rife,
A "Zoetrope, or Wheel of Life."

Captain Reece

New volumes came across the sea
From MISTER MUDIE's libraree;
The Times and *Saturday Review*
Beguiled the leisure of the crew.

Kind-hearted CAPTAIN REECE, R.N.,
Was quite devoted to his men;
In point of fact, good CAPTAIN REECE
Beatified *The Mantelpiece*.

One summer eve, at half-past ten,
He said (addressing all his men):
"Come, tell me, please, what I can do
To please and gratify my crew?

"By any reasonable plan
I'll make you happy, if I can;
My own convenience count as *nil*;
It is my duty, and I will."

Then up and answered WILLIAM LEE
(The kindly captain's coxswain he,
A nervous, shy, low-spoken man),
He cleared his throat and thus began:

"You have a daughter, CAPTAIN REECE,
Ten female cousins and a niece,
A ma, if what I'm told is true,
Six sisters, and an aunt or two.

"Now, somehow, sir, it seems to me,
More friendly-like we all should be
If you united of 'em to
Unmarried members of the crew.

Captain Reece

"If you'd ameliorate our life,
Let each select from them a wife;
And as for nervous me, old pal,
Give me your own enchanting gal!"

Good CAPTAIN REECE, that worthy man,
Debated on his coxswain's plan:
"I quite agree," he said, "O BILL;
It is my duty, and I will.

"My daughter, that enchanting gurl,
Has just been promised to an earl,
And all my other familee,
To peers of various degree.

"But what are dukes and viscounts to
The happiness of all my crew?
The word I gave you I'll fulfil;
It is my duty, and I will.

"As you desire it shall befall,
I'll settle thousands on you all,
And I shall be, despite my hoard,
The only bachelor on board."

The boatswain of *The Mantelpiece*,
He blushed and spoke to CAPTAIN REECE.
"I beg your honour's leave," he said,
"If you would wish to go and wed,

"I have a widowed mother who
Would be the very thing for you—
She long has loved you from afar,
She washes for you, CAPTAIN R."

Captain Reece

The captain saw the dame that day—
Addressed her in his playful way—
"And did it want a wedding ring?
It was a tempting ickle sing!

"Well, well, the chaplain I will seek,
We'll all be married this day week—
At yonder church upon the hill;
It is my duty, and I will!"

The sisters, cousins, aunts, and niece,
And widowed ma of CAPTAIN REECE,
Attended there as they were bid;
It was their duty, and they did.

THE DARNED MOUNSEER

I SHIPPED, d'ye see, in a Revenue sloop,
    And, off Cape Finisteere,
        A merchantman we see,
        A Frenchman, going free,
    So we made for the bold Mounseer,
        D'ye see?
    We made for the bold Mounseer!
But she proved to be a Frigate—and she up with her
      ports,
    And fires with a thirty-two!
        It come uncommon near,
        But we answered with a cheer,
    Which paralysed the Parley-voo,
        D'ye see?
    Which paralysed the Parley-voo!

6

The Darned Mounseer

Then our Captain he up and he says, says he,
  "That chap we need not fear,—
    We can take her, if we like,
    She is sartin for to strike,
For she's only a darned Mounseer,
    D'ye see?
She's only a darned Mounseer!
But to fight a French fal-lal—it's like hittin' of a gal—
  It's a lubberly thing for to do;
    For we, with all our faults,
    Why, we're sturdy British salts,
While she's but a Parley-voo,
    D'ye see?
A miserable Parley-voo!"

So we up with our helm, and we scuds before the breeze,
  As we gives a compassionating cheer;
    Froggee answers with a shout
    As he sees us go about,
Which was grateful of the poor Mounseer,
    D'ye see?
Which was grateful of the poor Mounseer!
And I'll wager in their joy they kissed each other's cheek
  (Which is what them furriners do),
    And they blessed their lucky stars
    We were hardy British tars
Who had pity on a poor Parley-voo,
    D'ye see?
Who had pity on a poor Parley-voo!

THE RIVAL CURATES

LIST while the poet trolls
   Of MR. CLAYTON HOOPER,
Who had a cure of souls
   At Spiffton-extra-Sooper.

He lived on curds and whey,
   And daily sang their praises,
And then he'd go and play
   With buttercups and daisies.

Wild crôquet HOOPER banned,
   And all the sports of Mammon,
He warred with cribbage, and
   He exorcised backgammon.

His helmet was a glance
   That spoke of holy gladness;
A saintly smile his lance,
   His shield a tear of sadness.

The Rival Curates

His Vicar smiled to see
    This armour on him buckled;
With pardonable glee
    He blessed himself and chuckled:

"In mildness to abound
    My curate's sole design is,
In all the country round
    There's none so mild as mine is!"

And HOOPER, disinclined
    His trumpet to be blowing,
Yet didn't think you'd find
    A milder curate going.

A friend arrived one day
    At Spiffton-extra-Sooper,
And in this shameful way
    He spoke to MR. HOOPER:

"You think your famous name
    For mildness can't be shaken,
That none can blot your fame—
    But, HOOPER, you're mistaken!

"Your mind is not as blank
    As that of HOPLEY PORTER,
Who holds a curate's rank
    At Assesmilk-cum-Worter.

"*He* plays the airy flute,
    And looks depressed and blighted,
Doves round about him 'toot,'
    And lambkins dance delighted.

The Rival Curates

"*He* labours more than you
    At worsted work, and frames it ;
In old maids' albums, too,
    Sticks seaweed—yes, and names it ! "

The tempter said his say,
    Which pierced him like a needle—
He summoned straight away
    His sexton and his beadle.

These men were men who could
    Hold liberal opinions :
On Sundays they were good—
    On week-days they were minions.

" To HOPLEY PORTER go,
    Your fare I will afford you—
Deal him a deadly blow,
    And blessings shall reward you.

The Rival Curates

"But stay—I do not like
    Undue assassination,
And so, before you strike,
    Make this communication:

"I'll give him this one chance—
    If he'll more gaily bear him,
Play crôquet, smoke, and dance,
    I willingly will spare him."

They went, those minions true,
    To Assesmilk-cum-Worter,
And told their errand to
    The REVEREND HOPLEY PORTER.

"What?" said that reverend gent,
    "Dance through my hours of leisure?
Smoke?—bathe myself with scent?—
    Play crôquet?   Oh, with pleasure!

The Rival Curates

"Wear all my hair in curl?
　　Stand at my door, and wink—so—
At every passing girl?
　　My brothers, I should think so!

"For years I've longed for some
　　Excuse for this revulsion:
Now that excuse has come—
　　I do it on compulsion!!!"

He smoked and winked away—
　　This REVEREND HOPLEY PORTER—
The deuce there was to pay
　　At Assesmilk-cum-Worter.

And HOOPER holds his ground,
　　In mildness daily growing—
They think him, all around,
　　The mildest curate going.

THE ENGLISHMAN

He is an Englishman !
       For he himself has said it,
       And it's greatly to his credit,
That he is an Englishman !
       For he might have been a Roosian,
       A French, or Turk, or Proosian,
Or perhaps Itali-an !
       But in spite of all temptations,
       To belong to other nations,
He remains an Englishman !
       Hurrah !
For the true-born Englishman !

ONLY A DANCING GIRL

ONLY a dancing girl,
　　With an unromantic style,
With borrowed colour and curl,
　　With fixed mechanical smile,
　　With many a hackneyed wile,
With ungrammatical lips,
And corns that mar her trips !

Hung from the " flies " in air,
　　She acts a palpable lie ;
She's as little a fairy there
　　As unpoetical I !
　　I hear you asking, Why—
Why in the world I sing
This tawdry, tinselled thing ?

14

Only a Dancing Girl

No airy fairy she,
  As she hangs in arsenic green,
From a highly impossible tree,
  In a highly impossible scene
  (Herself not over clean).
For fays don't suffer, I'm told,
From bunions, coughs, or cold.

And stately dames that bring
  Their daughters there to see,
Pronounce the "dancing thing"
  No better than she should be.
  With her skirt at her shameful knee,
And her painted, tainted phiz:
Ah, matron, which of us is?

(And, in sooth, it oft occurs
  That while these matrons sigh,
Their dresses are lower than hers,
  And sometimes half as high;
  And their hair is hair they buy.
And they use their glasses, too,
In a way she'd blush to do.)

But change her gold and green
  For a coarse merino gown,
And see her upon the scene
  Of her home, when coaxing down
  Her drunken father's frown,
In his squalid cheerless den:
She's a fairy truly, then!

THE DISAGREEABLE MAN

If you give me your attention, I will tell you what I am:
I'm a genuine philanthropist—all other kinds are sham.
Each little fault of temper and each social defect
In my erring fellow-creatures, I endeavour to correct.
To all their little weaknesses I open people's eyes,
And little plans to snub the self-sufficient I devise;
I love my fellow-creatures—I do all the good I can—
Yet everybody says I'm such a disagreeable man!
        And I can't think why!

To compliments inflated I've a withering reply,
And vanity I always do my best to mortify;
A charitable action I can skilfully dissect;
And interested motives I'm delighted to detect.
I know everybody's income and what everybody earns,
And I carefully compare it with the income-tax returns;
But to benefit humanity, however much I plan,
Yet everybody says I'm such a disagreeable man!
        And I can't think why!

16

The Disagreeable Man

I'm sure I'm no ascetic; I'm as pleasant as can be;
You'll always find me ready with a crushing repartee;
I've an irritating chuckle, I've a celebrated sneer,
I've an entertaining snigger, I've a fascinating leer;
To everybody's prejudice I know a thing or two;
I can tell a woman's age in half a minute—and I do—
But although I try to make myself as pleasant as I can,
Yet everybody says I'm such a disagreeable man!
      And I can't think why!

GENERAL JOHN

THE bravest names for fire and flames
    And all that mortal durst,
Were GENERAL JOHN and PRIVATE JAMES,
    Of the Sixty-seventy-first.

GENERAL JOHN was a soldier tried,
    A chief of warlike dons;
A haughty stride and a withering pride
    Were MAJOR-GENERAL JOHN'S.

A sneer would play on his martial phiz,
    Superior birth to show;
" Pish ! " was a favourite word of his,
    And he often said " Ho ! ho ! "

General John

FULL-PRIVATE JAMES described might be.
   As a man of a mournful mind ;
No characteristic trait had he
   Of any distinctive kind.

From the ranks, one day, cried PRIVATE JAMES,
   "Oh ! MAJOR-GENERAL JOHN,
I've doubts of our respective names,
   My mournful mind upon.

"A glimmering thought occurs to me
   (Its source I can't unearth),
But I've a kind of a notion we
   Were cruelly changed at birth.

"I've a strange idea that each other's names
   We've each of us here got on.
Such things have been," said PRIVATE JAMES.
   "They have !" sneered GENERAL JOHN.

General John

"My GENERAL JOHN, I swear upon
  My oath I think 'tis so——"
"Pish!" proudly sneered his GENERAL JOHN,
  And he also said "Ho! ho!"

"My GENERAL JOHN! my GENERAL JOHN!
  My GENERAL JOHN!" quoth he,
"This aristocratical sneer upon
  Your face I blush to see!

"No truly great or generous cove
  Deserving of them names,
Would sneer at a fixed idea that's drove
  In the mind of a PRIVATE JAMES!"

Said GENERAL JOHN, "Upon your claims
  No need your breath to waste;
If this is a joke, FULL-PRIVATE JAMES,
  It's a joke of doubtful taste.

General John

" But, being a man of doubtless worth,
   If you feel certain quite
That we were probably changed at birth,
   I'll venture to say you're right."

So GENERAL JOHN as PRIVATE JAMES
   Fell in, parade upon ;
And PRIVATE JAMES, by change of names,
   Was MAJOR-GENERAL JOHN.

THE COMING BY-AND-BY

SAD is that woman's lot who, year by year,
Sees, one by one, her beauties disappear;
As Time, grown weary of her heart-drawn sighs,
Impatiently begins to "dim her eyes"!—
Herself compelled, in life's uncertain gloamings,
To wreathe her wrinkled brow with well-saved "comb
    ings"—
Reduced, with rouge, lipsalve, and pearly grey,
To "make up" for lost time, as best she may!

    Silvered is the raven hair,
        Spreading is the parting straight,
    Mottled the complexion fair,
        Halting is the youthful gait,

The Coming By-and-by

Hollow is the laughter free,
    Spectacled the limpid eye,
Little will be left of me,
    In the coming by-and-by!

Fading is the taper waist—
    Shapeless grows the shapely limb,
And although securely laced,
    Spreading is the figure trim!
Stouter than I used to be,
    Still more corpulent grow I—
There will be too much of me
    In the coming by-and-by!

TO A LITTLE MAID

BY A POLICEMAN

COME with me, little maid!
Nay, shrink not, thus afraid—
    I'll harm thee not!
Fly not, my love, from me—
I have a home for thee—
    A fairy grot,
      Where mortal eye
      Can rarely pry,
There shall thy dwelling be!

List to me, while I tell
The pleasures of that cell,
    Oh, little maid!
What though its couch be rude—
Homely the only food
    Within its shade?
      No thought of care
      Can enter there,
No vulgar swain intrude!

To a Little Maid

Come with me, little maid,
Come to the rocky shade
    I love to sing;
Live with us, maiden rare—
Come, for we "want" thee there,
    Thou elfin thing,
      To work thy spell,
      In some cool cell
In stately Pentonville!

THE HIGHLY RESPECTABLE GONDOLIER

I STOLE the Prince, and I brought him here,
 And left him, gaily prattling
With a highly respectable Gondolier,
Who promised the Royal babe to rear,
And teach him the trade of a timoneer
 With his own beloved bratling.

  Both of the babes were strong and stout,
   And, considering all things, clever.
  Of that there is no manner of doubt—
  No probable, possible shadow of doubt—
   No possible doubt whatever.

Time sped, and when at the end of a year
 I sought that infant cherished,
That highly respectable Gondolier

The Highly Respectable Gondolier

Was lying a corpse on his humble bier—
I dropped a Grand Inquisitor's tear—
   That Gondolier had perished!

    A taste for drink, combined with gout,
      Had doubled him up for ever.
    Of *that* there is no manner of doubt—
    No probable, possible shadow of doubt—
      No possible doubt whatever.

But owing, I'm much disposed to fear,
    To his terrible taste for tippling,
That highly respectable Gondolier
Could never declare with a mind sincere
Which of the two was his offspring dear,
    And which the Royal stripling!

    Which was which he could never make out,
      Despite his best endeavour.
    Of *that* there is no manner of doubt—
    No probable, possible shadow of doubt—
      No possible doubt whatever.

The children followed his old career—
    (This statement can't be parried)
Of a highly respectable Gondolier:
Well, one of the two (who will soon be here)—
But *which* of the two is not quite clear—
    Is the Royal Prince you married!

    Search in and out and round about
      And you'll discover never
    A tale so free from every doubt—
    All probable, possible shadow of doubt—
      All possible doubt whatever!

JOHN AND FREDDY

JOHN courted lovely MARY ANN,
  So likewise did his brother, FREDDY.
FRED was a very soft young man,
  While JOHN, though quick, was most unsteady.

FRED was a graceful kind of youth,
  But JOHN was very much the strongest.
"Oh, dance away," said she, "in truth,
  I'll marry him who dances longest."

JOHN tries the maiden's taste to strike
  With gay, grotesque, outrageous dresses,
And dances comically, like
  CLODOCHE AND CO., at the Princess's.

But FREDDY tries another style,
  He knows some graceful steps and does 'em—
A breathing Poem—Woman's smile—
  A man all poesy and buzzem.

John and Freddy

Now FREDDY'S operatic *pas*—
   Now JOHNNY'S hornpipe seems entrapping:
Now FREDDY'S graceful *entrechats*—
   Now JOHNNY'S skilful "cellar-flapping."

For many hours—for many days—
   For many weeks performed each brother,
For each was active in his ways,
   And neither would give in to t'other.

After a month of this, they say
   (The maid was getting bored and moody)
A wandering curate passed that way
   And talked a lot of goody-goody.

"Oh my," said he, with solemn frown,
   "I tremble for each dancing *frater*,
Like unregenerated clown
   And harlequin at some the-ayter."

John and Freddy

He showed that men, in dancing, do
  Both impiously and absurdly,
And proved his proposition true,
  With Firstly, Secondly, and Thirdly.

For months both JOHN and FREDDY danced,
  The curate's protests little heeding;
For months the curate's words enhanced
  The sinfulness of their proceeding.

At length they bowed to Nature's rule—
  Their steps grew feeble and unsteady,
Till FREDDY fainted on a stool,
  And JOHNNY on the top of FREDDY.

"Decide!" quoth they, "let him be named,
  Who henceforth as his wife may rank you."
"I've changed my views," the maiden said,
  "I only marry curates, thank you!"

John and Freddy

Says FREDDY, " Here is goings on !
   To bust myself with rage I'm ready."
" I'll be a curate ! " whispers JOHN—
   " And I," exclaimed poetic FREDDY.

But while they read for it, these chaps,
   The curate booked the maiden bonny—
And when she's buried him, perhaps,
   She'll marry FREDERICK or JOHNNY.

THE FAIRY QUEEN'S SONG

OH, foolish fay,
   Think you because
Man's brave array
   My bosom thaws
I'd disobey
   Our fairy laws?
Because I fly
   In realms above,
In tendency
   To fall in love
Resemble I
   The amorous dove?

Oh, amorous dove!
  Type of Ovidius Naso!
    This heart of mine
    Is soft as thine,
  Although I dare not say so!

The Fairy Queen's Song

On fire that glows
    With heat intense
I turn the hose
    Of Common Sense,
And out it goes
    At small expense!
We must maintain
    Our fairy law;
That is the main
    On which to draw—
In that we gain
    A Captain Shaw.

Oh, Captain Shaw!
    Type of true love kept under!
Could thy Brigade
With cold cascade
Quench my great love, I wonder!

SIR GUY THE CRUSADER

Sir Guy was a doughty crusader,
    A muscular knight,
    Ever ready to fight,
A very determined invader,
    And Dickey de Lion's delight.

Lenore was a Saracen maiden,
    Brunette, statuesque,
    The reverse of grotesque,
Her pa was a bagman from Aden,
    Her mother she played in burlesque.

A *coryphée*, pretty and loyal,
    In amber and red
    The ballet she led;
Her mother performed at the Royal,
    Lenore at the Saracen's Head.

Sir Guy the Crusader

Of face and of figure majestic,
    She dazzled the cits—
    Ecstaticised pits;—
Her troubles were only domestic,
    But drove her half out of her wits.

Her father incessantly lashed her,
    On water and bread
    She was grudgingly fed;
Whenever her father he thrashed her
    Her mother sat down on her head.

Guy saw her, and loved her, with reason,
    For beauty so bright
    Sent him mad with delight;
He purchased a stall for the season,
    And sat in it every night.

Sir Guy the Crusader

His views were exceedingly proper,
  He wanted to wed,
  So he called at her shed
And saw her progenitor whop her—
  Her mother sit down on her head.

THE REST IS TOO AWFUL!

"So pretty," said he, "and so trusting!
  You brute of a dad,
  You unprincipled cad,
Your conduct is really disgusting,
  Come, come, now admit it's too bad!

"You're a turbaned old Turk, and malignant—
  Your daughter LENORE
  I intensely adore,
And I cannot help feeling indignant,
  A fact that I hinted before;

Sir Guy the Crusader

"To see a fond father employing
  A deuce of a knout
  For to bang her about,
To a sensitive lover's annoying."
  Said the bagman, "Crusader, get out."

Says Guy, "Shall a warrior laden
  With a big spiky knob,
  Sit in peace on his cob
While a beautiful Saracen maiden
  Is whipped by a Saracen snob?

"To London I'll go from my charmer."
  Which he did, with his loot
  (Seven hats and a flute),
And was nabbed for his Sydenham armour
  At Mr. Ben-Samuel's suit.

Sir Guy he was lodged in the Compter,
  Her pa, in a rage,
  Died (don't know his age),
His daughter, she married the prompter,
  Grew bulky and quitted the stage.

IS LIFE A BOON

Is life a boon?
    If so, it must befall
    That Death, whene'er he call,
Must call too soon.
    Though fourscore years he give,
    Yet one would pray to live
Another moon!
    What kind of plaint have I,
    Who perish in July?
    I might have had to die
Perchance in June!

Is life a thorn?
    Then count it not a whit!
    Man is well done with it;
Soon as he's born
    He should all means essay
    To put the plague away;
And I, war-worn,
    Poor captured fugitive,
    My life most gladly give—
    I might have had to live
Another morn!

HAUNTED

HAUNTED? Ay, in a social way,
By a body of ghosts in a dread array:
But no conventional spectres they—
    Appalling, grim, and tricky:
I quail at mine as I'd never quail
At a fine traditional spectre pale,
With a turnip head and a ghostly wail,
    And a splash of blood on the dicky!

Mine are horrible social ghosts,
Speeches and women and guests and hosts,
Weddings and morning calls and toasts,
    In every bad variety:
Ghosts that hover about the grave
Of all that's manly, free, and brave:
You'll find their names on the architrave
    Of that charnel-house, Society.

Haunted

Black Monday—black as its schoolroom ink—
With its dismal boys that snivel and think
Of nauseous messes to eat and drink,
    And a frozen tank to wash in.
That was the first that brought me grief
And made me weep, till I sought relief
In an emblematical handkerchief,
    To choke such baby bosh in.

First and worst in the grim array—
Ghosts of ghosts that have gone their way,
Which I wouldn't revive for a single day
    For all the wealth of PLUTUS—
Are the horrible ghosts that schooldays scared:
If the classical ghost that BRUTUS dared
Was the ghost of his " Cæsar " unprepared,
    I'm sure I pity BRUTUS.

I pass to critical seventeen:
The ghost of that terrible wedding scene,
When an elderly colonel stole my queen,
    And woke my dream of heaven:
No school-girl decked in her nursery curls
Was my gushing innocent queen of pearls;
If she wasn't a girl of a thousand girls,
    She was one of forty-seven!

I see the ghost of my first cigar—
Of the thence-arising family jar—
Of my maiden brief (I was at the bar),
    When I called the judge " Your wushup " !
Of reckless days and reckless nights,
With wrenched-off knockers, extinguished lights,
Unholy songs, and tipsy fights,
    Which I strove in vain to hush up.

Haunted

Ghosts of fraudulent joint-stock banks,
Ghosts of copy, "declined with thanks,"
Of novels returned in endless ranks,
    And thousands more, I suffer.
The only line to fitly grace
My humble tomb, when I've run my race,
Is " Reader, this is the resting-place
    Of an unsuccessful duffer."

I've fought them all, these ghosts of mine,
But the weapons I've used are sighs and brine,
And now that I'm nearly forty-nine,
    Old age is my only bogy;
For my hair is thinning away at the crown,
And the silver fights with the worn-out brown;
And a general verdict sets me down
    As an irreclaimable fogy.

THE MODERN MAJOR-GENERAL

I AM the very pattern of a modern Major-Gineral,
I've information vegetable, animal, and mineral;
I know the kings of England, and I quote the fights historical,
From Marathon to Waterloo, in order categorical;
I'm very well acquainted, too, with matters mathematical,
I understand equations, both the simple and quadratical;
About binomial theorem I'm teeming with a lot o' news,
With interesting facts about the square of the hypotenuse.
I'm very good at integral and differential calculus,
I know the scientific names of beings animalculous.
In short, in matters vegetable, animal, and mineral,
I am the very model of a modern Major-Gineral

The Modern Major-General

I know our mythic history—KING ARTHUR'S and SIR
    CARADOC'S,
I answer hard acrostics, I've a pretty taste for paradox ;
I quote in elegiacs all the crimes of HELIOGABALUS,
In conics I can floor peculiarities parabolous.
I tell undoubted RAPHAELS from GERARD DOWS and
    ZOFFANIES,
I know the croaking chorus from the "Frogs" of
    ARISTOPHANES ;
Then I can hum a fugue, of which I've heard the music's
    din afore,
And whistle all the airs from that confounded nonsense
    "Pinafore."
Then I can write a washing-bill in Babylonic cuneiform,
And tell you every detail of CARACTACUS's uniform.
In short, in matters vegetable, animal, and mineral,
I am the very model of a modern Major-Gineral.

In fact, when I know what is meant by "mamelon" and
    "ravelin,"
When I can tell at sight a Chassepôt rifle from a javelin,
When such affairs as *sorties* and surprises I'm more wary at,
And when I know precisely what is meant by Commissariat,
When I have learnt what progress has been made in
    modern gunnery,
When I know more of tactics than a novice in a nunnery,
In short, when I've a smattering of elementary strategy,
You'll say a better Major-Gener*al* has never *sat* a gee—
For my military knowledge, though I'm plucky and
    adventury,
Has only been brought down to the beginning of the
    century.
But still in learning vegetable, animal, and mineral,
I am the very model of a modern Major-Gineral!

THE BISHOP AND THE 'BUSMAN

IT was a Bishop bold,
    And London was his see,
He was short and stout and round about
    And zealous as could be.

It also was a Jew,
    Who drove a Putney 'bus—
For flesh of swine however fine
    He did not care a cuss.

His name was HASH BAZ BEN,
    And JEDEDIAH too,
And SOLOMON and ZABULON—
    This 'bus-directing Jew.

44

The Bishop and the 'Busman

The Bishop said, said he,
  "I'll see what I can do
To Christianise and make you wise,
  You poor benighted Jew."

So every blessed day
  That 'bus he rode outside,
From Fulham town, both up and down,
  And loudly thus he cried:

"His name is HASH BAZ BEN,
  And JEDEDIAH too,
And SOLOMON and ZABULON—
  This 'bus-directing Jew."

At first the 'busman smiled,
  And rather liked the fun—
He merely smiled, that Hebrew child,
  And said, "Eccentric one!"

The Bishop and the 'Busman

And gay young dogs would wait
   To see the 'bus go by
(These gay young dogs, in striking togs),
   To hear the Bishop cry :

" Observe his grisly beard,
   His race it clearly shows,
He sticks no fork in ham or pork—
   Observe, my friends, his nose.

" His name is HASH BAZ BEN,
   And JEDEDIAH too,
And SOLOMON and ZABULON—
   This 'bus-directing Jew."

But though at first amused,
   Yet after seven years,
This Hebrew child got rather riled,
   And melted into tears.

He really almost feared
   To leave his poor abode,
His nose, and name, and beard became
   A byword on that road.

At length he swore an oath,
   The reason he would know—
" I'll call and see why ever he
   Does persecute me so !"

The Bishop and the 'Busman

The good old Bishop sat
  On his ancestral chair,
The 'busman came, sent up his name,
  And laid his grievance bare.

"Benighted Jew," he said
  (The good old Bishop did),
"Be Christian, you, instead of Jew—
  Become a Christian kid!

"I'll ne'er annoy you more."
  "Indeed?" replied the Jew;
"Shall I be freed?" "You will, indeed!"
  Then "Done!" said he, "with you!"

The organ which, in man,
  Between the eyebrows grows,
Fell from his face, and in its place
  He found a Christian nose.

The Bishop and the 'Busman

His tangled Hebrew beard,
    Which to his waist came down,
Was now a pair of whiskers fair—
    His name ADOLPHUS BROWN!

He wedded in a year
    That prelate's daughter JANE,
He's grown quite fair—has auburn hair–
    His wife is far from plain.

THE HEAVY DRAGOON

If you want a receipt for that popular mystery,
  Known to the world as a Heavy Dragoon,
Take all the remarkable people in history,
  Rattle them off to a popular tune!
The pluck of LORD NELSON on board of the *Victory*—
  Genius of BISMARCK devising a plan;
The humour of FIELDING (which sounds contradictory)—
  Coolness of PAGET about to trepan—
The grace of MOZART, that unparalleled musico—
  Wit of MACAULAY, who wrote of QUEEN ANNE—
The pathos of PADDY, as rendered by BOUCICAULT—
  Style of the BISHOP OF SODOR AND MAN—
The dash of a D'ORSAY, divested of quackery—
Narrative powers of DICKENS and THACKERAY—

The Heavy Dragoon

VICTOR EMMANUEL—peak-haunting PEVERIL—
THOMAS AQUINAS, and DOCTOR SACHEVERELL—
  TUPPER and TENNYSON—DANIEL DEFOE—
  ANTHONY TROLLOPE and MISTER GUIZOT!
        Take of these elements all that is fusible,
        Melt 'em all down in a pipkin or crucible,
        Set 'em to simmer and take off the scum,
        And a Heavy Dragoon is the residuum!

If you want a receipt for this soldierlike paragon,
  Get at the wealth of the CZAR (if you can)—
The family pride of a Spaniard from Arragon—
  Force of MEPHISTO pronouncing a ban—
A smack of LORD WATERFORD, reckless and rollicky—
  Swagger of RODERICK, heading his clan—
The keen penetration of PADDINGTON POLLAKY—
  Grace of an Odalisque on a divan—
The genius strategic of CÆSAR or HANNIBAL—
Skill of LORD WOLSELEY in thrashing a cannibal—
Flavour of HAMLET—the STRANGER, a touch of him—
Little of MANFRED (but not very much of him)—
  Beadle of Burlington—RICHARDSON'S show—
  MR. MICAWBER and MADAME TUSSAUD!
        Take of these elements all that is fusible—
        Melt 'em all down in a pipkin or crucible—
        Set 'em to simmer and take off the scum,
        And a Heavy Dragoon is the residuum!

THE TROUBADOUR

A TROUBADOUR he played
  Without a castle wall,
Within, a hapless maid
  Responded to his call.

"Oh, willow, woe is me!
  Alack and well-a-day!
If I were only free
  I'd hie me far away!"

Unknown her face and name,
  But this he knew right well,
The maiden's wailing came
  From out a dungeon cell.

The Troubadour

A hapless woman lay
   Within that prison grim—
That fact, I've heard him say,
   Was quite enough for him.

"I will not sit or lie,
   Or eat or drink, I vow,
Till thou art free as I,
   Or I as pent as thou!"

Her tears then ceased to flow,
   Her wails no longer rang,
And tuneful in her woe
   The prisoned maiden sang:

"Oh, stranger, as you play
   I recognise your touch;
And all that I can say,
   Is thank you very much!"

He seized his clarion straight,
   And blew thereat, until
A warder oped the gate,
   "Oh, what might be your will?"

"I've come, sir knave, to see
   The master of these halls:
A maid unwillingly
   Lies prisoned in their walls."

With barely stifled sigh
   That porter drooped his head,
With teardrops in his eye,
   "A many, sir," he said.

The Troubadour

He stayed to hear no more,
  But pushed that porter by,
And shortly stood before
  Sir Hugh de Peckham Rye.

Sir Hugh he darkly frowned,
  "What would you, sir, with me?"
The troubadour he downed
  Upon his bended knee.

"I've come, de Peckham Rye,
  To do a Christian task,
You ask me what would I?
  It is not much I ask.

"Release these maidens, sir,
  Whom you dominion o'er—
Particularly her
  Upon the second floor!

"And if you don't, my lord"—
  He here stood bolt upright.
And tapped a tailor's sword—
  "Come out at once and fight!"

53

The Troubadour

SIR HUGH he called—and ran
  The warden from the gate,
"Go, show this gentleman
  The maid in forty-eight."

By many a cell they passed
  And stopped at length before
A portal, bolted fast:
  The man unlocked the door.

He called inside the gate
  With coarse and brutal shout,
"Come, step it, forty-eight!"
  And forty-eight stepped out.

"They gets it pretty hot,
  The maidens wot we cotch—
Two years this lady's got
  For collaring a wotch."

The Troubadour

"Oh, ah!—indeed—I see,"
  The troubadour exclaimed—
"If I may make so free,
  How is this castle named?"

The warden's eyelids fill,
  And, sighing, he replied,
"Of gloomy Pentonville
  This is the Female Side!"

The minstrel did not wait
  The warden stout to thank,
But recollected straight
  He'd business at the Bank.

PROPER PRIDE

THE Sun, whose rays
Are all ablaze
   With ever-living glory,
Will not deny
His majesty—
   He scorns to tell a story:
He won't exclaim,
"I blush for shame,
   So kindly be indulgent,"
But, fierce and bold,
In fiery gold,
   He glories all effulgent!

I mean to rule the earth,
   As he the sky—
We really know our worth,
   The Sun and I!

Proper Pride

Observe his flame,
That placid dame,
   The Moon's Celestial Highness;
There's not a trace .
Upon her face
   Of diffidence or shyness:
She borrows light
That, through the night,
   Mankind may all acclaim her!
And, truth to tell,
She lights up well,
   So I, for one, don't blame her!

Ah, pray make no mistake,
   We are not shy;
We're very wide awake,
   The Moon and I!

FERDINANDO AND ELVIRA

OR, THE GENTLE PIEMAN

PART I

At a pleasant evening party I had taken down to supper
One whom I will call Elvira, and we talked of love and
    Tupper,

Mr. Tupper and the poets, very lightly with them dealing,
For I've always been distinguished for a strong poetic
    feeling.

Then we let off paper crackers, each of which contained a
    motto,
And she listened while I read them, till her mother told
    her not to.

Then she whispered, "To the ball-room we had better,
    dear, be walking;
If we stop down here much longer, really people will be
    talking."

Ferdinando and Elvira

There were noblemen in coronets, and military cousins,
There were captains by the hundred, there were baronets
    by dozens.

Yet she heeded not their offers, but dismissed them with
    a blessing ;
Then she let down all her back hair which had taken long
    in dressing.

Then she had convulsive sobbings in her agitated throttle,
Then she wiped her pretty eyes and smelt her pretty
    smelling-bottle.

So I whispered, "Dear ELVIRA, say—what can the matter
    be with you ?
Does anything you've eaten, darling POPSY, disagree with
    you ?"

But spite of all I said, her sobs grew more and more dis-
    tressing,
And she tore her pretty back hair, which had taken long
    in dressing.

Then she gazed upon the carpet, at the ceiling then above
    me,
And she whispered, "FERDINANDO, do you really, *really*
    love me ?"

"Love you ?" said I, then I sighed, and then I gazed
    upon her sweetly—
For I think I do this sort of thing particularly neatly—

"Send me to the Arctic regions, or illimitable azure,
On a scientific goose-chase, with my COXWELL or my
    GLAISHER.

Ferdinando and Elvira

"Tell me whither I may hie me, tell me, dear one, that I
   may know—
Is it up the highest Andes? down a horrible volcano?"

But she said, "It isn't polar bears, or hot volcanic grottoes,
Only find out who it is that writes those lovely cracker
   mottoes!"

PART II

"Tell me, HENRY WADSWORTH, ALFRED, POET CLOSE, or
   MISTER TUPPER,
Do you write the bonbon mottoes my ELVIRA pulls at
   supper?"

But HENRY WADSWORTH smiled, and said he had not had
   that honour;
And ALFRED, too, disclaimed the words that told so much
   upon her.

"MISTER MARTIN TUPPER, POET CLOSE, I beg of you
   inform us";
But my question seemed to throw them both into a rage
   enormous.

MISTER CLOSE expressed a wish that he could only get
   anigh to me.
And MISTER MARTIN TUPPER sent the following reply to
   me:—

"A fool is bent upon a twig, but wise men dread a bandit."
Which I think must have been clever, for I didn't understand it.

Seven weary years I wandered—Patagonia, China, Norway,
Till at last I sank exhausted at a pastrycook his doorway.

Ferdinando and Elvira

There were fuchsias and geraniums, and daffodils and
    myrtle,
So I entered, and I ordered half a basin of mock turtle.

He was plump and he was chubby, he was smooth and he
    was rosy,
And his little wife was pretty, and particularly cosy.

And he chirped and sang, and skipped about, and laughed
    with laughter hearty—
He was wonderfully active for so very stout a party.

And I said, "Oh, gentle pieman, who so very, very merry?
Is it purity of conscience, or your one-and-seven sherry?"

But he answered, "I'm so happy—no profession could be
    dearer—
If I am not humming 'Tra! la! la!' I'm singing, 'Tirer,
    lirer!'

"First I go and make the patties, and the puddings and
    the jellies,
Then I make a sugar birdcage, which upon a table swell
    is;

Ferdinando and Elvira

"Then I polish all the silver, which a supper-table
    lacquers;
Then I write the pretty mottoes which you find inside the
    crackers "—

"Found at last!" I madly shouted.   "Gentle pieman,
    you astound me!"
Then I waved the turtle soup enthusiastically round me.

And I shouted and I danced until he'd quite a crowd
    around him—
And I rushed away, exclaiming, "I have found him! I
    have found him!"

And I heard the gentle pieman in the road behind me
    trilling,
"'Tira! lira!' stop him, stop him!   'Tra! la! la!' the
    soup's a shilling!"

But until I reached ELVIRA's home, I never, never waited,
And ELVIRA to her FERDINAND 's irrevocably mated!

THE POLICEMAN'S LOT

WHEN a felon's not engaged in his employment
   Or maturing his felonious little plans,
His capacity for innocent enjoyment
   Is just as great as any honest man's.
Our feelings we with difficulty smother
   When constabulary duty's to be done:
Ah, take one consideration with another,
   A policeman's lot is not a happy one!

When the enterprising burglar isn't burgling,
   When the cut-throat isn't occupied in crime,
He loves to hear the little brook a-gurgling,
   And listen to the merry village chime.
When the coster's finished jumping on his mother,
   He loves to lie a-basking in the sun:
Ah, take one consideration with another,
   The policeman's lot is not a happy one!

LORENZO DE LARDY

Dalilah de Dardy adored
    The very correctest of cards,
Lorenzo de Lardy, a lord—
    He was one of Her Majesty's Guards.

Dalilah de Dardy was fat,
    Dalilah de Dardy was old—
(No doubt in the world about that)
    But Dalilah de Dardy had gold.

Lorenzo de Lardy was tall,
    The flower of maidenly pets,
Young ladies would love at his call,
    But Lorenzo de Lardy had debts.

Lorenzo de Lardy

His money-position was queer,
    And one of his favourite freaks
Was to hide himself three times a year,
    In Paris, for several weeks.

Many days didn't pass him before
    He fanned himself into a flame,
For a beautiful "Dam du Comptwore,"
    And this was her singular name:

Alice Eulalie Coraline
    Euphrosine Colombina Thérèse
Juliette Stephanie Celestine
    Charlotte Russe de la Sauce Mayonnaise.

She booked all the orders and tin,
    Accoutred in showy fal-lal,
At a two-fifty Restaurant, in
    The glittering Palais Royal.

Lorenzo de Lardy

He'd gaze in her orbit of blue,
   Her hand he would tenderly squeeze,
But the words of her tongue that he knew
   Were limited strictly to these:

"CORALINE CELESTINE EULALIE,
   Houp là! Je vous aime, oui, mossoo,
Combien donnez moi aujourd'hui
   Bonjour, Mademoiselle, parlez voo."

MADEMOISELLE DE LA SAUCE MAYONNAISE
   Was a witty and beautiful miss,
Extremely correct in her ways,
   But her English consisted of this:

"Oh my! pretty man, if you please,
   Blom boodin, biftek, currie lamb,
Bouldogue, two franc half, quite ze cheese,
   Rosbif, me spik Angleesh, godam."

A waiter, for seasons before,
   Had basked in her beautiful gaze,
And burnt to dismember MILOR,
   He loved DE LA SAUCE MAYONNAISE.

He said to her, "Méchante THÉRÈSE,
   Avec désespoir tu m'accables.
Penses-tu, DE LA SAUCE MAYONNAISE,
   Ses intentions sont honorables?

"Flirtez toujours, ma belle, si tu ôses——
   Je me vengerai ainsi, ma chère,
Je lui dirai de quoi l'on compose
   Vol au vent à la Financière!"

Lorenzo de Lardy

Lord Lardy knew nothing of this—
    The waiter's devotion ignored,
But he gazed on the beautiful miss,
    And never seemed weary or bored.

The waiter would screw up his nerve,
    His fingers he'd snap and he'd dance—
And Lord Lardy would smile and observe,
    "How strange are the customs of France!"

Well, after delaying a space,
    His tradesmen no longer would wait:
Returning to England apace,
    He yielded himself to his fate.

Lord Lardy espoused, with a groan,
    Miss Dardy's developing charms,
And agreed to tag on to his own,
    Her name and her newly-found arms.

Lorenzo de Lardy

The waiter he knelt at the toes
   Of an ugly and thin coryphée,
Who danced in the hindermost rows
   At the Théatre des Variétés.

MADEMOISELLE DE LA SAUCE MAYONNAISE
   Didn't yield to a gnawing despair
But married a soldier, and plays
   As a pretty and pert Vivandière.

THE BAFFLED GRUMBLER

WHENE'ER I poke
Sarcastic joke
   Replete with malice spiteful,
The people vile
Politely smile
    And vote me quite delightful!
Now, when a wight
Sits up all night
   Ill-natured jokes devising,
And all his wiles
Are met with smiles,
    It's hard, there's no disguising!
Oh, don't the days seem lank and long
When all goes right and nothing goes wrong,
And isn't your life extremely flat
With nothing whatever to grumble at.!

The Baffled Grumbler

When German bands
From music stands
Play Wagner imper*fect*ly—
I bid them go—
They don't say no,
But off they trot directly!
The organ boys
They stop their noise
With readiness surprising,
And grinning herds
Of hurdy-gurds
Retire apologising!
Oh, don't the days seem lank and long
When all goes right and nothing goes wrong,
And isn't your life extremely flat
With nothing whatever to grumble at!

I've offered gold,
In sums untold,
To all who'd contradict me—
I've said I'd pay
A pound a day
To any one who kicked me—
I've bribed with toys
Great vulgar boys
To utter something spiteful,
But, bless you, no!
They *will* be so
Confoundedly politeful!
In short, these aggravating lads,
They tickle my tastes, they feed my fads,
They give me this and they give me that,
And I've nothing whatever to grumble at!

DISILLUSIONED

BY AN EX-ENTHUSIAST

OH, that my soul its gods could see
As years ago they seemed to me
    When first I painted them;
Invested with the circumstance
Of old conventional romance:
    Exploded theorem!

The bard who could, all men above,
Inflame my soul with songs of love,
    And, with his verse, inspire
The craven soul who feared to die
With all the glow of chivalry
    And old heroic fire;

Disillusioned

I found him in a beerhouse tap
Awaking from a gin-born nap,
   With pipe and sloven dress ;
Amusing chums, who fooled his bent,
With muddy, maudlin sentiment,
   And tipsy foolishness !

The novelist, whose painting pen
To legions of fictitious men
   A real existence lends,
Brain-people whom we rarely fail,
Whene'er we hear their names, to hail
   As old and welcome friends ;

I found in clumsy snuffy suit,
In seedy glove, and blucher boot,
   Uncomfortably big.
Particularly commonplace,
With vulgar, coarse, stockbroking face,
   And spectacles and wig.

My favourite actor who, at will,
With mimic woe my eyes could fill
   With unaccustomed brine :
A being who appeared to me
(Before I knew him well) to be
   A song incarnadine ;

I found a coarse unpleasant man
With speckled chin—unhealthy, wan—
   Of self-importance full :
Existing in an atmosphere
That reeked of gin and pipes and beer—
   Conceited, fractious, dull.

Disillusioned

The warrior whose ennobled name
Is woven with his country's fame,
   Triumphant over all,
I found weak, palsied, bloated, blear;
His province seemed to be, to leer
   At bonnets in Pall Mall.

Would that ye always shone, who write,
Bathed in your own innate limelight,
   And ye who battles wage,
Or that in darkness I had died
Before my soul had ever sighed
   To see you off the stage!

THE HOUSE OF PEERS

WHEN Britain really ruled the waves—
   (In good Queen Bess's time)
The House of Peers made no pretence
To intellectual eminence,
   Or scholarship sublime;
Yet Britain won her proudest bays
In good Queen Bess's glorious days!

When Wellington thrashed Bonaparte,
   As every child can tell,
The House of Peers, throughout the war,
Did nothing in particular,
   And did it very well;
Yet Britain set the world ablaze
In good King George's glorious days!

The House of Peers

And while the House of Peers withholds
   Its legislative hand,
And noble statesmen do not itch
To interfere with matters which
   They do not understand,
As bright will shine Great Britain's rays,
As in King George's glorious days!

BABETTE'S LOVE

Babette she was a fisher gal,
  With jupon striped and cap in crimps.
She passed her days inside the Halle,
  Or catching little nimble shrimps.
Yet she was sweet as flowers in May,
With no professional bouquet.

Jacot was, of the Customs bold,
  An officer, at gay Boulogne,
He loved Babette—his love he told,
  And sighed, " Oh, soyez vous my own ! "
But " Non ! " said she, " Jacot, my pet,
Vous êtes trop scraggy pour Babette.

76

Babette's Love

"Of one alone I nightly dream,
  An able mariner is he,
And gaily serves the Gen'ral Steam-
  Boat Navigation Companee.
I'll marry him, if he but will—
His name, I rather think, is BILL.

"I see him when he's not aware,
  Upon our hospitable coast,
Reclining with an easy air
  Upon the *Port* against a post,
A-thinking of, I'll dare to say,
His native Chelsea far away!"

"Oh, mon!" exclaimed the Customs bold,
  "Mes yeux!" he said (which means "my eye")
"Oh, chère!" he also cried, I'm told,
  "Par Jove," he added, with a sigh.
"Oh, mon! oh, chère! mes yeux! par Jove!
Je n'aime pas cet enticing cove!"

The *Panther's* captain stood hard by,
  He was a man of morals strict
If e'er a sailor winked his eye,
  Straightway he had that sailor licked,
Mast-headed all (such was his code)
Who dashed or jiggered, blessed or blowed.

He wept to think a tar of his
  Should lean so gracefully on posts,
He sighed and sobbed to think of this,
  On foreign, French, and friendly coasts.
"It's human natur', p'raps—if so,
Oh, isn't human natur' low!"

Babette's Love

He called his BILL, who pulled his curl,
   He said, "My BILL, I understand
You've captivated some young gurl
   On this here French and foreign land.
Her tender heart your beauties jog—
They do, you know they do, you dog.

"You have a graceful way, I learn,
   Of leaning airily on posts,
By which you've been and caused to burn
   A tender flame on these here coasts.
A fisher gurl, I much regret,—
Her age, sixteen—her name, BABETTE.

"You'll marry her, you gentle tar—
   Your union I myself will bless,
And when you matrimonied are,
   I will appoint her stewardess."
But WILLIAM hitched himself and sighed,
And cleared his throat. and thus replied:

Babette's Love

"Not so: unless you're fond of strife,
 You'd better mind your own affairs,
I have an able-bodied wife
 Awaiting me at Wapping Stairs;
If all this here to her I tell,
She'll larrup you and me as well

"Skin-deep, and valued at a pin,
 Is beauty such as VENUS owns—
Her beauty is beneath her skin,
 And lies in layers on her bones.
The other sailors of the crew
They always calls her 'Whopping Sue!'"

"Oho!" the Captain said, "I see!
 And is she then so very strong?"
"She'd take your honour's scruff," said he
 "And pitch you over to Bolong!"
"I pardon you," the Captain said,
"The fair BABETTE you needn't wed."

Babette's Love

Perhaps the Customs had his will,
    And coaxed the scornful girl to wed,
Perhaps the Captain and his BILL,
    And WILLIAM's little wife are dead;
Or p'raps they're all alive and well:
I cannot, cannot, cannot tell.

A MERRY MADRIGAL

BRIGHTLY dawns our wedding day ;
  Joyous hour, we give thee greeting !
  Whither, whither art thou fleeting ?
Fickle moment, prithee stay !
  What though mortal joys be hollow ?
  Pleasures come, if sorrows follow.
Though the tocsin sound, ere long,
 Ding dong ! Ding dong !
  Yet until the shadows fall
  Over one and over all,
  Sing a merry madrigal—
     Fal la !

Let us dry the ready tear ;
  Though the hours are surely creeping,
  Little need for woeful weeping
Till the sad sundown is near.
  All must sip the cup of sorrow,
  I to-day and thou to-morrow :
This the close of every song—
 Ding dong ! Ding dong !
  What though solemn shadows fall,
  Sooner, later, over all ?
  Sing a merry madrigal—
     Fal la !

TO MY BRIDE

(WHOEVER SHE MAY BE)

OH! little maid!—(I do not know your name,
　Or who you are, so, as a safe precaution
I'll add)—Oh, buxom widow! married dame!
　(As one of these must be your present portion)
　　Listen, while I unveil prophetic lore for you,
　　And sing the fate that Fortune has in store for you.

You'll marry soon—within a year or twain—
　A bachelor of *circa* two-and-thirty,
Tall, gentlemanly, but extremely plain,
　And, when you're intimate, you call him "BERTIE."
　　Neat—dresses well; his temper has been classified
　　As hasty; but he's very quickly pacified.

To My Bride

You'll find him working mildly at the Bar,
   After a touch at two or three professions,
From easy affluence extremely far,
    A brief or two on Circuit—"soup" at Sessions;
      A pound or two from whist and backing horses,
      And, say, three hundred from his own resources.

Quiet in harness; free from serious vice,
   His faults are not particularly shady;
You'll never find him "*shy*"—for, once or twice
    Already, he's been driven by a lady,
      Who parts with him—perhaps a poor excuse for him—
      Because she hasn't any further use for him.

Oh! bride of mine—tall, dumpy, dark, or fair!
   Oh! widow—wife, maybe, or blushing maiden,
I've told *your* fortune: solved the gravest care
    With which *your* mind has hitherto been laden.
      I've prophesied correctly, never doubt it;
      Now tell me mine—and please be quick about it!

You—only you—can tell me, an you will,
   To whom I'm destined shortly to be mated,
Will she run up a heavy *modiste's* bill?
    If so, I want to hear her income stated.
      (This is a point which interests me greatly),
      To quote the bard, "Oh! have I seen her lately?"

Say, must I wait till husband number one
   Is comfortably stowed away at Woking?
How is her hair most usually done?
    And tell me, please, will she object to smoking?
      The colour of her eyes, too, you may mention:
      Come, Sibyl, prophesy—I'm all attention.

THE DUKE AND THE DUCHESS

THE DUKE.

SMALL titles and orders
For Mayors and Recorders
    I get—and they're highly delighted.
M.P.s baronetted,
Sham Colonels gazetted,
    And second-rate Aldermen knighted.
Foundation-stone laying
I find very paying,
    It adds a large sum to my makings.
At charity dinners
The best of speech-spinners,
    I get ten per cent on the takings!

THE DUCHESS.

I present any lady
Whose conduct is shady
    Or smacking of doubtful propriety;
When Virtue would quash her
I take and whitewash her
    And launch her in first-rate society.

The Duke and the Duchess

        I recommend acres
        Of clumsy dressmakers—
            Their fit and their finishing touches;
        A sum in addition
        They pay for permission
            To say that they make for the Duchess!

THE DUKE.   Those pressing prevailers,
        The ready-made tailors,
            Quote me as their great double-barrel;
        I allow them to do so,
        Though ROBINSON CRUSOE
            Would jib at their wearing apparel!
        I sit, by selection,
        Upon the direction
            Of several Companies bubble;
        As soon as they're floated
        I'm freely bank-noted—
            I'm pretty well paid for my trouble!

THE DUCHESS. At middle-class party
        I play at *écarté*—
            And I'm by no means a beginner;
        To one of my station
        The remuneration—
            Five guineas a night and my dinner.
        I write letters blatant
        On medicines patent—
            And use any other you mustn't;
        And vow my complexion
        Derives its perfection
            From somebody's soap — which it
            doesn't.

The Duke and the Duchess

THE DUKE.
We're ready as witness
To any one's fitness
  To fill any place or preferment;
We're often in waiting
At junket or *fêting*,
  And sometimes attend an interment.
In short, if you'd kindle
The spark of a swindle,
  Lure simpletons into your clutches,
Or hoodwink a debtor,
You cannot do better
  Than trot out a Duke or a Duchess!

THE FOLLY OF BROWN

By a General Agent

I KNEW a boor—a clownish card
    (His only friends were pigs and cows and
The poultry of a small farmyard),
    Who came into two hundred thousand.

Good fortune worked no change in BROWN,
    Though she's a mighty social chymist;
He was a clown—and by a clown
    I do not mean a pantomimist.

It left him quiet, calm, and cool,
    Though hardly knowing what a crown was—
You can't imagine what a fool
    Poor rich uneducated BROWN was!

The Folly of Brown

He scouted all who wished to come
  And give him monetary schooling;
And I propose to give you some
  Idea of his insensate fooling.

I formed a company or two—
  (Of course I don't know what the rest meant,
I formed them solely with a view
  To help him to a sound investment).

Their objects were—their only cares—
  To justify their Boards in showing
A handsome dividend on shares
  And keep their good promoter going.

But no—the lout sticks to his brass,
  Though shares at par I freely proffer:
Yet—will it be believed?—the ass
  Declines, with thanks, my well-meant offer!

The Folly of Brown

He adds, with bumpkin's stolid grin
  (A weakly intellect denoting),
He'd rather not invest it in
  A company of my promoting!

"You have two hundred 'thou' or more,"
  Said I. "You'll waste it, lose it, lend it;
Come, take my furnished second floor,
  I'll gladly show you how to spend it."

But will it be believed that he,
  With grin upon his face of poppy,
Declined my aid, while thanking me
  For what he called my "philanthroppy"?

Some blind, suspicious fools rejoice
  In doubting friends who wouldn't harm them;
They will not hear the charmer's voice,
  However wisely he may charm them!

I showed him that his coat, all dust,
  Top boots and cords provoked compassion,
And proved that men of station must
  Conform to the decrees of fashion.

I showed him where to buy his hat
  To coat him, trouser him, and boot him;
But no—he wouldn't hear of that—
  "He didn't think the style would suit him!"

The Folly of Brown

I offered him a county seat,
  And made no end of an oration ;
I made it certainty complete,
  And introduced the deputation.

But no—the clown my prospect blights—
  (The worth of birth it surely teaches !)
"Why should I want to spend my nights
  In Parliament, a-making speeches?

"I haven't never been to school—
  I ain't had not no eddication—
And I should surely be a fool
  To publish that to all the nation !"

I offered him a trotting horse—
  No hack had ever trotted faster—
I also offered him, of course,
  A rare and curious "old master."

I offered to procure him weeds—
  Wines fit for one in his position—
But, though an ass in all his deeds,
  He'd learnt the meaning of "commission."

He called me "thief" the other day,
  And daily from his door he thrusts me ;
Much more of this, and soon I may
  Begin to think that BROWN mistrusts me.

The Folly of Brown

So deaf to all sound Reason's rule
    This poor uneducated clown is,
You can*not* fancy what a fool
    Poor rich uneducated BROWN is.

EHEU FUGACES—!

THE air is charged with amatory numbers—
  Soft madrigals, and dreamy lovers' lays.
Peace, peace, old heart! Why waken from its slumbers
  The aching memory of the old, old days?

Time was when Love and I were well acquainted;
  Time was when we walked ever hand in hand;
A saintly youth, with worldly thought untainted,
  None better loved than I in all the land!
Time was, when maidens of the noblest station,
  Forsaking even military men,
Would gaze upon me, rapt in adoration—
  Ah me, I was a fair young curate then!

92

Eheu Fugaces—!

Had I a headache? sighed the maids assembled;
   Had I a cold? welled forth the silent tear;
Did I look pale? then half a parish trembled;
   And when I coughed all thought the end was near!
I had no care—no jealous doubts hung o'er me—
   For I was loved beyond all other men.
Fled gilded dukes and belted earls before me—
   Ah me, I was a pale young curate then!

SIR MACKLIN

OF all the youths I ever saw
  None were so wicked, vain, or silly,
So lost to shame and Sabbath law
  As worldly TOM, and BOB, and BILLY.

For every Sabbath day they walked
  (Such was their gay and thoughtless natur')
In parks or gardens, where they talked
  From three to six, or even later.

SIR MACKLIN was a priest severe
  In conduct and in conversation,
It did a sinner good to hear
  Him deal in ratiocination.

He could in every action show
  Some sin, and nobody could doubt him.
He argued high, he argued low,
  He also argued round about him.

Sir Macklin

He wept to think each thoughtless youth
   Contained of wickedness a skinful,
And burnt to teach the awful truth,
   That walking out on Sunday's sinful.

"Oh, youths," said he, "I grieve to find
   The course of life you've been and hit on—
Sit down," said he, "and never mind
   The pennies for the chairs you sit on.

"My opening head is 'Kensington,'
   How walking there the sinner hardens;
Which when I have enlarged upon,
   I go to 'Secondly'—its Gardens.

"My 'Thirdly' comprehendeth 'Hyde,'
   Of Secrecy the guilts and shameses;
My 'Fourthly'—'Park'—its verdure wide—
   My 'Fifthly' comprehends 'St. James's.'

Sir Macklin

" That matter settled I shall reach
    The 'Sixthly' in my solemn tether,
And show that what is true of each,
    Is also true of all, together.

" Then I shall demonstrate to you,
    According to the rules of Whately,
That what is true of all, is true
    Of each, considered separately."

In lavish stream his accents flow,
    TOM, BOB, and BILLY dare not flout him ;
He argued high, he argued low,
    He also argued round about him.

" Ha, ha ! " he said, " you loathe your ways,
    Repentance on your souls is dawning,
In agony your hands you raise."
    (And so they did, for they were yawning.)

Sir Macklin

To "Twenty-firstly" on they go,
  The lads do not attempt to scout him;
He argued high, he argued low,
  He also argued round about him.

"Ho, ho!" he cries, "you bow your crests—
  My eloquence has set you weeping;
In shame you bend upon your breasts!"
  (They bent their heads, for they were sleeping.)

He proved them this—he proved them that
  This good but wearisome ascetic;
He jumped and thumped upon his hat,
  He was so very energetic.

His bishop at this moment chanced
  To pass, and found the road encumbered;
He noticed how the Churchman danced,
  And how his congregation slumbered.

Sir Macklin

The hundred and eleventh head
   The priest completed of his stricture ;
"Oh, bosh!" the worthy bishop said,
   And walked him off, as in the picture.

THEY'LL NONE OF 'EM BE MISSED

As some day it may happen that a victim must be found,
  I've got a little list—I've got a little list
Of social offenders who might well be underground,
  And who never would be missed—who never would be
    missed !
There's the pestilential nuisances who write for auto-
    graphs—
All people who have flabby hands and irritating laughs—
All children who are up in dates, and floor you with 'em
    flat—
All persons who in shaking hands, shake hands with you
    like *that*—
And all third persons who on spoiling *tête-à-têtes* insist—
  They'd none of 'em be missed—they'd none of 'em be
    missed !

There's the nigger serenader, and the others of his race,
  And the piano organist—I've got him on the list !
And the people who eat peppermint and puff it in your
    face,
  They never would be missed—they never would be
    missed !

They'll None of 'Em be Missed

Then the idiot who praises, with enthusiastic tone,
All centuries but this, and every country but his own;
And the lady from the provinces, who dresses like a guy,
And who "doesn't think she waltzes, but would rather
    like to try";
And that *fin-de-siècle* anomaly, the scorching motorist—
    I don't think he'd be missed—I'm *sure* he'd not be
    missed!

And that *Nisi Prius* nuisance, who just now is rather rife,
    The Judicial humorist—I've got *him* on the list!
All funny fellows, comic men, and clowns of private life—
    They'd none of 'em be missed—they'd none of 'em be
    missed!
And apologetic statesmen of the compromising kind,
Such as—What-d'ye-call-him—Thing'em-Bob, and likewise
    —Never-mind,
And 'St—'st—'st—and What's-his-name, and also—You-
    know-who—
(The task of filling up the blanks I'd rather leave to *you!*)
But it really doesn't matter whom you put upon the list,
    For they'd none of 'em be missed—they'd none of 'em
    be missed!

THE YARN OF THE "NANCY BELL"

'Twas on the shores that round our coast
From Deal to Ramsgate span,
That I found alone on a piece of stone
An elderly naval man.

His hair was weedy, his beard was long,
And weedy and long was he,
And I heard this wight on the shore recite,
In a singular minor key:

"Oh, I am a cook and a captain bold,
And the mate of the *Nancy* brig,
And a bo'sun tight, and a midshipmite,
And the crew of the captain's gig."

The Yarn of the " Nancy Bell "

And he shook his fists and he tore his hair,
  Till I really felt afraid,
For I couldn't help thinking the man had been drinking,
  And so I simply said:

"Oh, elderly man, it's little I know
  Of the duties of men of the sea,
But I'll eat my hand if I understand
  How you can possibly be

" At once a cook, and a captain bold,
  And the mate of the *Nancy* brig,
And a bo'sun tight, and a midshipmite,
  And the crew of the captain's gig."

Then he gave a hitch to his trousers, which
  Is a trick all seamen larn,
And having got rid of a thumping quid,
  He spun this painful yarn:

" 'Twas in the good ship *Nancy Bell*
  That we sailed to the Indian sea,
And there on a reef we come to grief,
  Which has often occurred to me.

" And pretty nigh all o' the crew was drowned
  (There was seventy-seven o' soul),
And only ten of the *Nancy's* men
  Said 'Here !' to the muster-roll.

" There was me and the cook and the captain bold,
  And the mate of the *Nancy* brig,
And the bo'sun tight, and a midshipmite,
  And the crew of the captain's gig.

The Yarn of the "Nancy Bell"

"For a month we'd neither wittles nor drink,
  Till a-hungry we did feel,
So we drawed a lot, and accordin' shot
  The captain for our meal.

"The next lot fell to the *Nancy's* mate,
  And a delicate dish he made;
Then our appetite with the midshipmite
  We seven survivors stayed.

"And then we murdered the bo'sun tight,
  And he much resembled pig;
Then we wittled free, did the cook and me,
  On the crew of the captain's gig.

"Then only the cook and me was left,
  And the delicate question, 'Which
Of us two goes to the kettle?' arose
  And we argued it out as sich.

"For I loved that cook as a brother, I did,
  And the cook he worshipped me;
But we'd both be blowed if we'd either be stowed
  In the other chap's hold, you see.

"'I'll be eat if you dines off me,' says TOM,
  'Yes, that,' says I, 'you'll be,'—
'I'm boiled if I die, my friend,' quoth I,
  And 'Exactly so,' quoth he.

'Says he, 'Dear JAMES, to murder me
  Were a foolish thing to do,
For don't you see that you can't cook *me*,
  While I can—and will—cook *you*!'

The Yarn of the "Nancy Bell"

"So he boils the water, and takes the salt
  And the pepper in portions true
(Which he never forgot), and some chopped shalot,
  And some sage and parsley too.

" 'Come here,' says he, with a proper pride,
  Which his smiling features tell,
" 'Twill soothing be if I let you see,
  How extremely nice you'll smell.'

"And he stirred it round and round and round,
  And he sniffed at the foaming froth;
When I ups with his heels, and smothers his squeals
  In the scum of the boiling broth.

The Yarn of the " Nancy Bell "

" And I eat that cook in a week or less,
    And——as I eating be
The last of his chops, why, I almost drops,
    For a wessel in sight I see !

         *   *   *   *   *

" And I never grin, and I never smile,
    And I never larf nor play,
But I sit and croak, and a single joke
    I have——which is to say :

" Oh, I am a cook and a captain bold,
    And the mate of the *Nancy* brig,
And a bo'sun tight, *and* a midshipmite,
    And the crew of the captain's gig ! "

GIRL GRADUATES

THEY intend to send a wire
    To the moon;
And they'll set the Thames on fire
    Very soon;
Then they learn to make silk purses
    With their rigs
From the ears of LADY CIRCE'S
    Piggy-wigs.
And weasels at their slumbers
    They'll trepan;
To get sunbeams from cu*cum*bers
    They've a plan.
They've a firmly rooted notion
They can cross the Polar Ocean,
And they'll find Perpetual Motion
    If they can!

    These are the phenomena
    That every pretty domina
      Hopes that we shall see
      At this Universitee!

Girl Graduates

As for fashion, they forswear it,
    So they say,
And the circle—they will square it
    Some fine day ;
Then the little pigs they're teaching
    For to fly ;
And the niggers they'll be bleaching
    By-and-by !
Each newly joined aspirant
    To the clan
Must repudiate the tyrant
    Known as Man ;
They mock at him and flout him,
For they do not care about him,
And they're " going to do without him "
    If they can !

These are the phenomena
That every pretty domina
    Hopes that we shall see
    At this Universitee !

THE BISHOP OF RUM-TI-FOO

FROM east and south the holy clan
Of Bishops gathered, to a man;
To Synod, called Pan-Anglican,
    In flocking crowds they came.
Among them was a Bishop, who
Had lately been appointed to
The balmy isle of Rum-ti-Foo,
    And PETER was his name.

His people—twenty-three in sum—
They played the eloquent tum-tum,
And lived on scalps served up in rum—
    The only sauce they knew.
When first good Bishop PETER came
(For PETER was that Bishop's name),
To humour them, he did the same
    As they of Rum-ti-Foo.

The Bishop of Rum-ti-Foo

His flock, I've often heard him tell,
(His name was PETER) loved him well,
And summoned by the sound of bell,
 In crowds together came.
"Oh, massa, why you go away?
Oh, Massa PETER, please to stay."
(They called him PETER, people say,
 Because it was his name.)

He told them all good boys to be,
And sailed away across the sea,
At London Bridge that Bishop he
 Arrived one Tuesday night—
And as forthwith he homeward strode
To his Pan-Anglican abode,
He passed along the Borough Road
 And saw a gruesome sight.

He saw a crowd assembled round
A person dancing on the ground,
Who straight began to leap and bound
 With all his might and main.
To see that dancing man he stopped,
Who twirled and wriggled, skipped and hopped,
Then down incontinently dropped,
 And then sprang up again.

The Bishop chuckled at the sight,
"This style of dancing would delight
A simple Rum-ti-Foozleite,
 I'll learn it if I can,
To please the tribe when I get back."
He begged the man to teach his knack.
"Right Reverend Sir, in half a crack,"
 Replied that dancing man.

The Bishop of Rum-ti-Foo

The dancing man he worked away—
And taught the Bishop every day—
The dancer skipped like any fay—
    Good PETER did the same.
The Bishop buckled to his task
With *battements*, cuts, and *pas de basque*
(I'll tell you, if you care to ask,
    That PETER was his name).

"Come, walk like this," the dancer said,
"Stick out your toes—stick in your head,
Stalk on with quick, galvanic tread—
    Your fingers thus extend;
The attitude's considered quaint."
The weary Bishop, feeling faint,
Replied, "I do not say it ain't,
    But Time, my Christian friend."

"We now proceed to something new—
Dance as the PAYNES and LAURIS do,
Like this—one, two—one, two—one, two."
    The Bishop, never proud,

The Bishop of Rum-ti-Foo

But in an overwhelming heat
(His name was PETER, I repeat)
Performed the PAYNE and LAURI feat,
    And puffed his thanks aloud.

Another game the dancer planned—
" Just take your ankle in your hand,
And try, my lord, if you can stand—
    Your body stiff and stark.
If, when revisiting your see,
You learnt to hop on shore—like me—
The novelty would striking be,
    And must attract remark."

" No," said the worthy Bishop, " No:
That is a length to which, I trow,
Colonial Bishops cannot go.
    You may express surprise
At finding Bishops deal in pride—
But, if that trick I ever tried,
I should appear undignified
    In Rum-ti-Foozle's eyes.

The Bishop of Rum-ti-Foo

"The islanders of Rum-ti-Foo
Are well-conducted persons, who
Approve a joke as much as you,
    And laugh at it as such;
But if they saw their Bishop land,
His leg supported in his hand,
The joke they wouldn't understand—
    'Twould pain them very much!"

BRAID THE RAVEN HAIR

BRAID the raven hair,
   Weave the supple tress,
Deck the maiden fair
   In her loveliness;
Paint the pretty face,
   Dye the coral lip,
Emphasise the grace
   Of her ladyship!
Art and nature, thus allied,
Go to make a pretty bride!

Sit with downcast eye,
   Let it brim with dew;
Try if you can cry,
   We will do so, too.
When you're summoned, start
   Like a frightened roe;
Flutter, little heart,
   Colour, come and go!
Modesty at marriage tide
Well becomes a pretty bride!

THE PRECOCIOUS BABY

A VERY TRUE TALE

(To be sung to the Air of the " Whistling Oyster.")

AN elderly person—a prophet by trade—
  With his quips and tips
  On withered old lips,
He married a young and a beautiful maid ;
  The cunning old blade,
  Though rather decayed,
He married a beautiful, beautiful maid.

She was only eighteen, and as fair as could be,
  With her tempting smiles
  And maidenly wiles,

The Precocious Baby

And he was a trifle of seventy-three :
    Now what she could see
    Is a puzzle to me,
In a prophet of seventy—seventy-three !

Of all their acquaintances bidden (or bade)
    With their loud high jinks
    And underbred winks
None thought they'd a family have—but they had ;
    A singular lad
    Who drove 'em half mad,
He proved such a horribly fast little cad.

For when he was born he astonished all by,
    With their " Law, dear me ! "
    " Did ever you see."
He'd a weed in his mouth and a glass in his eye,
    A hat all awry—
    An octagon tie,
And a miniature—miniature glass in his eye.

He grumbled at wearing a frock and a cap,
    With his " Oh dear, no ! "
    And his " Hang it ! 'oo know ! "
And he turned up his nose at his excellent pap—
    " My friends, it's a tap
    Dat is not worf a rap."
(Now this was remarkably excellent pap.)

He'd chuck his nurse under the chin, and he'd say,
    With his " Fal, lal, lal "—
    " 'Oo doosed fine gal ! "

The Precocious Baby

This shocking precocity drove 'em away :
    " A month from to-day
    Is as long as I'll stay—
Then I'd wish, if you please, for to go, if I may."

His father, a simple old gentleman, he
    With nursery rhyme
    And " Once on a time,"
Would tell him the story of " Little Bo-P,"
    " So pretty was she,
    So pretty and wee,
As pretty, as pretty, as pretty could be."

But the babe, with a dig that would startle an ox,
    With his " C'ck ! Oh my !—
    Go along wiz 'oo, fie ! "
Would exclaim, " I'm afraid 'oo a socking ole fox."
    Now a father it shocks,
    And it whitens his locks
When his little babe calls him a shocking old fox.

The name of his father he'd couple and pair
    (With his ill-bred laugh,
    And insolent chaff)
With those of the nursery heroines rare ;
    Virginia the fair,
    Or Good Goldenhair,
Till the nuisance was more than a prophet could bear.

" There's Jill and White Cat " (said the bold little brat,
    With his loud, " Ha, ha ! ")
    " 'Oo sly ickle pa !

The Precocious Baby

Wiz 'oo Beauty, Bo-Peep, and 'oo Mrs. Jack Sprat!
    I've noticed 'oo pat
    My pretty White Cat—
I sink dear mamma ought to know about dat !"

He early determined to marry and wive,
    For better or worse
    With his elderly nurse—
Which the poor little boy didn't live to contrive :
    His health didn't thrive—
    No longer alive,
He died an enfeebled old dotard at five !

The Precocious Baby

MORAL

Now elderly men of the bachelor crew,
With wrinkled hose
And spectacled nose,
Don't marry at all—you may take it as true
If ever you do
The step you will rue,
For your babes will be elderly—elderly too.

THE WORKING MONARCH

Rising early in the morning,
    We proceed to light the fire,
Then our Majesty adorning
    In its work-a-day attire,
        We embark without delay
        On the duties of the day.

First, we polish off some batches
Of political despatches,
        And foreign politicians circumvent;
Then, if business isn't heavy,
We may hold a Royal *levée,*
        Or ratify some Acts of Parliament:
Then we probably review the household troops—
With the usual "Shalloo humps" and "Shalloo hoops!"
Or receive with ceremonial and state
An interesting Eastern Potentate.
        After that we generally
        Go and dress our private *valet*—

The Working Monarch

(It's a rather nervous duty—he a touchy little man)—
    Write some letters literary
    For our private secretary—
(He is shaky in his spelling, so we help him if we can.)
    Then, in view of cravings inner,
    We go down and order dinner;
Or we polish the Regalia and the Coronation Plate—
    Spend an hour in titivating
    All our Gentlemen-in-Waiting;
Or we run on little errands for the Ministers of State.
      Oh, philosophers may sing
      Of the troubles of a King,
    Yet the duties are delightful, and the privileges great;
      But the privilege and pleasure
      That we treasure beyond measure
    Is to run on little errands for the Ministers of State!

After luncheon (making merry
On a bun and glass of sherry),
    If we've nothing in particular to do,
We may make a Proclamation,
Or receive a Deputation—
    Then we possibly create a Peer or two.
Then we help a fellow-creature on his path
With the Garter or the Thistle or the Bath:
Or we dress and toddle off in semi-State
To a festival, a function, or a *fête*.
    Then we go and stand as sentry
    At the Palace (private entry),
Marching hither, marching thither, up and down and to
      and fro,
    While the warrior on duty
    Goes in search of beer and beauty
(And it generally happens that he hasn't far to go).
    He relieves us, if he's able,
    Just in time to lay the table,

The Working Monarch

Then we dine and serve the coffee; and at half-past twelve
      or one,
    With a pleasure that's emphatic;
    Then we seek our little attic
With the gratifying feeling that our duty has been done.
      Oh, philosophers may sing
      Of the troubles of a King,
    But of pleasures there are many and of troubles there
      are none;
      And the culminating pleasure
      That we treasure beyond measure
Is the gratifying feeling that our duty has been done!

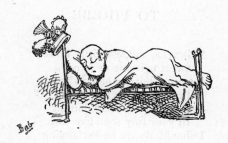

TO PHŒBE

"Gentle, modest, little flower,
    Sweet epitome of May,
Love me but for half-an-hour,
    Love me, love me, little fay."
Sentences so fiercely flaming
    In your tiny shell-like ear,
I should always be exclaiming
    If I loved you, Phœbe, dear.

"Smiles that thrill from any distance
    Shed upon me while I sing!
Please ecstaticise existence,
    Love me, oh thou fairy thing!"
Words like these, outpouring sadly,
    You'd perpetually hear,
If I loved you, fondly, madly;—
    But I do not, Phœbe, dear.

THE APE AND THE LADY

A LADY fair, of lineage high,
Was loved by an Ape, in the days gone by——
The Maid was radiant as the sun,
The Ape was a most unsightly one——
    So it would not do——
    His scheme fell through ;
For the Maid, when his love took formal shape,
    Expressed such terror
    At his monstrous error,
That he stammered an apology and made his 'scape,
The picture of a disconcerted Ape.

The Ape and the Lady

With a view to rise in the social scale,
He shaved his bristles, and he docked his tail,
He grew moustachios, and he took his tub,
    And he paid a guinea to a toilet club.
      But it would not do,
      The scheme fell through—
For the Maid was Beauty's fairest Queen,
      With golden tresses,
      Like a real princess's,
While the Ape, despite his razor keen,
Was the apiest Ape that ever was seen!

He bought white ties, and he bought dress suits,
He crammed his feet into bright tight boots,
And to start his life on a brand-new plan,
He christened himself Darwinian Man!
      But it would not do,
      The scheme fell through—
For the Maiden fair, whom the monkey craved,
      Was a radiant Being,
      With a brain far-seeing—
While a Man, however well-behaved,
At best is only a monkey shaved!

BAINES CAREW, GENTLEMAN

Of all the good attorneys who
    Have placed their names upon the roll,
But few could equal Baines Carew
    For tender-heartedness and soul.

Whene'er he heard a tale of woe
    From client A or client B,
His grief would overcome him so,
    He'd scarce have strength to take his fee.

It laid him up for many days,
    When duty led him to distrain ;
And serving writs, although it pays,
    Gave him excruciating pain.

Baines Carew, Gentleman

He made out costs, distrained for rent,
  Foreclosed and sued, with moistened eye—
No bill of costs could represent
  The value of such sympathy.

No charges can approximate
  The worth of sympathy with woe ;—
Although I think I ought to state
  He did his best to make them so.

Of all the many clients who
  Had mustered round his legal flag,
No single client of the crew
  Was half so dear as CAPTAIN BAGG.

Now CAPTAIN BAGG had bowed him to
  A heavy matrimonial yoke :
His wifey had of faults a few—
  She never could resist a joke.

Her chaff at first he meekly bore,
  Till unendurable it grew.
"To stop this persecution sore
  I will consult my friend CAREW.

"And when CAREW's advice I've got,
  Divorce *a mensâ* I shall try."
(A legal separation—not
  A *vinculo conjugii*.)

"O BAINES CAREW, my woe I've kept
  A secret hitherto, you know ; "—
(And BAINES CAREW, ESQUIRE, he wept
  To hear that BAGG had any woe).

Baines Carew, Gentleman

"My case, indeed, is passing sad,
  My wife—whom I considered true—
With brutal conduct drives me mad."
  "I am appalled," said BAINES CAREW.

"What! sound the matrimonial knell
  Of worthy people such as these!
Why was I an attorney?   Well—
  Go on to the *sævitia*, please."

"Domestic bliss has proved my bane,
  A harder case you never heard,
My wife (in other matters sane)
  Pretends that I'm a Dicky Bird!

"She makes me sing, 'Too-whit, too-wee!'
  And stand upon a rounded stick,
And always introduces me
  To every one as 'Pretty Dick'!"

Baines Carew, Gentleman

"Oh dear," said weeping BAINES CAREW,
  "This is the direst case I know"—
"I'm grieved," said BAGG, "at paining you
  To COBB and POLTERTHWAITE I'll go.

"To COBB's cold calculating ear
  My gruesome sorrows I'll impart"—
"No; stop," said BAINES, "I'll dry my tear
  And steel my sympathetic heart!"

"She makes me perch upon a tree,
  Rewarding me with, 'Sweety—nice!'
And threatens to exhibit me
  With four or five performing mice."

"Restrain my tears I wish I could"
  (Said BAINES), "I don't know what to do."
Said CAPTAIN BAGG, "You're very good."
  "Oh, not at all," said BAINES CAREW.

Baines Carew, Gentleman

"She makes me fire a gun," said BAGG;
  "And at a preconcerted word
Climb up a ladder with a flag,
  Like any street-performing bird.

"She places sugar in my way—
  In public places calls me 'Sweet!'—
She gives me groundsel every day,
  And hard canary seed to eat."

"Oh, woe! oh, sad! oh, dire to tell!"
  (Said BAINES), "Be good enough to stop."
And senseless on the floor he fell
  With unpremeditated flop.

Said CAPTAIN BAGG, "Well, really I
  Am grieved to think it pains you so.
I thank you for your sympathy;
  But, hang it—come—I say, you know!"

But BAINES lay flat upon the floor,
  Convulsed with sympathetic sob—
The Captain toddled off next door,
  And gave the case to MR. COBB.

ONLY ROSES

To a garden full of posies
   Cometh one to gather flowers ;
    And he wanders through its bowers
Toying with the wanton roses,
   Who, uprising from their beds,
    Hold on high their shameless heads
With their pretty lips a-pouting,
Never doubting—never doubting
   That for Cytherean posies
    He would gather aught but roses.

In a nest of weeds and nettles,
   Lay a violet, half hidden ;
    Hoping that his glance unbidden
Yet might fall upon her petals.
   Though she lived alone, apart,
    Hope lay nestling at her heart,
But, alas ! the cruel awaking
Set her little heart a-breaking,
   For he gathered for his posies
    Only roses—only roses !

Thomas Winterbottom Hance

THOMAS WINTERBOTTOM HANCE

In all the towns and cities fair
　　On Merry England's broad expanse,
No swordsman ever could compare
　　With Thomas Winterbottom Hance.

The dauntless lad could fairly hew
　　A silken handkerchief in twain,
Divide a leg of mutton, too—
　　And this without unwholesome strain.

On whole half-sheep, with cunning trick,
　　His sabre sometimes he'd employ—
No bar of lead, however thick,
　　Had terrors for the stalwart boy.

Thomas Winterbottom Hance

At Dover daily he'd prepare
    To hew and slash, behind, before—
Which aggravated MONSIEUR PIERRE,
    Who watched him from the Calais shore.

It caused good PIERRE to swear and dance,
    The sight annoyed and vexed him so;
He was the bravest man in France—
    He said so, and he ought to know.

'Regardez, donc, ce cochon gros—
    Ce polisson!　Oh, sacré bleu!
Son sabre, son plomb, et ses gigots!
    Comme cela m'ennuye, enfin, mon Dieu!

Thomas Winterbottom Hance

"Il sait que les foulards de soie
  Give no retaliating whack—
Les gigots morts n'ont pas de quoi—
  Le plomb don't ever hit you back."

But every day the zealous lad
  Cut lead and mutton more and more;
And every day, poor PIERRE, half mad,
  Shrieked loud defiance from his shore.

HANCE had a mother, poor and old,
  A simple, harmless village dame,
Who crowed and clapped as people told
  Of WINTERBOTTOM's rising fame.

She said, " I'll be upon the spot
  To see my TOMMY's sabre-play";
And so she left her leafy cot,
  And walked to Dover in a day.

PIERRE had a doting mother, who
  Had heard of his defiant rage:
His ma was nearly eighty-two,
  And rather dressy for her age.

At HANCE's doings every morn,
  With sheer delight *his* mother cried;
And MONSIEUR PIERRE's contemptuous scorn
  Filled *his* mamma with proper pride.

But HANCE's powers began to fail—
  His constitution was not strong—
And PIERRE, who once was stout and hale,
  Grew thin from shouting all day long.

Thomas Winterbottom Hance

Their mothers saw them pale and wan,
    Maternal anguish tore each breast,
And so they met to find a plan
    To set their offsprings' minds at rest.

Said Mrs. Hance, "Of course I shrinks
    From bloodshed, ma'am, as you're aware,
But still they'd better meet, I thinks."
    "Assurément!" said Madame Pierre.

A sunny spot in sunny France
    Was hit upon for this affair;
The ground was picked by Mrs. Hance,
    The stakes were pitched by Madame Pierre.

Said Mrs. H., "Your work you see—
    Go in, my noble boy, and win."
"En garde, mon fils!" said Madame P.
    "Allons!" "Go on!" "En garde!" "Begin!"

Thomas Winterbottom Hance

Loud sneered the doughty man of France,
  "Ho! ho! Ho! ho! Ha! ha! Ha! ha!"
"The French for 'Pish!'" said THOMAS HANCE.
  Said PIERRE, "L'Anglais, Monsieur, pour 'bah!'"

Said MRS. H., "Come, one! two! three!—
  We're sittin' here to see all fair";
"C'est magnifique!" said MADAME P.,
  "Mais, parbleu! ce n'est pas la guerre!"

"Je scorn un foe si lâche que vous,"
  Said PIERRE, the doughty son of France.
"I fight not coward foe like you!"
  Said our undaunted TOMMY HANCE.

"The French for 'Pooh!'" our TOMMY cried.
  "L'Anglais pour 'Va!'" the Frenchman crowed
And so, with undiminished pride,
  Each went on his respective road.

THE ROVER'S APOLOGY

OH, gentlemen, listen, I pray ;
  Though I own that my heart has been ranging,
Of nature the laws I obey,
  For nature is constantly changing.
The moon in her phases is found,
  The time and the wind and the weather,
The months in succession come round,
  And you don't find two Mondays together.
    Consider the moral, I pray,
      Nor bring a young fellow to sorrow,
    Who loves this young lady to-day,
      And loves that young lady to-morrow !

You cannot eat breakfast all day.
  Nor is it the act of a sinner,
When breakfast is taken away,
  To turn your attention to dinner ;

The Rover's Apology

And it's not in the range of belief
    That you could hold him as a glutton,
Who, when he is tired of beef,
    Determines to tackle the mutton.
      But this I am ready to say,
        If it will diminish their sorrow,
    I'll marry this lady to-day,
      And I'll marry that lady to-morrow!

A DISCONTENTED SUGAR BROKER

A GENTLEMAN of City fame
  Now claims your kind attention;
West India broking was his game,
  His name I shall not mention;
    No one of finely pointed sense
    Would violate a confidence,
      And shall *I* go
      And do it? No.
  His name I shall not mention.

He had a trusty wife and true,
  And very cosy quarters,
A manager, a boy or two,
  Six clerks, and seven porters.
    A broker must be doing well
    (As any lunatic can tell)
      Who can employ
      An active boy,
  Six clerks, and seven porters.

A Discontented Sugar Broker

His knocker advertised no dun,
  No losses made him sulky,
He had one sorrow—only one—
  He was extremely bulky.
    A man must be, I beg to state,
    Exceptionally fortunate
        Who owns his chief
        And only grief
Is being very bulky.

"This load," he'd say, "I cannot bear,
  I'm nineteen stone or twenty!
Henceforward I'll go in for air
  And exercise in plenty."
    Most people think that, should it come,
    They can reduce a bulging tum
        To measures fair
        By taking air
And exercise in plenty.

In every weather, every day,
  Dry, muddy, wet, or gritty,
He took to dancing all the way
  From Brompton to the City.
    You do not often get the chance
    Of seeing sugar-brokers dance
        From their abode
        In Fulham Road
Through Brompton to the City.

He braved the gay and guileless laugh
  Of children with their nusses,
The loud uneducated chaff
  Of clerks on omnibuses.

A Discontented Sugar Broker

Against all minor things that rack
A nicely balanced mind, I'll back
The noisy chaff
And ill-bred laugh
Of clerks on omnibuses.

His friends, who heard his money chink,
And saw the house he rented,
And knew his wife, could never think
What made him discontented.
It never struck their simple minds
That fads are of eccentric kinds,
Nor would they own
That fat alone
Could make one discontented.

"Your riches know no kind of pause,
Your trade is fast advancing,
You dance—but not for joy, because
You weep as you are dancing.

A Discontented Sugar Broker

To dance implies that man is glad,
To weep implies that man is sad.
But here are you
Who do the two—
You weep as you are dancing!"

His mania soon got noised about
And into all the papers—
His size increased beyond a doubt
For all his reckless capers:

It may seem singular to you,
But all his friends admit it true—
The more he found
His figure round,
The more he cut his capers.

His bulk increased—no matter that—
He tried the more to toss it—
He never spoke of it as "fat"
But "adipose deposit."
Upon my word, it seems to me
Unpardonable vanity
(And worse than that)
To call your fat
An "adipose deposit."

A Discontented Sugar Broker

At length his brawny knees gave way,
   And on the carpet sinking,
Upon his shapeless back he lay
   And kicked away like winking.
     Instead of seeing in his state
     The finger of unswerving Fate,
      He laboured still
      To work his will,
   And kicked away like winking.

His friends, disgusted with him now,
   Away in silence wended—
I hardly like to tell you how
   This dreadful story ended.
     The shocking sequel to impart,
     I must employ the limner's art—
      If you would know,
      This sketch will show
How his exertions ended.

MORAL

I hate to preach—I hate to prate—
   I'm no fanatic croaker,
But learn contentment from the fate
   Of this West India broker.
     He'd everything a man of taste
     Could ever want, except a waist :
      And discontent
      His size anent,
And bootless perseverance blind,
Completely wrecked the peace of mind
   Of this West India broker.

AN APPEAL

OH ! is there not one maiden breast
    Which does not feel the moral beauty
Of making worldly interest
    Subordinate to sense of duty ?
Who would not give up willingly
    All matrimonial ambition
To rescue such a one as I
    From his unfortunate position ?

Oh, is there not one maiden here,
    Whose homely face and bad complexion
Have caused all hopes to disappear
    Of ever winning man's affection ?
To such a one, if such there be,
    I swear by heaven's arch above you,
If you will cast your eyes on me,—
    However plain you be—I'll love you !

THE PANTOMIME "SUPER" TO HIS MASK

VAST, empty shell!
Impertinent, preposterous abortion:
With vacant stare,
And ragged hair,
And every feature out of all proportion!
Embodiment of echoing inanity,
Excellent type of simpering insanity,
Unwieldy, clumsy nightmare of humanity,
I ring thy knell!

To-night thou diest,
Beast that destroy'st my heaven-born identity!
Twelve weeks of nights
Before the lights,
Swamped in thine own preposterous nonentity,
I've been ill-treated, cursed, and thrashed diurnally,
Credited for the smile you wear externally—
I feel disposed to smash thy face, infernally,
As there thou liest!

The Pantomime "Super" to his Mask .

I've been thy brain :
I've been the brain that lit thy dull concavity !
    The human race
    Invest *my* face
With thine expression of unchecked depravity :
Invested with a ghastly reciprocity,
I've been responsible for thy monstrosity,
I, for thy wanton, blundering ferocity—
    But not again !

    'Tis time to toll
Thy knell, and that of follies pantomimical :
    A twelve weeks' run,
    And thou hast done
All thou canst do to make thyself inimical.
Adieu, embodiment of all inanity !
Excellent type of simpering insanity !
Unwieldy, clumsy nightmare of humanity !
    Freed is thy soul !

    (*The Mask respondeth.*)

    Oh ! master mine,
Look thou within thee, ere again ill-using me.
    Art thou aware
    Of nothing there
Which might abuse thee, as thou art abusing me ?
A brain that mourns *thine* unredeemed rascality ?
A soul that weeps at *thy* threadbare morality ?
Both grieving that *their* individuality
    Is merged in thine ?

THE REWARD OF MERIT

DR. BELVILLE was regarded as the CRICHTON of his age:
His tragedies were reckoned much too thoughtful for
 the stage;
His poems held a noble rank, although it's very true
That, being very proper, they were read by very few.
He was a famous Painter, too, and shone upon the "line,"
And even MR. RUSKIN came and worshipped at his shrine;
But, alas, the school he followed was heroically high—
The kind of Art men rave about, but very seldom buy;
   And everybody said
    "How can he be repaid—
This very great—this very good—this very gifted man?"
But nobody could hit upon a practicable plan!

The Reward of Merit

He was a great Inventor, and discovered, all alone,
A plan for making everybody's fortune but his own ;
For, in business, an Inventor's little better than a fool,
And my highly-gifted friend was no exception to the rule.
His poems—people read them in the Quarterly Reviews—
His pictures—they engraved them in the *Illustrated News*—
His inventions—they, perhaps, might have enriched him
    by degrees,
But all his little income went in Patent Office fees ;
        And everybody said
        "How can he be repaid—
This very great—this very good—this very gifted man ? "
But nobody could hit upon a practicable plan !

At last the point was given up in absolute despair,
When a distant cousin died, and he became a millionaire,
With a county seat in Parliament, a moor or two of grouse,
And a taste for making inconvenient speeches in the House !
Then it flashed upon Britannia that the fittest of rewards
Was, to take him from the Commons and to put him in
    the Lords !
And who so fit to sit in it, deny it if you can,
As this very great—this very good—this very gifted man ?
       (Though I'm more than half afraid
       That it sometimes may be said
That we never should have revelled in that source of
    proper pride,
However great his merits—if his cousin hadn't died !)

THE GHOST, THE GALLANT, THE GAEL,
AND THE GOBLIN

O'ER unreclaimed suburban clay
    Some years ago were hobblin',
An elderly ghost of easy ways,
    And an influential goblin.
The ghost was a sombre spectral shape,
    A fine old five-act fogy,
The goblin imp, a lithe young ape,
    A fine low-comedy bogy.

And as they exercised their joints,
    Promoting quick digestion,
They talked on several curious points,
    And raised this pregnant question :
"Which of us two is Number One—
    The ghostie, or the goblin ? "
And o'er the point they raised in fun
    They fairly fell a-squabblin'.

The Ghost, the Gallant, the Gael, the Goblin

They'd barely speak, and each, in fine,
   Grew more and more reflective,
Each thought his own particular line
   By far the more effective.
At length they settled some one should
   By each of them be haunted,
And so arranged that either could
   Exert his prowess vaunted.

" The Quaint against the Statuesque "—
   By competition lawful—
The goblin backed the Quaint Grotesque,
   The ghost the Grandly Awful.
" Now," said the goblin, " here's my plan—
   In attitude commanding,
I see a stalwart Englishman
   By yonder tailor's standing.

" The very fittest man on earth
   My influence to try on—
Of gentle, p'raps of noble birth,
   And dauntless as a lion !
Now wrap yourself within your shroud—
   Remain in easy hearing—
Observe—you'll hear him scream aloud
   When I begin appearing ! "

The imp with yell unearthly—wild—
   Threw off his dark enclosure :
His dauntless victim looked and smiled
   With singular composure.
For hours he tried to daunt the youth,
   For days, indeed, but vainly—
The stripling smiled !—to tell the truth,
   The stripling smiled inanely.

The Ghost, the Gallant, the Gael, the Goblin

For weeks the goblin weird and wild,
   That noble stripling haunted;
For weeks the stripling stood and smiled
   Unmoved and all undaunted.
The sombre ghost exclaimed, "Your plan
   Has failed you, goblin, plainly:
Now watch yon hardy Hieland man,
   So stalwart and ungainly.

"These are the men who chase the roe,
   Whose footsteps never falter,
Who bring with them where'er they go,
   A smack of old SIR WALTER.
Of such as he, the men sublime
   Who lead their troops victorious,
Whose deeds go down to after-time,
   Enshrined in annals glorious!

The Ghost, the Gallant, the Gael, the Goblin

"Of such as he the bard has said
  'Hech thrawfu' raltie rawkie!
Wi' thecht ta' croonie clapperhead
  And fash' wi' unco pawkie!'
He'll faint away when I appear
  Upon his native heather;
Or p'raps he'll only scream with fear,
  Or p'raps the two together."

The spectre showed himself, alone,
  To do his ghostly battling,
With curdling groan and dismal moan
  And lots of chains a-rattling!
But no—the chiel's stout Gaelic stuff
  Withstood all ghostly harrying,
His fingers closed upon the snuff
  Which upwards he was carrying.

The Ghost, the Gallant, the Gael, the Goblin

For days that ghost declined to stir,
    A foggy, shapeless giant—
For weeks that splendid officer
    Stared back again defiant!
Just as the Englishman returned
    The goblin's vulgar staring,
Just so the Scotchman boldly spurned
    The ghost's unmannered scaring.

For several years the ghostly twain
    These Britons bold have haunted,
But all their efforts are in vain—
    Their victims stand undaunted.
Unto this day the imp and ghost
    (Whose powers the imp derided)
Stand each at his allotted post—
    The bet is undecided.

THE MAGNET AND THE CHURN

A MAGNET hung in a hardware shop,
And all around was a loving crop
Of scissors and needles, nails and knives,
Offering love for all their lives ;
But for iron the Magnet felt no whim,
Though he charmed iron, it charmed not him,
From needles and nails and knives he'd turn,
For he'd set his love on a Silver Churn !
          His most æsthetic,
          Very magnetic
     Fancy took this turn—
          "If I can wheedle
          A knife or needle,
     Why not a Silver Churn ?"

The Magnet and the Churn

And Iron and Steel expressed surprise,
The needles opened their well-drilled eyes,
The pen-knives felt "shut up," no doubt,
The scissors declared themselves "cut out,"
The kettles they boiled with rage, 'tis said,
While every nail went off its head,
And hither and thither began to roam,
Till a hammer came up—and drove it home.
    While this magnetic
    Peripatetic
Lover he lived to learn,
    By no endeavour,
    Can Magnet ever
Attract a Silver Churn!

King Borria Bungalee Boo

KING BORRIA BUNGALEE BOO

King Borria Bungalee Boo
  Was a man-eating African swell;
His sigh was a hullaballoo,
  His whisper a horrible yell—
  A horrible, horrible yell!

Four subjects, and all of them male,
  To Borria doubled the knee,
They were once on a far larger scale,
  But he'd eaten the balance, you see
  ("Scale" and "balance" is punning, you see).

King Borria Bungalee Boo

There was haughty PISH-TUSH-POOH-BAH,
   There was lumbering DOODLE-DUM-DEH.
Despairing ALACK-A-DEY-AH,
   And good little TOOTLE-TUM-TEH–
   Exemplary TOOTLE-TUM-TEH.

One day there was grief in the crew,
   For they hadn't a morsel of meat,
And BORRIA BUNGALEE BOO
   Was dying for something to eat—
   "Come, provide me with something to eat!

"ALACK-A-DEY, famished I feel;
   Oh, good little TOOTLE-TUM-TEH,
Where on earth shall I look for a meal?
   For I haven't had dinner to-day!—
   Not a morsel of dinner to-day!

"Dear TOOTLE-TUM, what shall we do?
   Come, get us a meal, or in truth,
If you don't we shall have to eat you,
   Oh, adorable friend of our youth!
   Thou beloved little friend of our youth!"

King Borria Bungalee Boo

And he answered, "Oh, BUNGALEE BOO,
 For a moment I hope you will wait,—
TIPPY-WIPPITY TOL-THE-ROL-LOO
 Is the Queen of a neighbouring state—
 A remarkably neighbouring state.

"TIPPY-WIPPITY TOL-THE-ROL-LOO,
 She would pickle deliciously cold—
And her four pretty Amazons, too,
 Are enticing, and not very old—
 Twenty-seven is not very old.

" There is neat little TITTY-FOL-LEH,
 There is rollicking TRAL-THE-RAL-LAH,
There is jocular WAGGETY-WEH,
 There is musical DOH-REH-MI-FAH—
 There's the nightingale DOH-REH-MI-FAH ! "

So the forces of BUNGALEE BOO
 Marched forth in a terrible row,
And the ladies who fought for QUEEN LOO
 Prepared to encounter the foe—
 This dreadful insatiate foe !

King Borria Bungalee Boo

But they sharpened no weapons at all,
    And they poisoned no arrows—not they;
They made ready to conquer or fall
    In a totally different way—
    A perfectly different way.

With a crimson and pearly-white dye
    They endeavoured to make themselves fair ;
With black they encircled each eye,
    And with yellow they painted their hair.
    (It was wool, but they thought it was hair.)

The warriors met in the field :
    And the men of KING BORRIA said,
"Amazonians, immediately yield !"
    And their arrows they drew to the head—
    Yes, drew them right up to the head.

But jocular WAGGETY-WEH
    Ogled DOODLE-DUM-DEH (which was wrong),
And neat little TITTY-FOL-LEH
    Said, "TOOTLE-TUM, you go along !
    You naughty old dear, go along !"

And rollicking TRAL-THE-RAL-LAH
    Tapped ALACK-A-DEY-AH with her fan ;
And musical DOH-REH-MI-FAH
    Said, "Pish, go away, you bad man !
    Go away, you delightful young man !"

And the Amazons simpered and sighed,
    And they ogled, and giggled, and flushed,
And they opened their pretty eyes wide,
    And they chuckled, and flirted, and blushed
    (At least, if they could, they'd have blushed).

King Borria Bungalee Boo

But haughty PISH-TUSH-POOH-BAH
  Said, " ALACK-A-DEY, what does this mean ? "
And despairing ALACK-A-DEY-AH
  Said, " They think us uncommonly green—
  Ha ! ha ! most uncommonly green ! "

Even blundering DOODLE-DUM-DEH
  Was insensible quite to their leers,
And said good little TOOTLE-TUM-TEH,
  " It's your blood that we're wanting, my dears—
  We have come for our dinners, my dears ! "

And the Queen of the Amazons fell
  To BORRIA BUNGALEE BOO,—
In a mouthful he gulped, with a yell,
  TIPPY-WIPPITY TOL-THE-ROL-LOO—
  The pretty QUEEN 'TOL-THE-ROL-LOO.

King Borria Bungalee Boo

And neat little TITTY-FOL-LEH
　　Was eaten by PISH-POOH-BAH,
And light-hearted WAGGETY-WEH
　　By dismal ALACK-A-DEY-AH—
　　Despairing ALACK-A-DEY-AH.

And rollicking TRAL-THE-RAL-LAH
　　Was eaten by DOODLE-DUM-DEH,
And musical DOH-REH-MI-FAH
　　By good little TOOTLE-TUM-TEH—
　　Exemplary TOOTLE-TUM-TEH.

THE FAMILY FOOL

OH! a private buffoon is a light-hearted loon,
　　If you listen to popular rumour;
From morning to night he's so joyous and bright,
　　And he bubbles with wit and good humour!
He's so quaint and so terse, both in prose and in verse;
　　Yet though people forgive his transgression,
There are one or two rules that all Family Fools
　　Must observe, if they love their profession.
　　　　　There are one or two rules,
　　　　　　Half-a-dozen, maybe,
　　　　　That all family fools,
　　　　　　Of whatever degree,
　　　Must observe if they love their profession.

If you wish to succeed as a jester, you'll need
　　To consider each person's auricular:
What is all right for B would quite scandalise C
　　(For C is so very particular);

The Family Fool

And D may be dull, and E's very thick skull
  Is as empty of brains as a ladle ;
While F is F sharp, and will cry with a carp,
    That he's known your best joke from his cradle !
      When your humour they flout,
        You can't let yourself go ;
      And it *does* put you out
        When a person says, " Oh !
    I have known that old joke from my cradle !"

If your master is surly, from getting up early
  (And tempers are short in the morning),
An inopportune joke is enough to provoke
  Him to give you, at once, a month's warning.
Then if you refrain, he is at you again,
  For he likes to get value for money :
He'll ask then and there, with an insolent stare,
  " If you know that you're paid to be funny ? "
      It adds to the tasks
        Of a merryman's place,
      When your principal asks,
        With a scowl on his face,
    If you know that you're paid to be funny ?

Comes a Bishop, maybe, or a solemn D.D.—
  Oh, beware of his anger provoking !
Better not pull his hair—don't stick pins in his chair ;
  He won't understand practical joking.
If the jests that you crack have an orthodox smack,
  You may get a bland smile from these sages ;
But should it, by chance, be imported from France,
  Half-a-crown is stopped out of your wages !
      It's a general rule,
        Though your zeal it may quench,
      If the Family Fool
        Makes a joke that's *too* French,
    Half-a-crown is stopped out of his wages !

The Family Fool

Though your head it may rack with a bilious attack,
  And your senses with toothache you're losing,
And you're mopy and flat—they don't fine you for that
  If you're properly quaint and amusing!
Though your wife ran away with a soldier that day,
  And took with her your trifle of money;
Bless your heart, they don't mind—they're exceedingly
    kind—
  They don't blame you—as long as you're funny!
      It's a comfort to feel
        If your partner should flit,
      Though *you* suffer a deal,
        They don't mind it a bit—
  They don't blame you—so long as you're funny!

THE PERIWINKLE GIRL

I'VE often thought that headstrong youths
    Of decent education,
Determine all-important truths,
    With strange precipitation.

The ever-ready victims they,
    Of logical illusions,
And in a self-assertive way
    They jump at strange conclusions.

Now take my case: Ere sorrow could
    My ample forehead wrinkle,
I had determined that I should
    Not care to be a winkle.

The Periwinkle Girl

"A winkle," I would oft advance
  With readiness provoking,
"Can seldom flirt, and never dance,
  Or soothe his mind by smoking."

In short, I spurned the shelly joy,
  And spoke with strange decision—
Men pointed to me as a boy
  Who held them in derision.

But I was young—too young, by far—
  Or I had been more wary,
I knew not then that winkles are
  The stock-in-trade of MARY.

I had not watched her sunlight blithe
  As o'er their shells it dances—
I've seen those winkles almost writhe
  Beneath her beaming glances.

Of slighting all the winkly brood
  I surely had been chary,
If I had known they formed the food
  And stock-in-trade of MARY.

Both high and low and great and small
  Fell prostrate at her tootsies,
They all were noblemen, and all
  Had balances at COUTTS'S.

Dukes with the lovely maiden dealt,
  DUKE BAILEY and DUKE HUMPHY,
Who ate her winkles till they felt
  Exceedingly uncomfy.

The Periwinkle Girl

DUKE BAILEY greatest wealth computes,
  And sticks, they say, at no-thing,
He wears a pair of golden boots
  And silver underclothing.

DUKE HUMPHY, as I understand,
  Though mentally acuter,
His boots are only silver, and
  His underclothing pewter.

A third adorer had the girl,
  A man of lowly station—
A miserable grov'ling Earl
  Besought her approbation.

This humble cad she did refuse
  With much contempt and loathing,
He wore a pair of leather shoes
  And cambric underclothing!

The Periwinkle Girl

"Ha! ha!" she cried. "Upon my word!
   Well, really—come, I never!
Oh, go along, it's too absurd!
   My goodness! Did you ever?

"Two Dukes would Mary make a bride,
   And from her foes defend her"—
"Well, not exactly that," they cried,
   "We offer guilty splendour.

"We do not offer marriage rite,
   So please dismiss the notion!"
"Oh dear," said she, "that alters quite
   The state of my emotion."

The Earl he up and says, says he,
   "Dismiss them to their orgies,
For I am game to marry thee
   Quite reg'lar at St. George's."

(He'd had, it happily befell,
   A decent education,
His views would have befitted well
   A far superior station.)

His sterling worth had worked a cure,
   She never heard him grumble;
She saw his soul was good and pure,
   Although his rank was humble.

The Periwinkle Girl

Her views of earldoms and their lot,
All underwent expansion—
Come, Virtue in an earldom's cot!
Go, Vice in ducal mansion!

SANS SOUCI

I cannot tell what this love may be
That cometh to all but not to me.
It cannot be kind as they'd imply,
Or why do these gentle ladies sigh?
It cannot be joy and rapture deep,
Or why do these gentle ladies weep?
It cannot be blissful, as 'tis said,
Or why are their eyes so wondrous red?

Sans Souci

If love is a thorn, they show no wit
Who foolishly hug and foster it.
If love is a weed, how simple they
Who gather and gather it, day by day!
If love is a nettle that makes you smart,
Why do you wear it next your heart?
And if it be neither of these, say I,
Why do you sit and sob and sigh?

THOMSON GREEN AND HARRIET HALE

(To be sung to the Air of " An 'Orrible Tale.")

Oh list to this incredible tale
Of THOMSON GREEN and HARRIET HALE;
Its truth in one remark you'll sum—
"Twaddle twaddle twaddle twaddle twaddle twaddle
twum!"

Oh, THOMSON GREEN was an auctioneer,
And made three hundred pounds a year;
And HARRIET HALE, most strange to say,
Gave pianoforte lessons at a sovereign a day.

Oh, THOMSON GREEN, I may remark,
Met HARRIET HALE in Regent's Park,
Where he, in a casual kind of way,
Spoke of the extraordinary beauty of the day.

Thomson Green and Harriet Hale

They met again, and strange, though true,
He courted her for a month or two,
Then to her pa he said, says he,
"Old man, I love your daughter and your daughter
worships me!"

Their names were regularly banned,
The wedding day was settled, and
I've ascertained by dint of search
They were married on the quiet at St. Mary Abbot's
Church.

Oh, list to this incredible tale
Of THOMSON GREEN and HARRIET HALE,
Its truth in one remark you'll sum—
"Twaddle twaddle twaddle twaddle twaddle twaddle
twum!"

That very self-same afternoon
They started on their honeymoon,
And (oh, astonishment!) took flight
To a pretty little cottage close to Shanklin, Isle of Wight.

But now—you'll doubt my word, I know—
In a month they both returned, and lo!
Astounding fact! this happy pair
Took a gentlemanly residence in Canonbury Square!

They led a weird and reckless life,
They dined each day, this man and wife
(Pray disbelieve it, if you please),
On a joint of meat, a pudding, and a little bit of cheese.

In time came those maternal joys
Which take the form of girls or boys,
And strange to say of each they'd one—
A tiddy-iddy daughter, and a tiddy-iddy son!

Thomson Green and Harriet Hale

Oh, list to this incredible tale
Of THOMSON GREEN and HARRIET HALE,
Its truth in one remark you'll sum—
"Twaddle twaddle twaddle twaddle twaddle twaddle
twum!"

My name for truth is gone, I fear,
But, monstrous as it may appear,
They let their drawing-room one day
To an eligible person in the cotton-broking way.

Whenever THOMSON GREEN fell sick
His wife called in a doctor, quick,
From whom some words like these would come—
Fiat mist. sumendum haustus, in a *cochleyareum*.

For thirty years this curious pair
Hung out in Canonbury Square,
And somehow, wonderful to say,
They loved each other dearly in a quiet sort of way.

Thomson Green and Harriet Hale

Well, THOMSON GREEN fell ill and died;
For just a year his widow cried,
    And then her heart she gave away
To the eligible lodger in the cotton-broking way.

Oh, list to this incredible tale
Of THOMSON GREEN and HARRIET HALE,
    Its truth in one remark you'll sum—
"Twaddle twaddle twaddle twaddle twaddle twaddle
    twum!"

A RECIPE

TAKE a pair of sparkling eyes,
　　Hidden, ever and anon,
　　　　In a merciful eclipse—
Do not heed their mild surprise—
　　Having passed the Rubicon.
　　　　Take a pair of rosy lips;
Take a figure trimly planned—
　　Such as admiration whets
　　　　(Be particular in this);
Take a tender little hand,
　　Fringed with dainty fingerettes,
　　　　Press it—in parenthesis;—
Take all these, you lucky man—
Take and keep them, if you can.

Take a pretty little cot—
　　Quite a miniature affair—
　　　　Hung about with trellised vine,
Furnish it upon the spot
　　With the treasures rich and rare
　　　　I've endeavoured to define.
Live to love and love to live—
　　You will ripen at your ease,
　　　　Growing on the sunny side—
Fate has nothing more to give.
　　You're a dainty man to please
　　　　If you are not satisfied.
Take my counsel, happy man:
Act upon it, if you can!

Bab

BOB POLTER

Bob Polter was a navvy, and
   His hands were coarse, and dirty too,
His homely face was rough and tanned,
   His time of life was thirty-two.

He lived among a working clan
   (A wife he hadn't got at all),
A decent, steady, sober man——
   No saint, however—not at all

Bob Polter

He smoked, but in a modest way,
   Because he thought he needed it :
He drank a pot of beer a day,
   And sometimes he exceeded it.

At times he'd pass with other men
   A loud convivial night or two,
With, very likely, now and then,
   On Saturdays, a fight or two.

But still he was a sober soul,
   A labour-never-shrinking man,
Who paid his way—upon the whole,
   A decent English working-man.

One day, when at the Nelson's Head
   (For which he may be blamed of you),
A holy man appeared and said,
   "Oh, ROBERT, I'm ashamed of you."

Bob Polter

He laid his hand on ROBERT'S beer
    Before he could drink up any,
And on the floor, with sigh and tear,
    He poured the pot of "thruppenny."

"Oh, ROBERT, at this very bar,
    A truth you'll be discovering,
A good and evil genius are
    Around your noddle hovering.

"They both are here to bid you shun
    The other one's society,
For Total Abstinence is one,
    The other, Inebriety."

He waved his hand—a vapour came—
    A wizard, POLTER reckoned him:
A bogy rose and called his name,
    And with his finger beckoned him.

The monster's salient points to sum,
    His breath was hot as cautery;
His glowing nose suggested rum;
    His eyes were gin-and-watery.

His dress was torn—for dregs of ale
    And slops of gin had rusted it;
His pimpled face was wan and pale,
    Where filth had not encrusted it.

"Come, POLTER," said the fiend, "begin
    And keep the bowl a-flowing on—
A working-man needs pints of gin
    To keep his clockwork going on."

Bob Polter

Bob shuddered: "Ah, you've made a miss,
    If you take me for one of you—
You filthy brute, get out of this—
    Bob Polter don't want none of you."

The demon gave a drunken shriek,
    And crept away in stealthiness,
And lo, instead, a person sleek
    Who seemed to burst with healthiness.

"In me, as your adviser hints,
    Of Abstinence you've got a type—
Of Mr. Tweedie's pretty prints
    I am the happy prototype.

Bob Polter

"If you abjure the social toast,
    And pipes, and such frivolities,
You possibly some day may boast
    My prepossessing qualities!"

Bob rubbed his eyes, and made 'em blink,
    "You almost make me tremble, you!
If I abjure fermented drink,
    Shall I, indeed, resemble you?

"And will my whiskers curl so tight?
    My cheeks grow smug and muttony?
My face become so pink and white?
    My coat so blue and buttony?

"Will trousers, such as yours, array
    Extremities inferior?
Will chubbiness assert its sway
    All over my exterior?

"In this, my unenlightened state,
    To work in heavy boots I comes—
Will pumps henceforward decorate
    My tiddle toddle tootsicums?

"And shall I get so plump and fresh,
    And look no longer seedily?
My skin will henceforth fit my flesh
    So tightly and so TWEEDIE-ly?"

The phantom said, "You'll have all this,
    You'll have no kind of huffiness,
Your life will be one chubby bliss,
    One long unruffled puffiness!"

Bob Polter

"Be off," said irritated Bob,
  "Why come you here to bother one?
You pharisaical old snob,
  You're wuss, almost, than t'other one!

"I takes my pipe—I takes my pot,
  And drunk I'm never seen to be
I'm no teetotaller or sot,
  And as I am I mean to be!"

THE MERRYMAN AND HIS MAID

HE.   I HAVE a song to sing, O!
SHE.   Sing me your song, O!
HE.   It is sung to the moon
               By a love-lorn loon,
        Who fled from the mocking throng, O!
It's the song of a merryman, moping mum,
Whose soul was sad, whose glance was glum,
Who sipped no sup, and who craved no crumb,
       As he sighed for the love of a ladye.
           Heighdy! heighdy!
            Misery me—lackadaydee!
He sipped no sup, and he craved no crumb,
       As he sighed for the love of a ladye!

SHE.   I have a song to sing, O!
HE.   Sing me your song, O!
SHE.   It is sung with the ring
              Of the song maids sing
       Who love with a love life-long, O!

The Merryman and his Maid

It's the song of a merrymaid, peerly proud,
Who loved a lord, and who laughed aloud
At the moan of the merryman, moping mum,
Whose soul was sore, whose glance was glum,
Who sipped no sup, and who craved no crumb,
    As he sighed for the love of a ladye !
        Heighdy ! heighdy !
        Misery me—lackadaydee !
He sipped no sup, and he craved no crumb,
    As he sighed for the love of a ladye !

HE.   I have a song to sing, O !
SHE.   Sing me your song, O !
HE.   It is sung to the knell
        Of a churchyard bell,
    And a doleful dirge, ding dong, O !
It's a song of a popinjay, bravely born,
Who turned up his noble nose with scorn
At the humble merrymaid, peerly proud,
Who loved that lord, and who laughed aloud
At the moan of the merryman, moping mum,
Whose soul was sad, whose glance was glum,
Who sipped no sup, and who craved no crumb,
    As he sighed for the love of a ladye !
        Heighdy ! heighdy !
        Misery me—lackadaydee !
He sipped no sup, and he craved no crumb,
    As he sighed for the love of a ladye !

SHE.   I have a song to sing, O !
HE.   Sing me your song, O !
SHE.   It is sung with a sigh
        And a tear in the eye,
    For it tells of a righted wrong, O !
It's a song of a merrymaid, once so gay,
Who turned on her heel and tripped away

The Merryman and his Maid

From the peacock popinjay, bravely born,
Who turned up his noble nose with scorn
At the humble heart that he did not prize;
And it tells how she begged, with downcast eyes,
For the love of a merryman, moping mum,
Whose soul was sad, whose glance was glum,
Who sipped no sup, and who craved no crumb,
    As he sighed for the love of a ladye!

Bотн.   Heighdy! heighdy!
          Misery me—lackadaydee!
His pains were o'er, and he sighed no more
    For he lived in the love of a ladye!

ELLEN M'JONES ABERDEEN

MACPHAIRSON CLONGLOCKETTY ANGUS
M'CLAN
Was the son of an elderly labouring man,
You've guessed him a Scotchman, shrewd reader, at sight,
And p'raps altogether, shrewd reader, you're right.

From the bonnie blue Forth to the hills of Deeside,
Round by Dingwall and Wrath to the mouth of the Clyde,
There wasn't a child or a woman or man
Who could pipe with CLONGLOCKETTY ANGUS M'CLAN.

Ellen M'Jones Aberdeen

No other could wake such detestable groans,
With reed and with chaunter—with bag and with drones:
All day and all night he delighted the chiels
With sniggering pibrochs and jiggety reels.

He'd clamber a mountain and squat on the ground,
And the neighbouring maidens would gather around
To list to his pipes and to gaze in his e'en,
Especially ELLEN M'JONES ABERDEEN.

All loved their M'CLAN, save a Sassenach brute,
Who came to the Highlands to fish and to shoot ;
He dressed himself up in a Highlander way,
Though his name it was PATTISON CORBY TORBAY.

TORBAY had incurred a good deal of expense
To make him a Scotchman in every sense ;
But this is a matter, you'll readily own,
That isn't a question of tailors alone.

A Sassenach chief may be bonily built,
He may purchase a sporran, a bonnet, and kilt ;
Stick a skean in his hose—wear an acre of stripes—
But he cannot assume an affection for pipes.

CLONGLOCKETTY'S pipings all night and all day
Quite frenzied poor PATTISON CORBY TORBAY ;
The girls were amused at his singular spleen,
Especially ELLEN M'JONES ABERDEEN.

Ellen M'Jones Aberdeen

" MACPHAIRSON CLONGLOCKETTY ANGUS, my lad,
With pibrochs and reels you are driving me mad ;
If you really must play on that cursed affair,
My goodness ! play something resembling an air."

Boiled over the blood of MACPHAIRSON M'CLAN—
The clan of Clonglocketty rose as one man ;
For all were enraged at the insult, I ween—
Especially ELLEN M'JONES ABERDEEN.

" Let's show," said M'CLAN, " to this Sassenach loon
That the bagpipes can play him a regular tune.
Let's see," said M'CLAN, as he thoughtfully sat,
" '*In My Cottage*' is easy—I'll practise at that."

Ellen M'Jones Aberdeen

He blew at his " Cottage," and blew with a will,
For a year, seven months, and a fortnight, until
(You'll hardly believe it) M'CLAN, I declare,
Elicited something resembling an air.

It was wild—it was fitful—as wild as the breeze—
It wandered about into several keys;
It was jerky, spasmodic, and harsh, I'm aware,
But still it distinctly suggested an air.

The Sassenach screamed, and the Sassenach danced,
He shrieked in his agony—bellowed and pranced;
And the maidens who gathered rejoiced at the scene,
Especially ELLEN M'JONES ABERDEEN.

Ellen M'Jones Aberdeen

" Hech gather, hech gather, hech gather around;
And fill a' yer lugs wi' the exquisite sound.
An air frae the bagpipes—beat that if ye can !
Hurrah for CLONGLOCKETTY ANGUS M'CLAN ! "

The fame of his piping spread over the land :
Respectable widows proposed for his hand,
And maidens came flocking to sit on the green—
Especially ELLEN M'JONES ABERDEEN.

One morning the fidgety Sassenach swore
He'd stand it no longer—he drew his claymore,
And (this was, I think, in extremely bad taste),
Divided CLONGLOCKETTY close to the waist.

Oh ! loud were the wailings for ANGUS M'CLAN—
Oh ! deep was the grief for that excellent man—
The maids stood aghast at the horrible scene,
Especially ELLEN M'JONES ABERDEEN.

It sorrowed poor PATTISON CORBY TORBAY
To find them " take on " in this serious way,
He pitied the poor little fluttering birds,
And solaced their souls with the following words :—

"Oh, maidens," said PATTISON, touching his hat,
" Don't snivel, my dears, for a fellow like that ;
Observe, I'm a very superior man,
A much better fellow than ANGUS M'CLAN."

Ellen M'Jones Aberdeen

They smiled when he winked and addressed them as
  " dears,"
And they all of them vowed, as they dried up their tears,
A pleasanter gentleman never was seen—
Especially ELLEN M'JONES ABERDEEN.

THE SUSCEPTIBLE CHANCELLOR

THE law is the true embodiment
Of everything that's excellent.
It has no kind of fault or flaw,
And I, my lords, embody the Law.
The constitutional guardian I
Of pretty young Wards in Chancery,
All very agreeable girls—and none
Is over the age of twenty-one.
    A pleasant occupation for
    A rather susceptible Chancellor!

But though the compliment implied
Inflates me with legitimate pride,
It nevertheless can't be denied
That it has its inconvenient side.
For I'm not so old, and not so plain,
And I'm quite prepared to marry again,

The Susceptible Chancellor

But there'd be the deuce to pay in the Lords
If I fell in love with one of my Wards:
    Which rather tries my temper, for
    I'm *such* a susceptible Chancellor!

And every one who'd marry a Ward
Must come to me for my accord:
So in my court I sit all day,
Giving agreeable girls away,
With one for him—and one for he—
And one for you—and one for ye—
And one for thou—and one for thee—
But never, oh never a one for me!
    Which is exasperating, for
    A highly susceptible Chancellor!

PETER THE WAG

POLICEMAN PETER FORTH I drag
   From his obscure retreat:
He was a merry, genial wag,
   Who loved a mad conceit.
If he were asked the time of day
   By country bumpkins green,
He not unfrequently would say,
   " A quarter past thirteen."

If ever you by word of mouth
   Enquired of MISTER FORTH
The way to somewhere in the South,
   He always sent you North.
With little boys his beat along
   He loved to stop and play;
He loved to send old ladies wrong,
   And teach their feet to stray.

                H

Peter the Wag

He would in frolic moments, when
    Such mischief bent upon,
Take Bishops up as betting men—
    Bid Ministers move on.
Then all the worthy boys he knew
    He regularly licked,
And always collared people who
    Had had their pockets picked.

He was not naturally bad,
    Or viciously inclined,
But from his early youth he had
    A waggish turn of mind.
The Men of London grimly scowled
    With indignation wild ;
The Men of London gruffly growled,
    But PETER calmly smiled.

Against this minion of the Crown
    The swelling murmurs grew—
From Camberwell to Kentish Town—
    From Rotherhithe to Kew.
Still humoured he his wagsome turn,
    And fed in various ways
The coward rage that dared to burn
    But did not dare to blaze.

Still, Retribution has her day
    Although her flight is slow :
One day that Crusher lost his way
    Near Poland Street, Soho.
The haughty youth, too proud to ask,
    To find his way resolved,
And in the tangle of his task
    Got more and more involved.

Peter the Wag

The Men of London, overjoyed,
    Came there to jeer their foe——
And flocking crowds completely cloyed
    The mazes of Soho.
The news, on telegraphic wires,
    Sped swiftly o'er the lea——
Excursion trains from distant shires
    Brought myriads to see.

For weeks he trod his self-made beats
    Through Newport, Gerrard, Bear,
Greek, Rupert, Frith, Dean, Poland Streets,
    And into Golden Square:
But all, alas, in vain, for when
    He tried to learn the way
Of little boys or grown-up men
    They none of them would say.

Their eyes would flash——their teeth would grind——
    Their lips would tightly curl——
They'd say, "Thy way thyself must find,
    Thou misdirecting churl!"

Peter the Wag

And, similarly, also, when
   He tried a foreign friend;
Italians answered, "Il balen"—
   The French, "No comprehend."

The Russ would say with gleaming eye
   "Sevastopol!" and groan.
The Greek said, "Τυπτω, τυπτομαι,
   Τυπτω, τυπτειν, τυπτων."
To wander thus for many a year
   That Crusher never ceased—
The Men of London dropped a tear,
   Their anger was appeased.

At length exploring gangs were sent
   To find poor FORTH's remains—
A handsome grant by Parliament
   Was voted for their pains.

Peter the Wag

To seek the poor policeman out
  Bold spirits volunteered,
And when at length they solved the doubt
  The Men of London cheered.

And in a yard, dark, dank, and drear,
  They found him, on the floor—
(It leads from Richmond Buildings—near
  The Royalty stage-door.)
With brandy cold and brandy hot
  They plied him, starved and wet,
And made him sergeant on the spot—
  The Men of London's pet!

WHEN A MERRY MAIDEN MARRIES

WHEN a merry maiden marries,
Sorrow goes and pleasure tarries;
    Every sound becomes a song,
    All is right and nothing's wrong!
From to-day and ever after
Let your tears be tears of laughter—
    Every sigh that finds a vent
    Be a sigh of sweet content!
When you marry merry maiden,
Then the air with love is laden;
    Every flower is a rose,
        Every goose becomes a swan,
    Every kind of trouble goes
        Where the last year's snows have gone;
    Sunlight takes the place of shade
    When you marry merry maid!

When a Merry Maiden Marries

When a merry maiden marries
Sorrow goes and pleasure tarries;
 Every sound becomes a song,
 All is right, and nothing's wrong.
Gnawing Care and aching Sorrow,
Get ye gone until to-morrow;
 Jealousies in grim array,
 Ye are things of yesterday!
When you marry merry maiden,
Then the air with joy is laden;
 All the corners of the earth
  Ring with music sweetly played,
 Worry is melodious mirth,
  Grief is joy in masquerade;
 Sullen night is laughing day—
 All the year is merry May!

THE THREE KINGS OF CHICKERABOO

THERE were three niggers of Chickeraboo—
PACIFICO, BANG-BANG, POPCHOP—who
Exclaimed, one terribly sultry day,
"Oh, let's be kings in a humble way."

The first was a highly-accomplished "bones,"
The next elicited banjo tones,
The third was a quiet, retiring chap,
Who danced an excellent break-down "flap."

"We niggers," said they, "have formed a plan
By which, whenever we like, we can
Extemporise kingdoms near the beach,
And then we'll collar a kingdom each.

The Three Kings of Chickeraboo

"Three casks, from somebody else's stores,
Shall represent our island shores,
Their sides the ocean wide shall lave,
Their heads just topping the briny wave.

"Great Britain's navy scours the sea,
And everywhere her ships they be ;
She'll recognise our rank, perhaps,
When she discovers we're Royal Chaps.

"If to her skirts you want to cling,
It's quite sufficient that you're a king ;
She does not push inquiry far
To learn what sort of king you are."

A ship of several thousand tons,
And mounting seventy-something guns,
Ploughed, every year, the ocean blue,
Discovering kings and countries new.

The brave REAR-ADMIRAL BAILEY PIP,
Commanding that magnificent ship,
Perceived one day, his glasses through,
The kings that came from Chickeraboo.

"Dear eyes ! " said ADMIRAL PIP, "I see
Three flourishing islands on our lee.
And, bless me ! most remarkable thing !
On every island stands a king !

"Come, lower the Admiral's gig," he cried,
"And over the dancing waves I'll glide ;
That low obeisance I may do
To those three kings of Chickeraboo ! "

The Three Kings of Chickeraboo

The Admiral pulled to the islands three;
The kings saluted him gracious*lee*.
The Admiral, pleased at his welcome warm,
Unrolled a printed Alliance form.

"Your Majesty, sign me this, I pray—
I come in a friendly kind of way—
I come, if you please, with the best intents,
And QUEEN VICTORIA'S compliments."

The kings were pleased as they well could be;
The most retiring of the three,
In a "cellar-flap" to his joy gave vent
With a banjo-bones accompaniment.

The great REAR-ADMIRAL BAILEY PIP
Embarked on board his jolly big ship,
Blue Peter flew from his lofty fore,
And off he sailed to his native shore.

The Three Kings of Chickeraboo

ADMIRAL PIP directly went
To the Lord at the head of the Government,
Who made him, by a stroke of a quill,
BARON DE PIPPE, of PIPPETONNEVILLE.

The College of Heralds permission yield
That he should quarter upon his shield
Three islands, *vert*, on a field of blue,
With the pregnant motto "Chickeraboo."

Ambassadors, yes, and attachés, too,
Are going to sail for Chickeraboo.
And, see, on the good ship's crowded deck,
A bishop, who's going out there on spec.

And let us all hope that blissful things
May come of alliance with darky kings,
And, may we never, whatever we do,
Declare a war with Chickeraboo!

THE BRITISH TAR

A BRITISH tar is a soaring soul,
   As free as a mountain bird,
His energetic fist should be ready to resist
   A dictatorial word.
His nose should pant and his lip should curl,
His cheeks should flame and his brow should furl,
His bosom should heave and his heart should glow,
And his fist be ever ready for a knock-down blow.

His eyes should flash with an inborn fire,
   His brow with scorn be rung;
He never should bow down to a domineering frown
   Or the tang of a tyrant tongue.
His foot should stamp and his throat should growl,
His hair should twirl and his face should scowl;
His eyes should flash and his breast protrude,
And this should be his customary attitude!

204

GENTLE ALICE BROWN

IT was a robber's daughter, and her name was ALICE BROWN,
Her father was the terror of a small Italian town;
Her mother was a foolish, weak, but amiable old thing;
But it isn't of her parents that I'm going for to sing.

As ALICE was a-sitting at her window-sill one day
A beautiful young gentleman he chanced to pass that way;
She cast her eyes upon him, and he looked so good and true,
That she thought, "I could be happy with a gentleman
    like you!"

And every morning passed her house that cream of gentlemen,
She knew she might expect him at a quarter unto ten,
A sorter in the Custom-house, it was his daily road
(The Custom-house was fifteen minutes' walk from her abode).

Gentle Alice Brown

But ALICE was a pious girl, who knew it wasn't wise
To look at strange young sorters with expressive purple eyes;
So she sought the village priest to whom her family con-
fessed—
The priest by whom their little sins were carefully assessed.

"Oh, holy father," ALICE said, "'twould grieve you, would
it not?
To discover that I was a most disreputable lot!
Of all unhappy sinners I'm the most unhappy one!"
The padre said, "Whatever have you been and gone and
done?"

"I have helped mamma to steal a little kiddy from its dad,
I've assisted dear papa in cutting up a little lad.
I've planned a little burglary and forged a little cheque,
And slain a little baby for the coral on its neck!"

The worthy pastor heaved a sigh, and dropped a silent
tear—
And said, "You mustn't judge yourself too heavily, my
dear—
It's wrong to murder babies, little corals for to fleece;
But sins like these one expiates at half-a-crown apiece.

"Girls will be girls—you're very young, and flighty in your
mind;
Old heads upon young shoulders we must not expect to
find:
We mustn't be too hard upon these little girlish tricks—
Let's see—five crimes at half-a-crown—exactly twelve-and-
six."

"Oh, father," little ALICE cried, "your kindness makes me
weep,
You do these little things for me so singularly cheap—
Your thoughtful liberality I never can forget;
But oh, there is another crime I haven't mentioned yet!"

Gentle Alice Brown

"A pleasant-looking gentleman, with pretty purple eyes,—
I've noticed at my window, as I've sat a-catching flies;
He passes by it every day as certain as can be—
I blush to say I've winked at him, and he has winked at me!

"For shame," said FATHER PAUL, "my erring daughter!
    On my word
This is the most distressing news that I have ever heard.
Why, naughty girl, your excellent papa has pledged your hand
To a promising young robber, the lieutenant of his band!

"This dreadful piece of news will pain your worthy
    parents so!
They are the most remunerative customers I know;
For many many years they've kept starvation from my doors,
I never knew so criminal a family as yours!

"The common country folk in this insipid neighbourhood
Have nothing to confess, they're so ridiculously good;
And if you marry any one respectable at all,
Why, you'll reform, and what will then become of FATHER
    PAUL?"

The worthy priest, he up and drew his cowl upon his crown,
And started off in haste to tell the news to ROBBER BROWN;
To tell him how his daughter, who was now for marriage fit,
Had winked upon a sorter, who reciprocated it.

Gentle Alice Brown

Good ROBBER BROWN he muffled up his anger pretty well,
He said, "I have a notion, and that notion I will tell;
I will nab this gay young sorter, terrify him into fits,
And get my gentle wife to chop him into little bits.

"I've studied human nature, and I know a thing or two;
Though a girl may fondly love a living gent, as many do,
A feeling of disgust upon her senses there will fall
When she looks upon his body chopped particularly small."

He traced that gallant sorter to a still suburban square;
He watched his opportunity and seized him unaware;
He took a life-preserver and he hit him on the head,
And MRS. BROWN dissected him before she went to bed.

And pretty little ALICE grew more settled in her mind,
She never more was guilty of a weakness of the kind,
Until at length good ROBBER BROWN bestowed her pretty
     hand
On the promising young robber, the lieutenant of his band.

A MAN WHO WOULD WOO A FAIR
MAID

A MAN who would woo a fair maid,
Should 'prentice himself to the trade ;
    And study all day,
    In methodical way,
How to flatter, cajole, and persuade.
He should 'prentice himself at fourteen.
And practise from morning to e'en ;
    And when he's of age,
    If he will, I'll engage,
He may capture the heart of a queen !
      It is purely a matter of skill,
      Which all may attain if they will :
        But every Jack
        He must study the knack
      If he wants to make sure of his Jill !

A Man who would Woo a Fair Maid

If he's made the best use of his time,
His twig he'll so carefully lime
    That every bird
    Will come down at his word,
Whatever its plumage and clime.
He must learn that the thrill of a touch
May mean little, or nothing, or much;
    It's an instrument rare,
    To be handled with care,
And ought to be treated as such.
    It is purely a matter of skill,
    Which all may attain if they will:
      But every Jack,
      He must study the knack
    If he wants to make sure of his Jill!

Then a glance may be timid or free;
It will vary in mighty degree,
    From an impudent stare
    To a look of despair
That no maid without pity can see.
And a glance of despair is no guide—
It may have its ridiculous side;
    It may draw you a tear
    Or a box on the ear;
You can never be sure till you've tried.
    It is purely a matter of skill,
    Which all may attain if they will:
      But every Jack
      He must study the knack
    If he wants to make sure of his Jill!

THE SORCERER'S SONG

OH ! my name is JOHN WELLINGTON WELLS—
I'm a dealer in magic and spells,
  In blessings and curses,
  And ever-filled purses,
In prophecies, witches, and knells !
If you want a proud foe to "make tracks"—
If you'd melt a rich uncle in wax—
  You've but to look in
  On our resident Djinn,
Number seventy, Simmery Axe.

We've a first-class assortment of magic ;
  And for raising a posthumous shade
With effects that are comic or tragic,
  There's no cheaper house in the trade.

The Sorcerer's Song

Love-philtre—we've quantities of it ;
  And for knowledge if any one burns,
We keep an extremely small prophet, a prophet
  Who brings us unbounded returns :
      For he can prophesy
      With a wink *of* his eye,
      Peep with security
      Into futurity,
      Sum up your history,
      Clear up a mystery,
      Humour proclivity
      For a nativity.
      With mirrors so magical,
      Tetrapods tragical,
      Bogies spectacular,
      Answers oracular,
      Facts astronomical,
      Solemn or comical,
      And, if you want it, he
Makes a reduction on taking a quantity !
        Oh !
  If any one anything lacks,
  He'll find it all ready in stacks,
    If he'll only look in
    On the resident Djinn,
Number seventy, Simmery Axe !

    He can raise you hosts,
          Of ghosts,
And that without reflectors ;
  And creepy things
        With wings,
And gaunt and grisly spectres !
  He can fill you crowds
        Of shrouds,
And horrify you vastly ;
  He can rack your brains
        With chains,

The Sorcerer's Song

And gibberings grim and ghastly.
  Then, if you plan it, he
  Changes organity
  With an urbanity,
  Full of Satanity,
  Vexes humanity
  With an inanity
  Fatal to vanity—
Driving your foes to the verge of insanity.
  Barring tautology,
  In demonology,
  'Lectro biology,
  Mystic nosology,
  Spirit philology,
  High class astrology,
  Such is his knowledge, he
Isn't the man to require an apology!
    Oh!
My name is JOHN WELLINGTON WELLS,
I'm a dealer in magic and spells,
  In blessings and curses,
  And ever-filled purses—
In prophecies, witches, and knells.
If any one anything lacks,
He'll find it all ready in stacks,
  If he'll only look in
  On the resident Djinn,
Number seventy, Simmery Axe!

THE BUMBOAT WOMAN'S STORY

I'M old, my dears, and shrivelled with age, and work, and grief,
My eyes are gone, and my teeth have been drawn by
    Time, the Thief!
For terrible sights I've seen, and dangers great I've run—
I'm nearly seventy now, and my work is almost done!

Ah! I've been young in my time, and I've played the
    deuce with men!
I'm speaking of ten years past—I was barely sixty then:
My cheeks were mellow and soft, and my eyes were large
    and sweet,
POLL PINEAPPLE'S eyes were the standing toast of the
    Royal Fleet!

The Bumboat Woman's Story

A bumboat woman was I, and I faithfully served the ships
With apples and cakes, and fowls and beer, and halfpenny
dips,
And beef for the generous mess, where the officers dine at
nights,
And fine fresh peppermint drops for the rollicking mid-
shipmites.

Of all the kind commanders who anchored in Portsmouth
Bay,
By far the sweetest of all was kind LIEUTENANT BELAYE.
LIEUTENANT BELAYE commanded the gunboat *Hot Cross
Bun*,
She was seven and seventy feet in length, and she carried
a gun.

With the laudable view of enhancing his country's naval
pride,
When people inquired her size, LIEUTENANT BELAYE replied,
"Oh, my ship, my ship is the first of the Hundred and
Twenty-ones!"
Which meant her tonnage, but people imagined it meant
her guns.

Whenever I went on board he would beckon me down
below,
"Come down, Little Buttercup, come" (for he loved to
call me so),
And he'd tell of the fights at sea in which he'd taken a part,
And so LIEUTENANT BELAYE won poor POLL PINEAPPLE's
heart!

But at length his orders came, and he said one day, said he,
"I'm ordered to sail with the *Hot Cross Bun* to the
German Sea."
And the Portsmouth maidens wept when they learnt the
evil day,
For every Portsmouth maid loved good LIEUTENANT BELAYE.

The Bumboat Woman's Story

And I went to a back back street, with plenty of cheap
    cheap shops,
And I bought an oilskin hat, and a second-hand suit of slops,
And I went to LIEUTENANT BELAYE (and he never sus-
    pected *me !*)
And I entered myself as a chap as wanted to go to sea.

We sailed that afternoon at the mystic hour of one,—
Remarkably nice young men were the crew of the *Hot*
    Cross Bun.
I'm sorry to say that I've heard that sailors sometimes
    swear,
But I never yet heard a *Bun* say anything wrong, I declare.

When Jack Tars meet, they meet with a " Messmate, ho !
    What cheer ? "
But here, on the *Hot Cross Bun*, it was " How do you do,
    my dear ? "
When Jack Tars growl, I believe they growl with a big
    big D—
But the strongest oath of the *Hot Cross Buns* was a mild
    " Dear me ! "

The Bumboat Woman's Story

Yet, though they were all well bred, you could scarcely
    call them slick :
Whenever a sea was on, they were all extremely sick ;
And whenever the weather was calm, and the wind was
    light and fair,
They spent more time than a sailor should on his back
    back hair.

They certainly shivered and shook when ordered aloft to run,
And they screamed when Lieutenant Belaye discharged
    his only gun.
And as he was proud of his gun—such pride is hardly
    wrong—
The Lieutenant was blazing away at intervals all day long.

They all agreed very well, though at times you heard it said
That Bill had a way of his own of making his lips look
    red—
That Joe looked quite his age—or somebody might declare
That Barnacle's long pig-tail was never his own own hair.

Belaye would admit that his men were of no great use to
    him,
"But then," he would say, "there is little to do on a gun-
    boat trim.
I can hand, and reef, and steer, and fire my big gun too—
And it *is* such a treat to sail with a gentle well-bred crew."

I saw him every day !   How the happy moments sped !
Reef topsails ! Make all taut ! There's dirty weather ahead !
(I do not mean that tempests threatened the *Hot Cross Bun:*
In *that* case, I don't know whatever we *should* have done !)

After a fortnight's cruise we put into port one day,
And off on leave for a week went kind Lieutenant Belaye,
And after a long long week had passed (and it seemed like
    a life),
Lieutenant Belaye returned to his ship with a fair young
    wife !

The Bumboat Woman's Story

He up, and he says, says he, "Oh, crew of the *Hot Cross Bun*,
Here is the wife of my heart, for the Church has made us one!"
And as he uttered the word, the crew went out of their wits,
And all fell down in so many separate fainting fits.

And then their hair came down, or off, as the case might be,
And lo! the rest of the crew were simple girls, like me,
Who all had fled from their homes in a sailor's blue array,
To follow the shifting fate of kind LIEUTENANT BELAYE!

It's strange to think that *I* should ever have loved young men,
But I'm speaking of ten years past—I was barely sixty then;
And now my cheeks are furrowed with grief and age, I trow!
And poor POLL PINEAPPLE's eyes have lost their lustre now!

THE FICKLE BREEZE

SIGHING softly to the river
  Comes the loving breeze,
Setting nature all a-quiver,
  Rustling through the trees !
And the brook in rippling measure
  Laughs for very love,
While the poplars, in their pleasure,
  Wave their arms above !
    River, river, little river,
    May thy loving prosper ever.
    Heaven speed thee, poplar tree,
    May thy wooing happy be !

Yet, the breeze is but a rover,
  When he wings away,
Brook and poplar mourn a lover !
  Sighing well-a-day !

The Fickle Breeze

Ah, the doing and undoing
   That the rogue could tell!
When the breeze is out a-wooing,
   Who can woo so well?
      Pretty brook, thy dream is over,
      For thy love is but a rover!
      Sad the lot of poplar trees,
      Courted by the fickle breeze!

THE TWO OGRES

Good children, list, if you're inclined,
    And wicked children too—
This pretty ballad is designed
    Especially for you.

Two ogres dwelt in Wickham Wold—
    Each *traits* distinctive had:
The younger was as good as gold,
    The elder was as bad.

The Two Ogres

A wicked, disobedient son
   Was JAMES M'ALPINE, and
A contrast to the elder one,
   Good APPLEBODY BLAND.

M'ALPINE—brutes like him are few—
   In greediness delights,
A melancholy victim to
   Unchastened appetites.

Good, well-bred children every day
   He ravenously ate,—
All boys were fish who found their way
   Into M'ALPINE'S net:

Boys whose good breeding is innate,
   Whose sums are always right;
And boys who don't expostulate
   When sent to bed at night;

And kindly boys who never search
   The nests of birds of song;
And serious boys for whom, in church,
   No sermon is too long.

Contrast with JAMES's greedy haste
   And comprehensive hand,
The nice discriminating taste
   Of APPLEBODY BLAND.

BLAND only eats bad boys, who swear—
   Who *can* behave, but *don't*—
Disgraceful lads who say "don't care,"
   And "shan't," and "can't," and "won't."

The Two Ogres

Who wet their shoes and learn to box,
    And say what isn't true,
Who bite their nails and jam their frocks,
    And make long noses too;

Who kick a nurse's aged shin,
    And sit in sulky mopes;
And boys who twirl poor kittens in
    Distracting zoëtropes.

But JAMES, when he was quite a youth,
    Had often been to school,
And though so bad, to tell the truth,
    He wasn't quite a fool.

The Two Ogres

At logic few with him could vie,
   To his peculiar sect
He could propose a fallacy
   With singular effect.

So, when his Mentors said, "Expound—
   Why eat good children—why?"
Upon his Mentors he would round
   With this absurd reply:

"I have been taught to love the good—
   The pure—the unalloyed—
And wicked boys, I've understood,
   I always should avoid.

"Why do I eat good children—why?
   Because I love them so!"
(But this was empty sophistry,
   As your Papa can show.)

Now, though the learning of his friends
   Was truly not immense,
They had a way of fitting ends
   By rule of common sense.

"Away, away!" his Mentors cried,
   "Thou uncongenial pest!
A quirk's a thing we can't abide,
   A quibble we detest!

"A fallacy in your reply
   Our intellect descries,
Although we don't pretend to spy
   Exactly where it lies.

The Two Ogres

"In misery and penal woes
    Must end a glutton's joys;
And learn how ogres punish those
    Who dare to eat good boys.

"Secured by fetter, cramp, and chain,
    And gagged securely—so—
You shall be placed in Drury Lane,
    Where only good lads go.

"Surrounded there by virtuous boys,
    You'll suffer torture wus
Than that which constantly annoys
    Disgraceful TANTALUS.

("If you would learn the woes that vex
    Poor TANTALUS, down there,
Pray borrow of Papa an ex-
    Purgated LEMPRIERE.)

225   I

The Two Ogres

"But as for BLAND who, as it seems,
    Eats only naughty boys,
We've planned a recompense that teems
    With gastronomic joys.

"Where wicked youths in crowds are stowed
    He shall unquestioned rule,
And have the run of Hackney Road
    Reformatory School!"

THE FIRST LORD'S SONG

WHEN I was a lad I served a term
As office boy to an Attorney's firm;
I cleaned the windows and I swept the floor,
And I polished up the handle of the big front door.
    I polished up that handle so successfullee,
    That now I am the Ruler of the Queen's Navee!

As office boy I made such a mark
That they gave me the post of a junior clerk;
I served the writs with a smile so bland,
And I copied all the letters in a big round hand.
    I copied all the letters in a hand so free,
    That now I am the Ruler of the Queen's Navee!

The First Lord's Song

In serving writs I made such a name
That an articled clerk I soon became;
I wore clean collars and a brand-new suit
For the Pass Examination at the Institute:
    And that Pass Examination did so well for me,
    That now I am the Ruler of the Queen's Navee!

Of legal knowledge I acquired such a grip
That they took me into the partnership,
And that junior partnership I ween,
Was the only ship that I ever had seen:
    But that kind of ship so suited me,
    That now I am the Ruler of the Queen's Navee!

I grew so rich that I was sent
By a pocket borough into Parliament;
I always voted at my Party's call,
And I never thought of thinking for myself at all.
    I thought so little, they rewarded me,
    By making me the Ruler of the Queen's Navee!

Now, landsmen all, whoever you may be,
If you want to rise to the top of the tree—
If your soul isn't fettered to an office stool,
Be careful to be guided by this golden rule—
    Stick close to your desks and *never go to sea*,
    And you all may be Rulers of the Queen's Navee!

LITTLE OLIVER

EARL JOYCE he was a kind old party
   Whom nothing ever could put out,
Though eighty-two, he still was hearty,
   Excepting as regarded gout.

He had one unexampled daughter,
   The LADY MINNIE-HAHA JOYCE,
Fair MINNIE-HAHA, "Laughing Water,"
   So called from her melodious voice.

By Nature planned for lover-capture,
   Her beauty every heart assailed ;
The good old nobleman with rapture
   Observed how widely she prevailed.

Little Oliver

Aloof from all the lordly flockings
    Of titled swells who worshipped her,
There stood, in pumps and cotton stockings,
    One humble lover—OLIVER.

He was no peer by Fortune petted,
    His name recalled no bygone age;
He was no lordling coronetted—
    Alas! he was a simple page!

With vain appeals he never bored her,
    But stood in silent sorrow by—
He knew how fondly he adored her,
    And knew, alas! how hopelessly!

Well grounded by a village tutor
    In languages alive and past,
He'd say unto himself, "Knee-suitor,
    Oh, do not go beyond your last!"

Little Oliver

But though his name could boast no handle,
    He could not every hope resign ;
As moths will hover round a candle,
    So hovered he about her shrine.

The brilliant candle dazed the moth well :
    One day she sang to her Papa
The air that MARIE sings with BOTHWELL
    In NEIDERMEYER'S opera.

(Therein a stable boy, it's stated,
    Devoutly loved a noble dame,
Who ardently reciprocated
    His rather injudicious flame.)

And then, before the piano closing
    (He listened coyly at the door),
She sang a song of her composing—
    I give one verse from half a score :

BALLAD

Why, pretty page, art ever sighing ?
Is sorrow in thy heartlet lying ?
    Come, set a-ringing
      Thy laugh entrancing,
    And ever singing
      And ever dancing.
    Ever singing, Tra ! la ! la !
    Ever dancing, Tra ! la ! la !
      Ever singing, ever dancing,
      Ever singing, Tra ! la ! la !

He skipped for joy like little muttons,
    He danced like Esmeralda's kid.
(She did not mean a boy in buttons,
    Although he fancied that she did.)

Little Oliver

Poor lad! convinced he thus would win her,
    He wore out many pairs of soles;
He danced when taking down the dinner—
    He danced when bringing up the coals.

He danced and sang (however laden)
    With his incessant "Tra! la! la!"
Which much surprised the noble maiden,
    And puzzled even her Papa.

He nourished now his flame and fanned it,
    He even danced at work below.
The upper servants wouldn't stand it,
    And Bowles the butler told him so.

At length on impulse acting blindly,
    His love he laid completely bare;
The gentle Earl received him kindly
    And told the lad to take a chair.

"Oh, sir," the suitor uttered sadly,
    "Don't give your indignation vent;
I fear you think I'm acting madly,
    Perhaps you think me insolent?"

Little Oliver

The kindly Earl repelled the notion ;
  His noble bosom heaved a sigh,
His fingers trembled with emotion,
  A tear stood in his mild blue eye :

For, oh ! the scene recalled too plainly
  The half-forgotten time when he,
A boy of nine, had worshipped vainly
  A governess of forty-three !

" My boy," he said, in tone consoling,
  " Give up this idle fancy—do—
The song you heard my daughter trolling
  Did not, indeed, refer to you.

" I feel for you, poor boy, acutely ;
  I would not wish to give you pain ;
Your pangs I estimate minutely,—
  I, too, have loved, and loved in vain.

" But still your humble rank and station
  For MINNIE surely are not meet "—
He said much more in conversation
  Which it were needless to repeat.

        I 2

Little Oliver

Now I'm prepared to bet a guinea,
    Were this a mere dramatic case,
The page would have eloped with MINNIE,
    But, no—he only left his place.

The simple Truth is my detective,
    With me Sensation can't abide;
The Likely beats the mere Effective,
    And Nature is my only guide.

MISTER WILLIAM

OH, listen to the tale of MISTER WILLIAM, if you please,
Whom naughty, naughty judges sent away beyond the seas.
He forged a party's will, which caused anxiety and strife,
Resulting in his getting penal servitude for life.

He was a kindly goodly man, and naturally prone,
Instead of taking others' gold, to give away his own.
But he had heard of Vice, and longed for only once to
    strike——
To plan *one* little wickedness—to see what it was like.

He argued with himself, and said, "A spotless man am I;
I can't be more respectable, however hard I try;
For six and thirty years I've always been as good as gold,
And now for half-an-hour I'll deal in infamy untold!

Mister William

" A baby who is wicked at the early age of one,
And then reforms—and dies at thirty-six a spotless son,
Is never, never saddled with his babyhood's defect,
But earns from worthy men consideration and respect.

"So one who never revelled in discreditable tricks
Until he reached the comfortable age of thirty-six,
Is free for half-an-hour to perpetrate a deed of shame,
Without incurring permanent disgrace, or even blame.

" That babies don't commit such crimes as forgery is true,
But little sins develop, if you leave 'em to accrue ;
And he who shuns all vices as successive seasons roll,
Should reap at length the benefit of so much self-control.

"The common sin of babyhood—objecting to be drest—
If you leave it to accumulate at compound interest,
For anything you know, may represent, if you're alive,
A burglary or murder at the age of thirty-five.

"Still, I wouldn't take advantage of this fact, but be content
With some pardonable folly—it's a mere experiment.
The greater the temptation to go wrong, the less the sin ;
So with something that's particularly tempting I'll begin.

"I would not steal a penny, for my income's very fair—
I do not want a penny—I have pennies and to spare—
And if I stole a penny from a money-bag or till,
The sin would be enormous—the temptation being *nil*.

"But if I broke asunder all such pettifogging bounds,
And forged a party's Will for (say) Five Hundred Thousand
        Pounds,
With such an irresistible temptation to a haul,
Of course the sin must be infinitesimally small.

Mister William

"There's WILSON who is dying—he has wealth from Stock
    and rent—
If I divert his riches from their natural descent,
I'm placed in a position to indulge each little whim."
So he diverted them—and they, in turn, diverted him.

Unfortunately, though, by some unpardonable flaw,
Temptation isn't recognised by Britain's Common Law;
Men found him out by some peculiarity of touch,
And WILLIAM got a "lifer," which annoyed him very much.

For ah! he never reconciled himself to life in gaol,
He fretted and he pined, and grew dispirited and pale;
He was numbered like a cabman, too, which told upon
    him so,
That his spirits, once so buoyant, grew uncomfortably low.

And sympathetic gaolers would remark, "It's very true,
He ain't been brought up common, like the likes of me
    and you."
So they took him into hospital, and gave him mutton chops,
And chocolate, and arrowroot, and buns, and malt and hops.

Mister William

Kind clergymen, besides, grew interested in his fate,
Affected by the details of his pitiable state.
They waited on the Secretary, somewhere in Whitehall,
Who said he would receive them any day they liked to call.

"Consider, sir, the hardship of this interesting case:
A prison life brings with it something very like disgrace;
It's telling on young WILLIAM, who's reduced to skin and
      bone—
Remember he's a gentleman, with money of his own.

"He had an ample income, and of course he stands in
      need
Of sherry with his dinner, and his customary weed;
No delicacies now can pass his gentlemanly lips—
He misses his sea-bathing and his continental trips.

"He says the other prisoners are commonplace and rude;
He says he cannot relish the disgusting prison food,
For when a boy they taught him to distinguish Good from
      Bad,
And other educational advantages he's had.

Mister William

"A burglar or garrotter, or, indeed, a common thief
Is very glad to batten on potatoes and on beef,
Or anything, in short, that prison kitchens can afford,—
A cut above the diet in a common workhouse ward.

"But beef and mutton-broth don't seem to suit our
      WILLIAM's whim,
A boon to other prisoners—a punishment to him:
It never was intended that the discipline of gaol
Should dash a convict's spirits, sir, or make him thin or
      pale."

"Good Gracious Me!" that sympathetic Secretary cried,
"Suppose in prison fetters MISTER WILLIAM should have
      died!
Dear me, of course!   Imprisonment for *Life* his sentence
      saith:
I'm very glad you mentioned it—it might have been For
      Death!

"Release him with a ticket—he'll be better then, no doubt,
And tell him I apologise."   So MISTER WILLIAM's out.
I hope he will be careful in his manuscripts, I'm sure,
And not begin experimentalising any more.

WOULD YOU KNOW?

WOULD you know the kind of maid
    Sets my heart a flame-a?
Eyes must be downcast and staid,
    Cheeks must flush for shame-a!
      She may neither dance nor sing,
      But, demure in everything,
      Hang her head in modest way
      With pouting lips that seem to say,
      "Kiss me, kiss me, kiss me, kiss me,
      Though I die of shame-a!"
Please you, that's the kind of maid
    Sets my heart a flame-a!

Would You Know?

When a maid is bold and gay
   With a tongue goes clang-a,
Flaunting it in brave array,
   Maiden may go hang-a!
      Sunflower gay and hollyhock
      Never shall my garden stock;
      Mine the blushing rose of May,
      With pouting lips that seem to say.
"Oh, kiss me, kiss me, kiss me, kiss me,
   Though I die for shame-a!"
Please you, that's the kind of maid
   Sets my heart a flame-a!

PASHA BAILEY BEN

A proud Pasha was Bailey Ben,
His wives were three, his tails were ten;
His form was dignified, but stout,
Men called him "Little Roundabout."

His Importance

Pale Pilgrims came from o'er the sea
To wait on Pasha Bailey B.,
All bearing presents in a crowd,
For B. was poor as well as proud.

His Presents

They brought him onions strung on ropes,
And cold boiled beef, and telescopes,
And balls of string, and shrimps, and guns,
And chops, and tacks, and hats, and buns.

Pasha Bailey Ben

More of them

They brought him white kid gloves, and pails,
And candlesticks, and potted quails,
And capstan-bars, and scales and weights,
And ornaments for empty grates.

Why I mention these

My tale is not of these—oh no!
I only mention them to show
The divers gifts that divers men
Brought o'er the sea to BAILEY BEN.

His Confidant

A confidant had BAILEY B.,
A gay Mongolian dog was he;
I am not good at Turkish names,
And so I call him SIMPLE JAMES.

His Confidant's Countenance

A dreadful legend you might trace
In SIMPLE JAMES'S honest face,
For there you read, in Nature's print,
"A Scoundrel of the Deepest Tint."

His Character

A deed of blood, or fire, or flames,
Was meat and drink to SIMPLE JAMES:
To hide his guilt he did not plan,
But owned himself a bad young man.

Pasha Bailey Ben

The Author to his Reader

And why on earth good BAILEY BEN
(The wisest, noblest, best of men)
Made SIMPLE JAMES his right-hand man
Is quite beyond my mental span.

The same, continued

But there—enough of gruesome deeds!
My heart, in thinking of them, bleeds;
And so let SIMPLE JAMES take wing,—
'Tis not of him I'm going to sing.

Pasha Bailey Ben

The Pasha's Clerk

Good PASHA BAILEY kept a clerk
(For BAILEY only made his mark),
His name was MATTHEW WYCOMBE COO,
A man of nearly forty-two.

His Accomplishments

No person that I ever knew
Could " yödel " half as well as Coo,
And Highlanders exclaimed, " Eh, weel ! "
When Coo began to dance a reel.

His Kindness to the Pasha's Wives

He used to dance and sing and play
In such an unaffected way,
He cheered the unexciting lives
Of PASHA BAILEY's lovely wives.

Pasha Bailey Ben

The Author to his Reader

But why should I encumber you
With histories of MATTHEW COO?
Let MATTHEW COO at once take wing,—
'Tis not of COO I'm going to sing.

The Author's Muse

Let me recall my wandering Muse;
She *shall* be steady if I choose—
She roves, instead of helping me
To tell the deeds of BAILEY B.

The Pasha's Visitor

One morning knocked, at half-past eight,
A tall Red Indian at his gate.
In Turkey, as you're p'raps aware,
Red Indians are extremely rare.

The Visitor's Outfit

Mocassins decked his graceful legs,
His eyes were black, and round as eggs,
And on his neck, instead of beads,
Hung several Catawampous seeds.

What the Visitor said

"Ho, ho!" he said, "thou pale-faced one,
Poor offspring of an Eastern sun,
You've *never* seen the Red Man skip
Upon the banks of Mississip!"

246

Pasha Bailey Ben

The Author's Moderation

To say that BAILEY oped his eyes
Would feebly paint his great surprise—
To say it almost made him die
Would be to paint it much too high.

The Author to his Reader

But why should I ransack my head
To tell you all that Indian said;
We'll let the Indian man take wing,—
'Tis not of him I'm going to sing.

The Reader to the Author

Come, come, I say, that's quite enough
Of this absurd disjointed stuff;
Now let's get on to that affair
About LIEUTENANT-COLONEL FLARE.

Bab

LIEUTENANT-COLONEL FLARE

THE earth has armies plenty,
    And semi-warlike bands,
I dare say there are twenty
    In European lands ;
But, oh ! in no direction
    You'd find one to compare
In brotherly affection
    With that of COLONEL FLARE.

His soldiers might be rated
    As military Pearls :
As unsophisticated
    As pretty little girls !

Lieutenant-Colonel Flare

They never smoked or ratted,
  Or talked of Sues or Polls;
The Sergeant-Major tatted,
  The others nursed their dolls.

He spent his days in teaching
  These truly solemn facts;
There's little use in preaching,
  Or circulating tracts.
(The vainest plan invented
  For stifling other creeds,
Unless it's supplemented
  With charitable *deeds*.)

He taught his soldiers kindly
  To give at Hunger's call:
"Oh, better far give blindly,
  Than never give at all!
Though sympathy be kindled
  By Imposition's game,
Oh, better far be swindled
  Than smother up its flame!"

His means were far from ample
  For pleasure or for dress,
Yet note this bright example
  Of single-heartedness:
Though ranking as a Colonel,
  His pay was but a groat,
While their reward diurnal
  Was—each a five-pound note.

Moreover,—this evinces
  His kindness, you'll allow,—
He fed them all like princes,
  And lived himself on cow.

Lieutenant-Colonel Flare

He set them all regaling
  On curious wines, and dear,
While he would sit pale-ale-ing,
  Or quaffing ginger-beer.

Then at his instigation
  (A pretty fancy this)
Their daily pay and ration
  He'd take in change for his;
They brought it to him weekly,
  And he without a groan,
Would take it from them meekly
  And give them all his own!

Lieutenant-Colonel Flare

Though not exactly knighted
    As knights, of course, should be,
Yet no one so delighted
    In harmless chivalry.
If peasant girl or ladye
    Beneath misfortunes sank,
Whate'er distinctions made he,
    They were not those of rank.

No maiden young and comely
    Who wanted good advice
(However poor or homely)
    Need ask him for it twice.

Lieutenant-Colonel Flare

He'd wipe away the blindness
　That comes of teary dew;
His sympathetic kindness
　No sort of limit knew.

He always hated dealing
　With men who schemed or planned;
A person harsh—unfeeling—
　The Colonel could not stand.
He hated cold, suspecting,
　Official men in blue,
Who pass their lives detecting
　The crimes that others do.

For men who'd shoot a sparrow,
　Or immolate a worm
Beneath a farmer's harrow,
　He could not find a term.
Humanely, ay, and knightly
　He dealt with such an one;
He took and tied him tightly,
　And blew him from a gun.

Lieutenant-Colonel Flare

The earth has armies plenty,
    And semi-warlike bands,
I'm certain there are twenty
    In European lands;
But, oh! in no direction
    You'd find one to compare
In brotherly affection
    With that of COLONEL FLARE.

SPECULATION

Comes a train of little ladies
   From scholastic trammels free,
Each a little bit afraid is,
   Wondering what the world can be !

Is it but a world of trouble—
   Sadness set to song ?
Is its beauty but a bubble
   Bound to break ere long ?

Are its palaces and pleasures
   Fantasies that fade ?
And the glory of its treasures
   Shadow of a shade ?

Schoolgirls we, eighteen and under,
   From scholastic trammels free,
And we wonder—how we wonder !—
   What on earth the world can be !

AH ME!

WHEN maiden loves, she sits and sighs,
　　She wanders to and fro;
Unbidden tear-drops fill her eyes,
And to all questions she replies,
　　With a sad heigho!
　　'Tis but a little word—"heigho!"
　　So soft, 'tis scarcely heard—"heigho!"
　　　An idle breath—
　　　Yet life and death
　　May hang upon a maid's "heigho!"

When maiden loves, she mopes apart,
　　As owl mopes on a tree;
Although she keenly feels the smart,
She cannot tell what ails her heart,
　　With its sad "Ah me!"
　　'Tis but a foolish sigh—"Ah me!"
　　Born but to droop and die—"Ah me!"
　　　Yet all the sense
　　　Of eloquence
　　Lies hidden in a maid's "Ah me!"

LOST MR. BLAKE

Mr. Blake was a regular out-and-out hardened sinner,
  Who was quite out of the pale of Christianity, so to speak:
He was in the habit of smoking a long pipe and drinking
    a glass of grog on Sunday after dinner,
  And seldom thought of going to church more than twice
    (or if Good Friday or Christmas Day happened to
    come in it) three times a week.

He was quite indifferent as to the particular kinds of dresses
  That the clergyman wore at the church where he used
    to go to pray,
And whatever he did in the way of relieving a chap's
    distresses,
  He always did in a nasty, sneaking, underhanded, hole-
    and-corner sort of way.

256

Lost Mr. Blake

I have known him indulge in profane, ungentlemanly emphatics,
  When the Protestant Church has been divided on the subject of the width of a chasuble's hem;
I have even known him to sneer at albs—and as for dalmatics,
  Words can't convey an idea of the contempt he expressed for *them*.

He didn't believe in persons who, not being well off themselves, are obliged to confine their charitable exertions to collecting money from wealthier people,
  And looked upon individuals of the former class as ecclesiastical hawks;
He used to say that he would no more think of interfering with his priest's robes than with his church or his steeple,
  And that he did not consider his soul imperilled because somebody over whom he had no influence whatever, chose to dress himself up like an ecclesiastical GUY FAWKES.

This shocking old vagabond was so unutterably shameless
  That he actually went a-courting a very respectable and pious middle-aged sister, by the name of BIGGS:
She was a rather attractive widow whose life, as such, had always been particularly blameless;
  Her first husband had left her a secure but moderate competence owing to some fortunate speculations in the matter of figs.

She was an excellent person in every way—and won the respect even of MRS. GRUNDY,
  She was a good housewife, too, and wouldn't have wasted a penny if she had owned the Koh-i-noor;

Lost Mr. Blake

She was just as strict as he was lax in her observance of
Sunday,
  And being a good economist, and charitable besides, she
  took all the bones and cold potatoes and broken
  pie-crusts and candle-ends (when she had quite done
  with them), and made them into an excellent soup
  for the deserving poor.

I am sorry to say that she rather took to BLAKE—that out-
cast of society;
  And when respectable brothers who were fond of her
  began to look dubious and to cough,
She would say, "Oh, my friends, it's because I hope to
bring this poor benighted soul back to virtue and
propriety"
  (And besides, the poor benighted soul, with all his faults,
  was uncommonly well off).

And when MR. BLAKE'S dissipated friends called his attention to the frown or the pout of her,
  Whenever he did anything which appeared to her to
  savour of an unmentionable place,
He would say she would be a very decent old girl when all
that nonsense was knocked out of her—
  And his method of knocking it out of her is one that
  covered him with disgrace.

She was fond of going to church services four times every
Sunday, and four or five times in the week, and never
seemed to pall of them,
  So he hunted out all the churches within a convenient
  distance that had services at different hours, so to
  speak;
And when he had married her he positively insisted upon
their going to all of them,
  So they contrived to do about twelve churches every
  Sunday, and, if they had luck, from twenty-two to
  twenty-three in the course of the week.

Lost Mr. Blake

She was fond of dropping his sovereigns ostentatiously into
    the plate, and she liked to see them stand out rather
    conspicuously against the commonplace half-crowns
    and shillings,
  So he took her to all the charity sermons, and if by any
    extraordinary chance there wasn't a charity sermon
    anywhere, he would drop a couple of sovereigns (one
    for him and one for her) into the poor-box at the
    door ;

VANITY.

And as he always deducted the sums thus given in charity
    from the housekeeping money, and the money he
    allowed her for her bonnets and frillings,
  She soon began to find that even charity, if you allow it
    to interfere with your personal luxuries, becomes an
    intolerable bore.

On Sundays she was always melancholy and anything but
    good society,
  For that day in her household was a day of sighings and
    sobbings and wringing of hands and shaking of heads:
She wouldn't hear of a button being sewn on a glove,
    because it was a work neither of necessity nor of
    piety,

Lost Mr. Blake

And strictly prohibited her servants from amusing themselves, or indeed doing anything at all except dusting
the drawing-rooms, cleaning the boots and shoes,
cooking the dinner, waiting generally on the family,
and making the beds.

But BLAKE even went farther than that, and said that, on
Sundays, people should do their own works of necessity,
and not delegate them to persons in a menial situation,
So he wouldn't allow his servants to do so much as
even answer a bell.
Here he is making his wife carry up the water for her bath
to the second floor, much against her inclination,—
And why in the world the gentleman who illustrates
these ballads has put him into a cocked hat is more
than I can tell.

After about three months of this sort of thing, taking the
smooth with the rough of it
   (Blacking her own boots and peeling her own potatoes
   was not her notion of connubial bliss),
MRS. BLAKE began to find that she had pretty nearly had
enough of it,
   And came, in course of time, to think that BLAKE'S own
   original line of conduct wasn't so much amiss.

Lost Mr. Blake

And now that wicked person—that detestable sinner
("Belial Blake" his friends and well-wishers call
him for his atrocities),
   And his poor deluded victim whom all her Christian
brothers dislike and pity so,
Go to the parish church only on Sunday morning and
afternoon and occasionally on a week-day, and spend
their evenings in connubial fondlings and affectionate
reciprocities,
   And I should like to know where in the world (or rather,
out of it) they expect to go!

THE DUKE OF PLAZA-TORO

IN enterprise of martial kind,
    When there was any fighting,
He led his regiment from behind
    (He found it less exciting).
But when away his regiment ran,
    His place was at the fore, O—
        That celebrated,
        Cultivated,
        Underrated
          Nobleman,
The Duke of Plaza-Toro!

The Duke of Plaza-Toro

In the first and foremost flight, ha, ha!
You always found that knight, ha, ha!
    That celebrated,
    Cultivated,
    Underrated
      Nobleman,
  The Duke of Plaza-Toro!

When, to evade Destruction's hand,
    To hide they all proceeded,
No soldier in that gallant band
    Hid half as well as he did.
He lay concealed throughout the war,
    And so preserved his gore, O!
    That unaffected,
    Undetected,
    Well connected
      Warrior,
  The Duke of Plaza-Toro!
In every doughty deed, ha, ha!
He always took the lead, ha, ha!
    That unaffected,
    Undetected,
    Well connected
      Warrior,
  The Duke of Plaza-Toro!

When told that they would all be shot
    Unless they left the service,
That hero hesitated not,
    So marvellous his nerve is.
He sent his resignation in,
    The first of all his corps, O!

The Duke of Plaza-Toro

That very knowing,
Overflowing,
Easy-going
Paladin,
The Duke of Plaza-Toro!
To men of grosser clay, ha, ha!
He always showed the way, ha, ha!
That very knowing,
Overflowing,
Easy-going
Paladin,
The Duke of Plaza-Toro!

THE BABY'S VENGEANCE

WEARY at heart and extremely ill
Was PALEY VOLLAIRE of Bromptonville,
In a dirty lodging, with fever down,
Close to the Polygon, Somers Town.

PALEY VOLLAIRE was an only son
(For why?   His mother had had but one),
And PALEY herited gold and grounds
Worth several hundred thousand pounds.

But he, like many a rich young man,
Through this magnificent fortune ran,
And nothing was left for his daily needs
But duplicate copies of mortgage-deeds.

Shabby and sorry and sorely sick,
He slept, and dreamt that the clock's "tick, tick,"
Was one of the Fates, with a long sharp knife,
Snicking off bits of his shortened life.

The Baby's Vengeance

He woke and counted the pips on the walls,
The outdoor passengers' loud footfalls,
And reckoned all over, and reckoned again,
The little white tufts on his counterpane.

A medical man to his bedside came
(I can't remember that doctor's name),
And said, " You'll die in a very short while
If you don't set sail for Madeira's isle."

" Go to Madeira? goodness me !
I haven't the money to pay your fee ! "
"Then, PALEY VOLLAIRE," said the leech, " good-bye ;
I'll come no more, for you're sure to die."

He sighed and he groaned and smote his breast ;
" Oh, send," said he, " for FREDERICK WEST,
Ere senses fade or my eyes grow dim :
I've a terrible tale to whisper him ! "

The Baby's Vengeance

Poor was FREDERICK's lot in life,—
A dustman he with a fair young wife,
A worthy man with a hard-earned store,
A hundred and seventy pounds—or more.

FREDERICK came, and he said, " Maybe
You'll say what you happen to want with me? "
" Wronged boy," said PALEY VOLLAIRE, " I will,
But don't you fidget yourself—sit still.

*　　　*　　　*　　　*　　　*

"'Tis now some thirty-seven years ago
    Since first began the plot that I'm revealing.
A fine young woman, wed·ten years or so,
    Lived with her husband down in Drum Lane, Ealing,
Herself by means of mangling reimbursing,
And now and then (at intervals) wet-nursing.

267

The Baby's Vengeance

"Two little babes dwelt in her humble cot:
  One was her own—the other only lent to her:
Her own she slighted. Tempted by a lot
  Of gold and silver regularly sent to her,
She ministered unto the little other
In the capacity of foster-mother.

"*I was her own.* Oh! how I lay and sobbed
  In my poor cradle—deeply, deeply cursing
The rich man's pampered bantling, who had robbed
  My only birthright—an attentive nursing!
Sometimes, in hatred of my foster-brother,
I gnashed my gums—which terrified my mother.

One darksome day (I should have mentioned that
  We were alike in dress and baby feature)
I *in* MY cradle having placed the brat,
  Crept into his—the pampered little creature!
It was imprudent—well, disgraceful maybe,
For, oh! I was a bad, black-hearted baby!

The Baby's Vengeance

"So rare a luxury was food, I think
   There was no wickedness I wouldn't try for it.
Now if I wanted anything to drink
   At any time, I only had to cry for it!
Once, if I dared to weep, the bottle lacking,
My blubbering involved a serious smacking!

"We grew up in the usual way—my friend,
   My foster-brother, daily growing thinner,
While gradually I began to mend,
   And thrived amazingly on double dinner.
And every one, besides my foster-mother,
Believed that either of us was the other.

"I came into his wealth—I bore his name,
   I bear it still—his property I squandered—
I mortgaged everything—and now (oh, shame!)
   Into a Somers Town shake-down I've wandered!
I am no PALEY—no VOLLAIRE—it's true, my boy!
The only rightful PALEY V. is *you*, my boy!

"And all I have is yours—and yours is mine.
   I still may place you in your true position:
Give me the pounds you've saved, and I'll resign
   My noble name, my rank, and my condition.
So for my sin in fraudulently owning
Your vasty wealth, I am at last atoning!"

    *   *   *   *   *

FREDERICK he was a simple soul,
He pulled from his pocket a bulky roll,
And gave to PALEY his hard-earned store,
A hundred and seventy pounds or more

269

The Baby's Vengeance

Bab

PALEY VOLLAIRE, with many a groan,
Gave FREDERICK all that he'd called his own,—
Two shirts and a sock, and a vest of jean,
A Wellington boot and a bamboo cane.

And FRED (entitled to all things there)
He took the fever from MR. VOLLAIRE,
Which killed poor FREDERICK WEST.   Meanwhile
VOLLAIRE sailed off to Madeira's isle.

THE ÆSTHETE

IF you're anxious for to shine in the high æsthetic line, as
    a man of culture rare,
You must get up all the germs of the transcendental terms,
    and plant them everywhere.
You must lie upon the daisies and discourse in novel
    phrases of your complicated state of mind
(The meaning doesn't matter if it's only idle chatter of a
    transcendental kind).
                    And every one will say,
                    As you walk your mystic way,
" If this young man expresses himself in terms too deep
    for *me*,
Why, what a very singularly deep young man this deep
    young man must be ! "

The Æsthete

Be eloquent in praise of the very dull old days which have
    long since passed away,
And convince 'em, if you can, that the reign of good
    QUEEN ANNE was Culture's palmiest day.
Of course you will pooh-pooh whatever's fresh and new,
    and declare it's crude and mean,
And that Art stopped short in the cultivated court of the
    EMPRESS JOSEPHINE.
              And every one will say,
              As you walk your mystic way,
" If that's not good enough for him which is good enough
    for *me*,
Why, what a very cultivated kind of youth this kind of
    youth must be ! "

Then a sentimental passion of a vegetable fashion must
    excite your languid spleen,
An attachment *à la* Plato for a bashful young potato, or a
    not-too-French French bean.
Though the Philistines may jostle, you will rank as an
    apostle in the high æsthetic band,
If you walk down Piccadilly with a poppy or a lily in your
    mediæval hand.
              And every one will say,
              As you walk your flowery way,
" If he's content with a vegetable love which would
    certainly not suit *me*,
Why, what a most particularly pure young man this pure
    young man must be ! "

THE CAPTAIN AND THE MERMAIDS

I SING a legend of the sea,
So hard-a-port upon your lee!
    A ship on starboard tack!
She's bound upon a private cruise—
(This is the kind of spice I use
    To give a salt-sea smack).

Behold, on every afternoon
(Save in a gale or strong monsoon)
    Great CAPTAIN CAPEL CLEGGS
(Great morally, though rather short)
Sat at an open weather-port
    And aired his shapely legs.

And Mermaids hung around in flocks,
On cable chains and distant rocks,
    To gaze upon those limbs;
For legs like his, of flesh and bone,
Are things "not generally known"
    To any Merman TIMBS.

But Mermen didn't seem to care
Much time (as far as I'm aware)
    With CLEGGS'S legs to spend;
Though Mermaids swam around all day
And gazed, exclaiming, "That's the way
    A gentleman should end!

The Captain and the Mermaids

"A pair of legs with well-cut knees
And calves and ankles such as these
　　Which we in rapture hail,
Are far more eloquent, it's clear,
When clothed in silk and kerseymere,
　　Than any nasty tail."

And CLEGGS—a worthy kind old boy—
Rejoiced to add to others' joy,
　　And, though he scarce knew why
(Perhaps to please the lookers-on),
He sat there every day—though con-
　　Stitutionally shy.

At first the Mermen sneered pooh-pooh.
But finally they jealous grew,
　　And sounded loud recalls;
But vainly.　So these fishy males
Declared they too would clothe their tails
　　In silken hose and smalls.

The Captain and the Mermaids

They set to work, these water-men,
And made their nether robes——but when
    They drew with dainty touch
The kerseymere upon their tails,
They found it scraped against their scales,
    And hurt them very much.

The silk, besides, with which they chose
To deck their tails, by way of hose
    (They never thought of shoon),
For such a use was much too thin,——
It tore against the caudal fin
    And "went in ladders" soon.

So they designed another plan:
They sent their most seductive man
    This note to CLEGGS to show——
"Our Monarch sends to CAPTAIN CLEGGS
His humble compliments, and begs
    He'll join him down below;

"We've pleasant homes below the sea——
Besides, if CAPTAIN CLEGGS should be
    (As our advices say)
A judge of Mermaids, he will find
Our lady-fish of every kind
    Inspection will repay."

Good CAPEL sent a kind reply,
For CAPEL thought he could descry
    An admirable plan
To study all their ways and laws——
(But not their lady-fish, because
    He was a married man).

The Captain and the Mermaids

The Merman sank—the Captain too
Jumped overboard, and dropped from view
    Like stone from catapult;
And when he reached the Merman's lair
He certainly was welcomed there,
    But, ah! with what result?

They didn't let him learn their law,
Or make a note of what he saw,
    Or interesting mem.:
The lady-fish he couldn't find,
But that, of course, he didn't mind—
    He didn't come for them.

For though when CAPTAIN CAPEL sank,
The Mermen drawn in double rank
    Gave him a hearty hail;
Yet when secure of CAPTAIN CLEGGS,
They cut off both his lovely legs,
    And gave him *such* a tail!

The Captain and the Mermaids

When CAPTAIN CLEGGS returned aboard,
His blithesome crew convulsive roar'd,
    To see him altered so.
The Admiralty did insist
That he upon the Half-pay list
    Immediately should go.

In vain declared the poor old salt,
" It's my misfortune—not my fault,"
    With tear and trembling lip—
In vain poor CAPEL begged and begged—
" A man must be completely legged
    Who rules a British ship."

Bab

So spake the stern First Lord aloud—
He was a wag, though very proud,
    And much rejoiced to say,
"You're only half a captain now—
And so, my worthy friend, I vow
    You'll only get half-pay."

SAID I TO MYSELF, SAID I

When I went to the Bar as a very young man
    (Said I to myself—said I),
I'll work on a new and original plan
    (Said I to myself—said I),
I'll never assume that a rogue or a thief
Is a gentleman worthy implicit belief,
Because his attorney has sent me a brief
    (Said I to myself—said I !)

I'll never throw dust in a juryman's eyes
    (Said I to myself—said I),
Or hoodwink a judge who is not over-wise
    (Said I to myself—said I),
Or assume that the witnesses summoned in force
In Exchequer, Queen's Bench, Common Pleas, or Divorce,
Have perjured themselves as a matter of course
    (Said I to myself—said I !)

Said I to Myself, Said I

Ere I go into court I will read my brief through
  (Said I to myself—said I),
And I'll never take work I'm unable to do
  (Said I to myself—said I).
My learned profession I'll never disgrace
By taking a fee with a grin on my face,
When I haven't been there to attend to the case
  (Said I to myself—said I !)

In other professions in which men engage
  (Said I to myself—said I),
The Army, the Navy, the Church, and the Stage
  (Said I to myself—said I),
Professional licence, if carried too far,
Your chance of promotion will certainly mar—
And I fancy the rule might apply to the Bar
  (Said I to myself—said I !)

ANNIE PROTHEROE

A LEGEND OF STRATFORD-LE-BOW

OH! listen to the tale of little ANNIE PROTHEROE,
She kept a small post-office in the neighbourhood of Bow,
She loved a skilled mechanic, who was famous in his day—
A gentle executioner whose name was GILBERT CLAY.

I think I hear you say, "A dreadful subject for your
     rhymes!"
O reader, do not shrink—he didn't live in modern times!
He lived so long ago (the sketch will show it at a glance)
That all his actions glitter with the limelight of Romance.

In busy times he laboured at his gentle craft all day—
"No doubt you mean his Cal-craft" you amusingly will
     say—
But, no—he didn't operate with common bits of string,
He was a Public Headsman, which is quite another thing.

Annie Protheroe

And when his work was over, they would ramble o'er the
    lea,
And sit beneath the frondage of an elderberry tree;
And ANNIE's simple prattle entertained him on his walk,
For public executions formed the subject of her talk.

And sometimes he'd explain to her, which charmed her
    very much,
How famous operators vary very much in touch,
And then, perhaps, he'd show how he himself performed
    the trick,
And illustrate his meaning with a poppy and a stick.

Or, if it rained, the little maid would stop at home, and
    look
At his favourable notices, all pasted in a book,
And then her cheek would flush—her swimming eyes
    would dance with joy
In a glow of admiration at the prowess of her boy.

Annie Protheroe

One summer eve, at supper-time, the gentle GILBERT said
(As he helped his pretty ANNIE to a slice of collared head),
"This collared head reminds me that to-morrow is the day
When I decapitate your former lover, PETER GRAY."

He saw his ANNIE tremble and he saw his ANNIE start,
Her changing colour trumpeted the flutter at her heart;
Young GILBERT's manly bosom rose and sank with jealous
      fear,
And he said, "O gentle ANNIE, what's the meaning of
      this here?"

And ANNIE answered, blushing in an interesting way,
"You think, no doubt, I'm sighing for that felon PETER
      GRAY:
That I was his young woman is unquestionably true,
But not since I began a-keeping company with you."

Then GILBERT, who was irritable, rose and loudly swore
He'd know the reason why if she refused to tell him more;
And she answered (all the woman in her flashing from her
      eyes),
"You mustn't ask no questions, and you won't be told no
      lies!

Annie Protheroe

"Few lovers have the privilege enjoyed, my dear, by you,
Of chopping off a rival's head and quartering him too!
Of vengeance, dear, to-morrow you will surely take your
    fill!"
And GILBERT ground his molars as he answered her, "I
    will!"

Young GILBERT rose from table with a stern determined
    look,
And, frowning, took an inexpensive hatchet from its hook;
And ANNIE watched his movements with an interested
    air—
For the morrow—for the morrow he was going to prepare!

He chipped it with a hammer and he chopped it with a
    bill,
He poured sulphuric acid on the edge of it, until
This terrible Avenger of the Majesty of Law
Was far less like a hatchet than a dissipated saw.

And ANNIE said, "O GILBERT, dear, I do not understand
Why ever you are injuring that hatchet in your hand?"
He said, "It is intended for to lacerate and flay
The neck of that unmitigated villain PETER GRAY!"

"Now, GILBERT," ANNIE answered, "wicked headsman,
    just beware—
I won't have PETER tortured with that horrible affair;
If you attempt to flay him, you will surely rue the day."
But GILBERT said, "Oh, shall I?" which was just his nasty
    way.

He saw a look of anger from her eyes distinctly dart,
For ANNIE was a *woman*, and had pity in her heart!
She wished him a good evening—he answered with a glare;
She only said, "Remember, for your ANNIE will be there!"

    *   *   *   *   *

Annie Protheroe

The morrow GILBERT boldly on the scaffold took his stand,
With a vizor on his face and with a hatchet in his hand,
And all the people noticed that the Engine of the Law
Was far less like a hatchet than a dissipated saw.

The felon very coolly loosed his collar and his stock,
And placed his wicked head upon the handy little block—
The hatchet was uplifted for to settle PETER GRAY,
When GILBERT plainly heard a woman's voice exclaiming, "Stay!"

'Twas ANNIE, gentle ANNIE, as you'll easily believe—
"O GILBERT, you must spare him, for I bring him a re
    prieve,
It came from our Home Secretary many weeks ago,
And passed through that post-office which I used to keep
    at Bow.

"I loved you, loved you madly, and you know it, GILBERT
    CLAY,
And having quite surrendered all idea of PETER GRAY,
I quietly suppressed it, as you'll clearly understand,
For I thought it might be awkward if he came and claimed
    my hand.

Annie Protheroe

"In anger at my secret (which I could not tell before)
To lacerate poor PETER GRAY vindictively you swore;
I told you if you used that blunted axe you'd rue the day,
And so you will, you monster, for I'll marry PETER GRAY!"

[*And so she did.*

SORRY HER LOT

SORRY her lot who loves too well,
    Heavy the heart that hopes but vainly,
Sad are the sighs that own the spell
    Uttered by eyes that speak too plainly;
      Heavy the sorrow that bows the head
      When Love is alive and Hope is dead!

Sad is the hour when sets the Sun —
    Dark is the night to Earth's poor daughters,
When to the ark the wearied one
    Flies from the empty waste of waters!
      Heavy the sorrow that bows the head
      When Love is alive and Hope is dead!

AN UNFORTUNATE LIKENESS

I've painted SHAKESPEARE all my life—
  "An infant" (even then at play),
"A boy," with stage-ambition rife,
  Then "Married to ANN HATHAWAY."

"The bard's first ticket night" (or "ben."),
  His "First appearance on the stage,"
His "Call before the curtain"—then
  "Rejoicings when he came of age."

The bard play-writing in his room,
  The bard a humble lawyer's clerk,
The bard a lawyer [1]—parson [2]—groom [3]—
  The bard deer-stealing, after dark.

[1] "Go with me to a notary—seal me there
  Your single bond."—*Merchant of Venice*, Act I., sc. 3.
[2] "And there she shall, at Friar Lawrence' cell,
  Be shrived and married."—*Romeo and Juliet*, Act II., sc. 4.
[3] "And give their fasting horses provender."
  —*Henry the Fifth*, Act IV., sc. 2.

An Unfortunate Likeness

The bard a tradesman [1]—and a Jew [2]—
    The bard a botanist [3]—a beak [4]—
The bard a skilled musician [5] too—
    A sheriff [6] and a surgeon [7] eke!

Yet critics say (a friendly stock)
    That, though with all my skill I try,
Yet even I can barely mock
    The glimmer of his wondrous eye!

One morning as a work I framed,
    There passed a person, walking hard:
"My gracious goodness," I exclaimed,
    "How very like my dear old bard!

"Oh, what a model he would make!"
    I rushed outside—impulsive me!—
"Forgive the liberty I take,
    But you're so very"—"Stop!" said he.

"You needn't waste your breath or time,—
    I know what you are going to say,—
That you're an artist, and that I'm
    Remarkably like SHAKESPEARE. Eh?

[1] "Let us, like merchants, show our foulest wares."
                —*Troilus and Cressida*, Act I., sc. 3.
[2] "Then must the Jew be merciful."
                —*Merchant of Venice*, Act IV., sc. 1.
[3]   "The spring, the summer,
  The childing autumn, angry winter, change
  Their wonted liveries."—*Midsummer Night's Dream*, Act IV., sc. 1.
[4] "In the county of Glo'ster, justice of the peace and *coram*."
                —*Merry Wives of Windsor*, Act I., sc. 1.
[5] "What lusty trumpet thus doth summon us?"
                —*King John*, Act V., sc. 2.
[6] "And I'll provide his executioner."
                —*Henry the Sixth* (Second Part), Act III., sc. 1.
[7] "The lioness had torn some flesh away,
  Which all this while had bled."—*As You Like It*, Act IV., sc. 3.

An Unfortunate Likeness

"You wish that I would sit to you?"
  I clasped him madly round the waist,
And breathlessly replied, "I do!"
  "All right," said he, "but please make haste."

I led him by his hallowed sleeve,
  And worked away at him apace,
I painted him till dewy eve,—
  There never was a nobler face!

"Oh, sir," I said, "a fortune grand
  Is yours, by dint of merest chance,—
To sport *his* brow at second-hand,
  To wear *his* cast-off countenance!

"To rub *his* eyes whene'er they ache—
  To wear *his* baldness ere you're old—
To clean *his* teeth when you awake—
  To blow *his* nose when you've a cold!"

His eyeballs glistened in his eyes—
  I sat and watched and smoked my pipe;
"Bravo!" I said, "I recognise
  The phrensy of your prototype!"

His scanty hair he wildly tore:
  "That's right," said I, "it shows your breed."
He danced—he stamped—he wildly swore—
  "Bless me, that's very fine indeed!"

"Sir," said the grand Shakespearian boy
  (Continuing to blaze away),
"You think my face a source of joy;
  That shows you know not what you say.

"Forgive these yells and cellar-flaps,
  I'm always thrown in some such state
When on his face well-meaning chaps
  This wretched man congratulate.

289   L

An Unfortunate Likeness

" For, oh ! this face—this pointed chin—
    This nose—this brow—these eyeballs too,
Have always been the origin
    Of all the woes I ever knew !

" If to the play my way I find,
    To see a grand Shakespearian piece,
I have no rest, no ease of mind
    Until the author's puppets cease !

" Men nudge each other—thus—and say,
    ' This certainly is SHAKESPEARE'S son,'
And merry wags (of course in play)
    Cry ' Author !' when the piece is done.

" In church the people stare at me,
    Their soul the sermon never binds ;
I catch them looking round to see,
    And thoughts of SHAKESPEARE fill their minds.

" And sculptors, fraught with cunning wile,
    Who find it difficult to crown
A bust with BROWN's insipid smile,
    Or TOMKINS's unmannered frown,

An Unfortunate Likeness

"Yet boldly make my face their own,
  When (oh, presumption !) they require
To animate a paving-stone
  With SHAKESPEARE'S intellectual fire.

" At parties where young ladies gaze,
  And I attempt to speak my joy,
'Hush, pray,' some lovely creature says,
  'The fond illusion don't destroy !'

"Whene'er I speak my soul is wrung
  With these or some such whisperings ;
''Tis pity that a SHAKESPEARE'S tongue
  Should say such un-Shakespearian things !'

"I should not thus be criticised
  Had I face of common wont :
Don't envy me—now, be advised !"
  And, now I think of it, I don't !

THE CONTEMPLATIVE SENTRY

WHEN all night long a chap remains
    On sentry-go, to chase monotony
He exercises of his brains,
    That is, assuming that he's got any.
Though never nurtured in the lap
    Of luxury, yet I admonish you,
I am an intellectual chap,
    And think of things that would astonish you.
        I often think it's comical
            How Nature always does contrive
        That every boy and every gal,
            That's born into the world alive,
        Is either a little Liberal,
            Or else a little Conservative!
                Fal lal la!

The Contemplative Sentry

When in that house M.P.'s divide,
  If they've a brain and cerebellum, too,
They've got to leave that brain outside,
  And vote just as their leaders tell 'em to.
But then the prospect of a lot
  Of statesmen, all in close proximity,
A-thinking for themselves, is what
  No man can face with equanimity.
    Then let's rejoice with loud Fal lal
      That Nature wisely does contrive
    That every boy and every gal,
      That's born into the world alive,
    Is either a little Liberal,
      Or else a little Conservative !
        Fal lal la !

GREGORY PARABLE, LL.D.

A LEAFY cot, where no dry rot
Had ever been by tenant seen,
Where ivy clung and wopses stung,
Where beeses hummed and drummed and strummed,
Where treeses grew and breezes blew—
A thatchy roof, quite waterproof,
Where countless herds of dicky-birds
Built twiggy beds to lay their heads
(My mother begs I'll make it " eggs,"
But though it's true that dickies do
Construct a nest with chirpy noise,
With view to rest their eggy joys,

294

Gregory Parable, LL.D.

'Neath eavy sheds, yet eggs and beds,
As I explain to her in vain
Five hundred times, are faulty rhymes)
'Neath such a cot, built on a plot
Of freehold land, dwelt MARY and
Her worthy father, named by me
GREGORY PARABLE, LL.D.

He knew no guile, this simple man,
No worldly wile, or plot, or plan,
Except that plot of freehold land
That held the cot, and MARY, and
Her worthy father, named by me
GREGORY PARABLE, LL.D.

A grave and learned scholar he,
Yet simple as a child could be.
He'd shirk his meal to sit and cram
A goodish deal of Eton Gram.
No man alive could him nonplus
With vocative of *filius*;
No man alive more fully knew
The passive of a verb or two;
None better knew the worth than he
Of words that end in *b, d, t.*
Upon his green in early spring
He might be seen endeavouring
To understand the hooks and crooks
Of HENRY and his Latin books;
Or calling for his " Cæsar on
The Gallic War," like any don;
Or, p'raps, expounding unto all
How mythic BALBUS built a wall.
So lived the sage who's named by me
GREGORY PARABLE, LL.D.

Gregory Parable, LL.D.

To him one autumn day there came
A lovely youth of mystic name :
He took a lodging in the house,
And fell a-dodging snipe and grouse,
For, oh ! that mild scholastic one
Let shooting for a single gun.

By three or four, when sport was o'er,
The Mystic One laid by his gun,
And made sheep's eyes of giant size,

Till after tea, at MARY P.
And MARY P. (so kind was she),
She, too, made eyes of giant size,
Whose every dart right through the heart
Appeared to run that Mystic One.
The Doctor's whim engrossing him,
He did not know they flirted so.
For, save at tea, "*musa musæ*,"
As I'm advised, monopolised
And rendered blind his giant mind.

Gregory Parable, LL.D.

But looking up above his cup
One afternoon, he saw them spoon.
"Aha!" quoth he, "you naughty lass.
As quaint old OVID says, 'Amas!'"

The Mystic Youth avowed the truth,
And, claiming ruth, he said, "In sooth
I love your daughter, aged man:
Refuse to join us if you can.
Treat not my offer, sir, with scorn,
I'm wealthy though I'm lowly born."
"Young sir," the aged scholar said,
"I never thought you meant to wed:
Engrossed completely with my books,
I little noticed lovers' looks.
I've lived so long away from man,
I do not know of any plan
By which to test a lover's worth,
Except, perhaps, the test of birth.
I've half forgotten in this wild
A father's duty to his child.
It is his place, I think it's said,
To see his daughters richly wed
To dignitaries of the earth—
If possible, of noble birth.
If noble birth is not at hand,
A father may, I understand
(And this affords a chance for you),
Be satisfied to wed her to
A BOUCICAULT or BARING—which
Means any one who's very rich.
Now, there's an Earl who lives hard by,—
My child and I will go and try
If he will make the maid his bride—
If not, to you she shall be tied."

They sought the Earl that very day;
The Sage began to say his say.

Gregory Parable, LL.D.

The Earl (a very wicked man,
Whose face bore Vice's blackest ban)
Cut short the scholar's simple tale,
And said in voice to make them quail,
"Pooh! go along! you're drunk, no doubt—
Here, PETERS, turn these people out!"

The Sage, rebuffed in mode uncouth,
Returning, met the Mystic Youth.
" My darling boy," the Scholar said,
"Take MARY—blessings on your head!"

The Mystic Boy undid his vest,
And took a parchment from his breast,
And said, " Now, by that noble brow,
I ne'er knew father such as thou!
The sterling rule of common sense
Now reaps its proper recompense.
Rejoice, my soul's unequalled Queen,
For I am DUKE OF GRETNA GREEN!"

THE PHILOSOPHIC PILL

I'VE wisdom from the East and from the West,
    That's subject to no academic rule; ·
You may find it in the jeering of a jest,
    Or distil it from the folly cf a fool.
I can teach you with a quip, if I've a mind;
    I can trick you into learning with a laugh;
Oh, winnow all my folly, and you'll find
    A grain or two of truth among the chaff!

I can set a braggart quailing with a quip,
    The upstart I can wither with a whim;
He may wear a merry laugh upon his lip,
    But his laughter has an echo that is grim.

The Philosophic Pill

When they're offered to the world in merry guise,
    Unpleasant truths are swallowed with a will—
For he who'd make his fellow·creatures wise
    Should always gild the philosophic pill !

The King of Canoodle-Dum

THE KING OF CANOODLE-DUM

THE story of FREDERICK GOWLER,
    A mariner of the sea,
Who quitted his ship, the *Howler*,
    A-sailing in Caribbee.
For many a day he wandered,
    Till he met, in a state of rum,
CALAMITY POP VON PEPPERMINT DROP,
    The King of Canoodle-Dum.

That monarch addressed him gaily,
    "Hum! Golly de do to-day?
Hum! Lily-white Buckra Sailee"—
    (You notice his playful way?)—
"What dickens you doin' here, sar?
    Why debbil you want to come?
Hum! Picaninnee, dere isn't no sea
    In City Canoodle-Dum!"

The King of Canoodle-Dum

And GOWLER he answered sadly,
  "Oh, mine is a doleful tale!
They've treated me werry badly
  In Lunnon, from where I hail.
I'm one of the Family Royal—
  No common Jack Tar you see;
I'm WILLIAM THE FOURTH, far up in the North,
  A King in my own countree!"

Bang-bang!   How the tom-toms thundered!
  Bang-bang!   How they thumped the gongs!
Bang-bang!   How the people wondered!
  Bang-bang!   At it, hammer and tongs!
Alliance with Kings of Europe
  Is an honour Canoodlers seek;
Her monarchs don't stop with PEPPERMINT DROP
  Every day in the week!

FRED told them that he was *un*done,
  For his people all went insane,
And fired the Tower of London,
  And Grinnidge's Naval Fane.
And some of them racked St. James's,
  And vented their rage upon
The Church of St. Paul, the Fishmongers' Hall,
  And the "Angel" at Islington.

CALAMITY POP implored him
  At Canoodle-Dum to remain
Till those people of his restored him
  To power and rank again.
CALAMITY POP he made him
  A Prince of Canoodle-Dum,
With a couple of caves, some beautiful slaves,
  And the run of the royal rum.

The King of Canoodle-Dum

Pop gave him his only daughter,
  Hum Pickety Wimple Tip:
Fred vowed that if over the water
  He went, in an English ship,
He'd make her his Queen,—though truly,
  It is an unusual thing
For a Caribbee brat who's as black as your hat
  To be wife of an English King.

And all the Canoodle-Dummers
  They copied his rolling walk,
His method of draining rummers,
  His emblematical talk.
For his dress and his graceful breeding,
  His delicate taste in rum,
And his nautical way, were the talk of the day
  In the Court of Canoodle-Dum.

The King of Canoodle-Dum

CALAMITY POP most wisely
  Determined in everything
To model his Court precisely
  On that of the English King;
And ordered that every lady
  And every lady's lord
Should masticate jacky (a kind of tobaccy)
  And scatter its juice abroad.

They signified wonder roundly
  At any astounding yarn,
By darning their dear eyes roundly
  ('Twas all that they had to darn).
They "hoisted their slacks," adjusting
  Garments of plantain-leaves
With nautical twitches (as if they wore—stitches,
  Instead of a dress like EVE's !)

They shivered their timbers proudly,
  At a phantom fore-lock dragged,
And called for a hornpipe loudly
  Whenever amusement flagged.

304

The King of Canoodle-Dum

"Hum! Golly! him Pop resemble,
   Him Britisher sov'reign, hum!
Calamity Pop Von Peppermint Drop,
   De King of Canoodle-Dum!"

The mariner's lively "Hollo!"
   Enlivened Canoodle's plain
(For blessings unnumbered follow
   In Civilisation's train).
But Fortune, who loves a bathos,
   A terrible ending planned,
For Admiral D. Chickabiddy, C.B.,
   Placed foot on Canoodle land!

That officer seized King Gowler;
   He threatened his royal brains,
And put him aboard the *Howler*,
   And fastened him down with chains.
The *Howler* she weighed her anchor,
   With Frederick nicely nailed,
And off to the North with William the Fourth
   That Admiral slowly sailed.

The King of Canoodle-Dum

CALAMITY said (with folly)
    "Hum! nebber want him again—
Him civilise all of us, golly!
    CALAMITY suck him brain!"
The people, however, were pained when
    They saw him aboard the ship,
But none of them wept for their FREDDY, except
    HUM PICKITY WIMPLE TIP.

BLUE BLOOD

Spurn not the nobly born
    With love affected,
Nor treat with virtuous scorn
    The well connected.
High rank involves no shame—
We boast an equal claim
With him of humble name
    To be respected!
      Blue blood! Blue blood!
        When virtuous love is sought,
          Thy power is naught,
      Though dating from the Flood,
        Blue blood!

Blue Blood

Spare us the bitter pain
  Of stern denials,
Nor with low-born disdain
  Augment our trials.
Hearts just as pure and fair
May beat in Belgrave Square
As in the lowly air
  Of Seven Dials !
    Blue blood ! Blue blood !
      Of what avail art thou
        To serve me now ?
      Though dating from the Flood,
        Blue blood !

FIRST LOVE

A CLERGYMAN in Berkshire dwelt,
 The REVEREND BERNARD POWLES,
And in his church there weekly knelt
 At least a hundred souls.

There little ELLEN you might see,
 The modest rustic belle;
In maidenly simplicity,
 She loved her BERNARD well.

Though ELLEN wore a plain silk gown
 Untrimmed with lace or fur,
Yet not a husband in the town
 But wished his wife like her.

First Love

Though sterner memories might fade,
  You never could forget
The child-form of that baby-maid,
  The Village Violet!

A simple frightened loveliness,
  Whose sacred spirit-part
Shrank timidly from worldly stress,
  And nestled in your heart.

POWLES woo'd with every well-worn plan
  And all the usual wiles
With which a well-schooled gentleman
  A simple heart beguiles.

The hackneyed compliments that bore
  World-folks like you and me,
Appeared to her as if they wore
  The crown of Poesy.

His winking eyelid sang a song
  Her heart could understand,
Eternity seemed scarce too long
  When BERNARD squeezed her hand.

He ordered down the martial crew
  Of GODFREY's Grenadiers,
And COOTE conspired with TINNEY to
  Ecstaticise her ears.

First Love

Beneath her window, veiled from eye,
  They nightly took their stand;
On birthdays supplemented by
  The Covent Garden band.

And little ELLEN, all alone,
  Enraptured sat above,
And thought how blest she was to own
  The wealth of POWLES's love.

I often, often wonder what
  Poor ELLEN saw in him;
For calculated he was *not*
  To please a woman's whim.

He wasn't good, despite the air
  An M.B. waistcoat gives;
Indeed, his dearest friends declare
  No greater humbug lives.

First Love

No kind of virtue decked this priest,
    He'd nothing to allure;
He wasn't handsome in the least,—
    He wasn't even poor.

No—he was cursed with acres fat
    (A Christian's direst ban),
And gold—yet, notwithstanding that,
    Poor ELLEN loved the man.

As unlike BERNARD as could be
    Was poor old AARON WOOD
(Disgraceful BERNARD's curate he):
    He was extremely good.

A BAYARD in his moral pluck
    Without reproach or fear,
A quiet venerable duck
    With fifty pounds a year.

First Love

No fault had he—no fad, except
    A tendency to strum,
In mode at which you would have wept,
    A dull harmonium.

He had no gold with which to hire
    The minstrels who could best
Convey a notion of the fire
    That raged within his breast.

And so, when COOTE and TINNEY's Own
    Had tootled all they knew,
And when the Guards, completely blown,
    Exhaustedly withdrew,

And NELL began to sleepy feel,
    Poor AARON then would come,
And underneath her window wheel
    His plain harmonium.

He woke her every morn at two,
    And having gained her ear,
In vivid colours AARON drew
    The sluggard's grim career.

He warbled Apiarian praise,
    And taught her in his chant
To shun the dog's pugnacious ways,
    And imitate the ant.

Still NELL seemed not, how much he played,
    To love him out and out,
Although the admirable maid
    Respected him, no doubt.

First Love

She told him of her early vow,
  And said as BERNARD's wife
It might be hers to show him how
  To rectify his life.

"You are so pure, so kind, so true,
  Your goodness shines so bright,
What use would ELLEN be to you?
  Believe me, you're all right."

She wished him happiness and health,
  And flew on lightning wings
To BERNARD with his dangerous wealth
  And all the woes it brings.

THE JUDGE'S SONG

When I, good friends, was called to the Bar,
  I'd an appetite fresh and hearty,
But I was, as many young barristers are,
  An impecunious party.
I'd a swallow-tail coat of a beautiful blue—
  A brief which was brought by a booby—
A couple of shirts and a collar or two,
  And a ring that looked like a ruby!

In Westminster Hall I danced a dance,
  Like a semi-despondent fury;
For I thought I should never hit on a chance
  Of addressing a British Jury—
But I soon got tired of third-class journeys,
  And dinners of bread and water;
So I fell in love with a rich attorney's
  Elderly, ugly daughter.

The Judge's Song

The rich attorney, he wiped his eyes,
    And replied to my fond professions :
" You shall reap the reward of your enterprise,
    At the Bailey and Middlesex Sessions.
You'll soon get used to her looks," said he,
    " And a very nice girl you'll find her—
She may very well pass for forty-three
    In the dusk, with a light behind her ! "

The rich attorney was as good as his word :
    The briefs came trooping gaily,
And every day my voice was heard
    At the Sessions or Ancient Bailey.
All thieves who could my fees afford
    Relied on my orations,
And many a burglar I've restored
    To his friends and his relations.

At length I became as rich as the GURNEYS—
    An incubus then I thought her,
So I threw over that rich attorney's
    Elderly, ugly daughter.
The rich attorney my character high
    Tried vainly to disparage—
And now, if you please, I'm ready to try
    This Breach of Promise of Marriage !

BRAVE ALUM BEY

Oh, big was the bosom of brave ALUM BEY,
And also the region that under it lay,
In safety and peril remarkably cool,
And he dwelt on the banks of the river Stamboul.

Each morning he went to his garden, to cull
A bunch of zenana or sprig of bul-bul,
And offered the bouquet, in exquisite bloom,
To BACKSHEESH, the daughter of RAHAT LAKOUM.

Brave Alum Bey

No maiden like BACKSHEESH could tastily cook
A kettle of kismet or joint of tchibouk,
As ALUM, brave fellow! sat pensively by,
With a bright sympathetic ka-bob in his eye.

Stern duty compelled him to leave her one day—
(A ship's supercargo was brave ALUM BEY)—
To pretty young BACKSHEESH he made a salaam,
And sailed to the isle of Seringapatam.

"O ALUM," said she, "think again, ere you go—
Hareems may arise and Moguls they may blow;
You may strike on a fez, or be drowned, which is wuss!"
But ALUM embraced her and spoke to her thus:

Cease weeping, fair BACKSHEESH! I willingly swear
Cork jackets and trousers I always will wear,
And I also throw in a large number of oaths
That I never—no, *never*—will take off my clothes!"

*   *   *   *   *

They left Madagascar away on their right,
And made Clapham Common the following night,
Then lay on their oars for a fortnight or two,
Becalmed in the ocean of Honololu.

One day ALUM saw, with alarm in his breast,
A cloud on the nor-sow-sow-nor-sow-nor-west;
The wind it arose, and the crew gave a scream,
For they knew it—they knew it!—the dreaded Hareem!!

The mast it went over, and so did the sails,
Brave ALUM threw over his casks and his bales;
The billows arose as the weather grew thick,
And all except ALUM were terribly sick.

Brave Alum Bey

The crew were but three, but they holloa'd for nine,
They howled and they blubbered with wail and with
    whine:
The skipper he fainted away in the fore,
For he hadn't the heart for to skip any more.

"Ho, coward!" said ALUM, "with heart of a child!
Thou son of a party whose grave is defiled!
Is ALUM in terror? is ALUM afeard?
Ho! ho! If you had one I'd laugh at your beard."

His eyeball it gleamed like a furnace of coke;
He boldly inflated his clothes as he spoke;
He daringly felt for the corks on his chest,
And he recklessly tightened the belt at his breast.

For he knew, the brave ALUM, that, happen what might,
With belts and cork-jacketing, *he* was all right;
Though others might sink, he was certain to swim,—
No Hareem whatever had terrors for him!

They begged him to spare from his personal store
A single cork garment—they asked for no more;
But he couldn't, because of the number of oaths
That he never—no, never!—would take off his clothes.

The billows dash o'er them and topple around,
They see they are pretty near sure to be drowned.
A terrible wave o'er the quarter-deck breaks,
And the vessel it sinks in a couple of shakes!

The dreadful Hareem, though it knows how to blow,
Expends all its strength in a minute or so;
When the vessel had foundered, as I have detailed,
The tempest subsided, and quiet prevailed.

Brave Alum Bey

One seized on a cork with a yelling " Ha ! ha ! "
(Its bottle had 'prisoned a pint of Pacha)—
Another a toothpick—another a tray—
" Alas ! it is useless ! " said brave ALUM BEY.

" To holloa and kick is a very bad plan :
Get it over, my tulips, as soon as you can ;
You'd better lay hold of a good lump of lead,
And cling to it tightly until you are dead.

" Just raise your hands over your pretty heads—so—
Right down to the bottom you're certain to go.
Ta ! ta ! I'm afraid we shall not meet again "—
For the truly courageous are truly humane.

Brave ALUM was picked up the very next day—
A man-o'-war sighted him smoking away ;
With hunger and cold he was ready to drop,
So they sent him below and they gave him a chop.

Brave Alum Bey

O reader, or readress, whichever you be,
You weep for the crew who have sunk in the sea?
O reader, or readress, read farther, and dry
The bright sympathetic ka-bob in your eye.

That ship had a grapple with three iron spikes,—
It's lowered, and, ha! on a something it strikes!
They haul it aboard with a British "heave-ho!"
And what it has fished the drawing will show.

There was WILSON, and PARKER, and TOMLINSON, too—
(The first was the captain, the others the crew)—
As lively and spry as a Malabar ape,
Quite pleased and surprised at their happy escape.

And ALUM, brave fellow, who stood in the fore,
And never expected to look on them more,
Was really delighted to see them again,
For the truly courageous are truly humane.

WHEN I FIRST PUT THIS UNIFORM ON

WHEN I first put this uniform on,
I said, as I looked in the glass,
    "It's one to a million
    That any civilian
My figure and form will surpass.
Gold lace has a charm for the fair,
And I've plenty of that, and to spare,
    While a lover's professions,
    When uttered in Hessians,
Are eloquent everywhere!"
    A fact that I counted upon,
    When I first put this uniform on!

When I First Put this Uniform On

I said, when I first put it on,
" It is plain to the veriest dunce
    That every beauty
    Will feel it her duty
To yield to its glamour at once.
They will see that I'm freely gold-laced
In a uniform handsome and chaste "—
    But the peripatetics
    Of long-haired æsthetics,
Are very much more to their taste—
      Which I never counted upon
      When I first put this uniform on !

SIR BARNABY BAMPTON BOO

THIS is SIR BARNABY BAMPTON BOO,
   Last of a noble race,
BARNABY BAMPTON, coming to woo,
   All at a deuce of a pace.
        BARNABY BAMPTON BOO,
        Here is a health to you:
   Here is wishing you luck, you elderly buck—
        BARNABY BAMPTON BOO!

The excellent women of Tuptonvee
   Knew SIR BARNABY BOO;
One of them surely his bride would be,
   But dickens a soul knew who.
        Women of Tuptonvee,
        Here is a health to ye:
   For a Baronet, dears, you would cut off your ears,
        Women of Tuptonvee!

Sir Barnaby Bampton Boo

Here are old MR. and MRS. DE PLOW
  (PETER his Christian name),
They kept seven oxen, a pig, and a cow—
  Farming it was their game.
        Worthy old PETER DE PLOW,
        Here is a health to thou :
    Your race isn't run, though you're seventy-one,
        Worthy old PETER DE PLOW !

To excellent MR. and MRS. DE PLOW
  Came SIR BARNABY BOO,
He asked for their daughter, and told 'em as how
  He was as rich as a Jew.
        BARNABY BAMPTON'S wealth,
        Here is your jolly good health :
    I'd never repine if you came to be mine,
        BARNABY BAMPTON'S wealth !

Sir Barnaby Bampton Boo

"O great SIR BARNABY BAMPTON BOO"
    (Said PLOW to that titled swell),
"My missus has given me daughters two—
    AMELIA and VOLATILE NELL!"
        AMELIA and VOLATILE NELL,
            I hope you're uncommonly well:
    You two pretty pearls—you extremely nice girls—
        AMELIA and VOLATILE NELL!

Bab

"AMELIA is passable only, in face,
    But, oh! she's a worthy girl;
Superior morals like hers would grace
    The home of a belted Earl."
        Morality, heavenly link!
        To you I'll eternally drink:
I'm awfully fond of that heavenly bond,
        Morality, heavenly link!

Sir Barnaby Bampton Boo

"Now NELLY's the prettier, p'raps, of my gals,
　But, oh! she's a wayward chit;
She dresses herself in her showy fal-lals,
　And doesn't read TUPPER a bit!"
　　　　O TUPPER, philosopher true,
　　　　How do you happen to do?
　　A publisher looks with respect on your books,
　　　　For they *do* sell, philosopher true!

The Bart. (I'll be hanged if I drink him again,
　Or care if he's ill or well),
He sneered at the goodness of MILLY THE PLAIN,
　And cottoned to VOLATILE NELL!
　　　　O VOLATILE NELLY DE P.!
　　　　Be hanged if I'll empty to thee:
　　I like worthy maids, not mere frivolous jades,
　　　　VOLATILE NELLY DE P.!

Sir Barnaby Bampton Boo

They bolted, the Bart. and his frivolous dear,
  And MILLY was left to pout;
For years they've got on very well, as I hear,
  But soon he will rue it, no doubt.
            O excellent MILLY DE PLOW,
            I really can't drink to you now;
      My head isn't strong, and the song has been long.
            Excellent MILLY DE PLOW!

SOLATIUM

Comes the broken flower—
    Comes the cheated maid—
Though the tempest lower,
    Rain and cloud will fade!
Take, O maid, these posies:
    Though thy beauty rare
Shame the blushing roses,
    They are passing fair!
        Wear the flowers till they fade;
        Happy be thy life, O maid!

O'er the season vernal,
    Time may cast a shade;
Sunshine, if eternal,
    Makes the roses fade:
Time may do his duty;
    Let the thief alone—
Winter hath a beauty
    That is all his own.
        Fairest days are sun and shade:
        Happy be thy life, O maid!

THE MODEST COUPLE

When man and maiden meet, I like to see a drooping eye,
I always droop my own—I am the shyest of the shy.
I'm also fond of bashfulness, and sitting down on thorns,
For modesty's a quality that womankind adorns.

Whenever I am introduced to any pretty maid,
My knees they knock together, just as if I were afraid;
I flutter, and I stammer, and I turn a pleasing red,
For to laugh, and flirt, and ogle I consider most ill-bred.

But still in all these matters, as in other things below,
There is a proper medium, as I'm about to show.
I do not recommend a newly-married pair to try
To carry on as Peter carried on with Sarah Bligh.

The Modest Couple

Betrothed they were when very young — before they'd
    learnt to speak
(For SARAH was but six days old, and PETER was a week);
Though little more than babies at those early ages, yet
They bashfully would faint when they occasionally met.

They blushed, and flushed, and fainted, till they reached
    the age of nine,
When PETER'S good papa (he was a Baron of the Rhine)
Determined to endeavour some sound argument to find
To bring these shy young people to a proper frame of mind.

He told them that as SARAH was to be his PETER'S bride,
They might at least consent to sit at table side by side;
He begged that they would now and then shake hands, till
    he was hoarse,
Which SARAH thought indelicate, and PETER very coarse.

The Modest Couple

And PETER in a tremble to the blushing maid would say,
"You must excuse papa, MISS BLIGH,—it is his mountain
    way."
Says SARAH, "His behaviour I'll endeavour to forget,
But your papa's the coarsest person that I ever met.

"He plighted us without our leave, when we were very
    young,
Before we had begun articulating with the tongue.
His underbred suggestions fill your SARAH with alarm;
Why, gracious me! he'll ask us next to walk out arm-in-
    arm!"

At length when SARAH reached the legal age of twenty-one,
The Baron he determined to unite her to his son;
And SARAH in a fainting-fit for weeks unconscious lay,
And PETER blushed so hard you might have heard him
    miles away.

And when the time arrived for taking SARAH to his heart,
They were married in two churches half-a-dozen miles apart
(Intending to escape all public ridicule and chaff),
And the service was conducted by electric telegraph.

The Modest Couple

And when it was concluded, and the priest had said his say,
Until the time arrived when they were both to drive away,
They never spoke or offered for to fondle or to fawn,
For *he* waited in the attic, and *she* waited on the lawn.

At length, when four o'clock arrived, and it was time to go,
The carriage was announced, but decent SARAH answered
       " No !
Upon my word, I'd rather sleep my everlasting nap,
Than go and ride alone with MR. PETER in a trap."

And PETER's over-sensitive and highly-polished mind
Wouldn't suffer him to sanction a proceeding of the kind ;
And further, he declared he suffered overwhelming shocks
At the bare idea of having any coachman on the box.

So PETER into one turn-out incontinently rushed,
While SARAH in a second trap sat modestly and blushed ;
And MR. NEWMAN's coachman, on authority I've heard,
Drove away in gallant style upon the coach-box of a third.

Now, though this modest couple in the matter of the car
Were very likely carrying a principle too far,
I hold their shy behaviour was more laudable in them
Than that of PETER's brother with MISS SARAH's sister EM

ALPHONSO, who in cool assurance all creation licks,
He up and said to EMMIE (who had impudence for six),
" MISS EMILY, I love you — will you marry ? Say the
    word ! "
And EMILY said, " Certainly, ALPHONSO, like a bird ! "

The Modest Couple

I do not recommend a newly-married pair to try
To carry on as PETER carried on with SARAH BLIGH,
But still their shy behaviour was more laudable in them
Than that of PETER's brother with MISS SARAH's sister EM

A NIGHTMARE

WHEN you're lying awake with a dismal headache, and
   repose is taboo'd by anxiety,
I conceive you may use any language you choose to indulge
   in without impropriety;
For your brain is on fire—the bedclothes conspire of usual
   slumber to plunder you:
First your counterpane goes and uncovers your toes, and
   your sheet slips demurely from under you;
Then the blanketing tickles—you feel like mixed pickles,
   so terribly sharp is the pricking,
And you're hot, and you're cross, and you tumble and toss
   till there's nothing 'twixt you and the ticking.

A Nightmare

Then the bedclothes all creep to the ground in a heap, and
    you pick 'em all up in a tangle;
Next your pillow resigns and politely declines to remain at
    its usual angle!
Well, you get some repose in the form of a doze, with hot
    eyeballs and head ever aching,
But your slumbering teems with such horrible dreams that
    you'd very much better be waking;
For you dream you are crossing the Channel, and tossing
    about in a steamer from Harwich,
Which is something between a large bathing-machine and
    a very small second-class carriage;
And you're giving a treat (penny ice and cold meat) to a
    party of friends and relations—
They're a ravenous horde—and they all came on board at
    Sloane Square and South Kensington Stations.
And bound on that journey you find your attorney (who
    started that morning from Devon);
He's a bit undersized, and you don't feel surprised when
    he tells you he's only eleven.
Well, you're driving like mad with this singular lad (by the
    bye the ship's now a four-wheeler),
And you're playing round games, and he calls you bad
    names when you tell him that " ties pay the dealer ";
But this you can't stand, so you throw up your hand, and
    you find you're as cold as an icicle,
In your shirt and your socks (the black silk with gold
    clocks), crossing Salisbury Plain on a bicycle:
And he and the crew are on bicycles too—which they've
    somehow or other invested in—
And he's telling the tars all the particu*lars* of a company
    he's interested in—
It's a scheme of devices, to get at low prices, all goods
    from cough mixtures to cables
(Which tickled the sailors) by treating retailers, as though
    they were all vege*ta*bles—
You get a good spadesman to plant a small tradesman
    (first take off his boots with a boot-tree),

A Nightmare

And his legs will take root, and his fingers will shoot, and
    they'll blossom and bud like a fruit-tree—
From the greengrocer tree you get grapes and green pea,
    cauliflower, pineapple, and cranberries,
While the pastry-cook plant cherry-brandy will grant—apple
    puffs, and three-corners, and banberries—
The shares are a penny, and ever so many are taken by
    ROTHSCHILD and BARING,
And just as a few are allotted to you, you awake with a
    shudder despairing—
You're a regular wreck, with a crick in your neck, and no
    wonder you snore, for your head's on the floor, and
    you've needles and pins from your soles to your
    shins, and your flesh is a-creep, for your left leg's
    asleep, and you've cramp in your toes, and a fly on
    your nose, and some fluff in your lung, and a feverish
    tongue, and a thirst that's intense, and a general sense
    that you haven't been sleeping in clover ;
But the darkness has passed, and it's daylight at last, and
    and the night has been long—ditto, ditto my song—
    and thank goodness they're both of them over !

THE MARTINET

SOME time ago, in simple verse,
    I sang the story true
Of CAPTAIN REECE, *The Mantelpiece*,
    And all her happy crew.

I showed how any captain may
    Attach his men to him,
If he but heeds their smallest needs,
    And studies every whim.

Now mark how, by Draconic rule
    And *hauteur* ill-advised,
The noblest crew upon the blue
    May be demoralised.

The Martinet

When his ungrateful country placed
    Kind REECE upon half-pay,
Without much claim SIR BERKELY came,
    And took command one day.

SIR BERKELY was a martinet—
    A stern unyielding soul—
Who ruled his ship by dint of whip
    And horrible black-hole.

A sailor who was overcome
    From having freely dined,
And chanced to reel when at the wheel,
    He instantly confined!

The Martinet

And tars who, when an action raged,
    Appeared alarmed or scared,
And those below who wished to go,
    He very seldom spared.

E'en he who smote his officer
    For punishment was booked,
And mutinies upon the seas
    He rarely overlooked.

In short, the happy *Mantelpiece*
    Where all had gone so well,
Beneath that fool SIR BERKELY'S rule
    Became a floating hell.

When first SIR BERKELY came aboard
    He read a speech to all,
And told them how he'd made a vow
    To act on duty's call.

Then WILLIAM LEE, he up and said
    (The captain's coxswain he):
"We've heard the speech your honour's made,
    And werry pleased we be.

"We won't pretend, my lad, as how
    We're glad to lose our REECE;
Urbane, polite, he suited quite
    The saucy *Mantelpiece*.

"But if your honour gives your mind
    To study all our ways,
With dance and song we'll jog along
    As in those happy days.

The Martinet

"I like your honour's looks, and feel
    You're worthy of your sword.
Your hand, my lad—I'm doosid glad
    To welcome you aboard!"

SIR BERKELY looked amazed, as though
    He did not understand.
"Don't shake your head," good WILLIAM said,
    "It is an honest hand.

"It's grasped a better hand than yourn—
    Come, gov'nor, I insist!"
The Captain stared—the coxswain glared—
    The hand became a fist!

The Martinet

"Down, upstart!" said the hardy salt;
    But BERKELY dodged his aim,
And made him go in chains below:
    The seamen murmured "Shame!"

He stopped all songs at 12 P.M.,
    Stopped hornpipes when at sea,
And swore his cot (or bunk) should not
    Be used by aught than he.

He never joined their daily mess,
    Nor asked them to his own,
But chaffed in gay and social way
    The officers alone.

The Martinet

His First Lieutenant, PETER, was
    As useless as could be,
A helpless stick, and always sick
    When there was any sea.

This First Lieutenant proved to be
    His foster-sister MAY,
·Who went to sea for love of he,
    In masculine array.

And when he learnt the curious fact,
    Did he emotion show,
Or dry her tears, or end her fears
    By marrying her?   No!

Or did he even try to soothe
    This maiden in her teens?
Oh no!—instead he made her wed
    The Sergeant of Marines!

The Martinet

Of course such Spartan discipline
    Would make an angel fret.
They drew a lot, and straightway shot
    This fearful martinet.

The Admiralty saw how ill
    They'd treated CAPTAIN REECE;
He was restored once more aboard
    The saucy *Mantelpiece.*

DON'T FORGET!

Now, Marco, dear,
My wishes hear:
   While you're away
It's understood
You will be good,
   And not too gay.
To every trace
Of maiden grace
   You will be blind,
And will not glance
By any chance
   On womankind!
If you are wise,
You'll shut your eyes
   Till we arrive,

Don't Forget !

And not address
A lady less
    Than forty-five ;
You'll please to frown
On every gown
    That you may see ;
And O, my pet,
You won't forget
    You've married me !

O, my darling, O, my pet,
Whatever else you may forget,
In yonder isle beyond the sea,
O, don't forget you've married me !

You'll lay your head
Upon your bed
    At set of sun.
You will not sing
Of anything
    To any one :
You'll sit and mope
All day, I hope,
    And shed a tear
Upon the life
Your little wife
    Is passing here !
And if so be
You think of me,
    Please tell the moon ;
I'll read it all
In rays that fall
    On the lagoon :

Don't Forget!

You'll be so kind
As tell the wind
   How you may be,
And send me words
By little birds
   To comfort me!

And O, my darling, O, my pet,
Whatever else you may forget,
In yonder isle beyond the sea,
O, don't forget you've married me!

THE SAILOR BOY TO HIS LASS

I GO away, this blessed day,
    To sail across the sea, MATILDA!
My vessel sails for various parts
    At twenty after three, MATILDA;
I hardly know where we may go,
    Or if it's near or far, MATILDA,
For CAPTAIN HYDE does not confide
    In any 'fore-mast tar, MATILDA!

The Sailor Boy to his Lass

Beneath my ban that mystic man
    Shall suffer, *coûte que coûte*, MATILDA!
What right has he to keep from me
    The Admiralty route, MATILDA?
Because, forsooth! I am a youth
    Of common sailors' lot, MATILDA!
Am I a man on human plan
    Designed, or am I not, MATILDA?

But there, my lass, we'll let that pass!
    With anxious love I burn, MATILDA.
I want to know if we shall go
    To church when I return, MATILDA?
Your eyes are red, you bow your head;
    It's pretty clear you thirst, MATILDA,
To name the day—What's that you say?—
    "You'll see me further first," MATILDA?

I can't mistake the signs you make,
    Although you barely speak, MATILDA;
Though pure and young, you thrust your tongue
    Right in your pretty cheek, MATILDA!
My dear, I fear I hear you sneer—
    I do—I'm sure I do, MATILDA—
With simple grace you make a face,
    Ejaculating, "Ugh!" MATILDA.

Oh, pause to think before you drink
    The dregs of Lethe's cup, MATILDA!
Remember, do, what I've gone through,
    Before you give me up, MATILDA!
Recall again the mental pain
    Of what I've had to do, MATILDA!
And be assured that I've endured
    It, all along of you, MATILDA!

The Sailor Boy to his Lass

Do you forget, my blithesome pet,
  How once with jealous rage, MATILDA,
I watched you walk and gaily talk
  With some one thrice your age, MATILDA?
You squatted free upon his knee,
  A sight that made me sad, MATILDA?
You pinched his cheek with friendly tweak,
  Which almost drove me mad, MATILDA!

I knew him not, but thought to spot
  Some man you wished to wed, MATILDA!
I took a gun, my darling one,
  And shot him through the head, MATILDA!
I'm made of stuff that's rough and gruff
  Enough, I own; but, ah, MATILDA!
It *did* annoy your poor old boy
  To find it was your pa, MATILDA!

The Sailor Boy to his Lass

I've passed a life of toil and strife,
   And disappointments deep, MATILDA ;
I've lain awake with dental ache
   Until I fell asleep, MATILDA ;
At times again I've missed a train,
   Or p'raps run short of tin, MATILDA,
And worn a boot on corns that shoot,
   Or, shaving, cut my chin, MATILDA !

But, oh ! no trains—no dental pains—
   Believe me when I say, MATILDA,
No corns that shoot—no pinching boot
   Upon a summer day, MATILDA—
It's my belief, could cause such grief
   As that I've suffered for, MATILDA,
My having shot in vital spot
   Your old progenitor, MATILDA !

Bethink you how I've kept the vow
   I made one winter day, MATILDA—
That, come what could, I never would
   Remain too long away, MATILDA.
And, oh ! the crimes with which, at times,
   I've charged my gentle mind, MATILDA,
To keep the vow I made—and now
   You treat me so unkind, MATILDA !

For when at sea off Caribbee,
   I felt my passion burn, MATILDA ;
By impulse egged, I went and begged
   The captain to return, MATILDA ;
And when, my pet, I couldn't get
   That captain to agree, MATILDA,
Right through a sort of open port
   I pitched him in the sea, MATILDA !

The Sailor Boy to his Lass

Remember, too, how all the crew,
    With indignation blind, MATILDA,
Distinctly swore they ne'er before
    Had thought me so unkind, MATILDA;
And how they'd shun me one by one—
    An unforgiving group, MATILDA—
I stopped their howls and sulky scowls
    By pizening their soup, MATILDA!

So pause to think, before you drink
    The dregs of Lethe's cup, MATILDA;
Remember, do, what I've gone through,
    Before you give me up, MATILDA.

The Sailor Boy to his Lass

Recall again the mental pain
　　Of what I've had to do, MATILDA,
And be assured that I've endured
　　It, all along of you, MATILDA!

THE SUICIDE'S GRAVE

On a tree by a river a little tomtit
      Sang "Willow, titwillow, titwillow!"
And I said to him, "Dicky-bird, why do you sit
      Singing 'Willow, titwillow, titwillow'?
Is it weakness of intellect, birdie?" I cried,
"Or a rather tough worm in your little inside?"
With a shake of his poor little head he replied,
      "Oh, willow, titwillow, titwillow!"

He slapped at his chest, as he sat on that bough,
      Singing "Willow, titwillow, titwillow!"
And a cold perspiration bespangled his brow,
      Oh, willow, titwillow, titwillow!

The Suicide's Grave

He sobbed and he sighed, and a gurgle he gave,
Then he threw himself into the billowy wave,
And an echo arose from the suicide's grave—
    "Oh, willow, titwillow, titwillow!"

Now I feel just as sure as I'm sure that my name
    Isn't Willow, titwillow, titwillow,
That 'twas blighted affection that made him exclaim,
    "Oh, willow, titwillow, titwillow!"
And if you remain callous and obdurate, I
Shall perish as he did, and you will know why,
Though I probably shall not exclaim as I die,
    "Oh, willow, titwillow, titwillow!"

THE REVEREND SIMON MAGUS

A RICH advowson, highly prized,
For private sale was advertised ;
And many a parson made a bid ;
The REVEREND SIMON MAGUS did.

He sought the agent's : " Agent, I
Have come prepared at once to buy
(If your demand is not too big)
The Cure of Otium-cum-Digge."

" Ah !" said the agent, "*there's* a berth—
The snuggest vicarage on earth ;
No sort of duty (so I hear),
And fifteen hundred pounds a year !

The Reverend Simon Magus

"If on the price we should agree,
The living soon will vacant be:
The good incumbent's ninety-five,
And cannot very long survive.

"See—here's his photograph—you see,
He's in his dotage." "Ah, dear me!
Poor soul!" said Simon. "His decease
Would be a merciful release!"

The agent laughed—the agent blinked—
The agent blew his nose and winked
And poked the parson's ribs in play—
It was that agent's vulgar way.

The REVEREND SIMON frowned: "I grieve
This light demeanour to perceive;
It's scarcely *comme il faut*, I think:
Now—pray oblige me—do not wink.

"Don't dig my waistcoat into holes—
Your mission is to sell the souls
Of human sheep and human kids
To that divine who highest bids.

"Do well in this, and on your head
Unnumbered honours will be shed."
The agent said, "Well, truth to tell,
I *have* been doing pretty well."

"You should," said SIMON, "at your age;
But now about the parsonage.
How many rooms does it contain?
Show me the photograph again.

The Reverend Simon Magus

"A poor apostle's humble house
Must not be too luxurious;
No stately halls with oaken floor—
It should be decent and no more.

"No billiard-rooms—no stately trees—
No croquêt-grounds or pineries."
"Ah!" sighed the agent, "very true:
This property won't do for you.

"All these about the house you'll find"—
"Well," said the parson, "never mind;
I'll manage to submit to these
Luxurious superfluities.

"A clergyman who does not shirk
The various calls of Christian work,
Will have no leisure to employ
These 'common forms' of worldly joy.

"To preach three times on Sabbath days—
To wean the lost from wicked ways—
The sick to soothe—the sane to wed—
The poor to feed with meat and bread;

"These are the various wholesome ways
In which I'll spend my nights and days:
My zeal will have no time to cool
At croquêt, archery, or pool."

The agent said, "From what I hear,
This living will not suit, I fear—
There are no poor, no sick at all;
For services there is no call."

The Reverend Simon Magus

The reverend gent looked grave.   "Dear me!
Then there is *no* 'society'?—
I mean, of course, no sinners there
Whose souls will be my special care?"

The cunning agent shook his head,
"No, none—except"—(the agent said)—
"The DUKE OF A., the EARL OF B.,
The MARQUIS C., and VISCOUNT D.

"But you will not be quite alone,
For, though they've chaplains of their own,
Of course this noble well-bred clan
Receive the parish clergyman."

"Oh, silence, sir!" said SIMON M.,
"Dukes—earls!   What should I care for them?
These worldly ranks I scorn and flout!"
"Of course," the agent said, "no doubt."

"Yet I might show these men of birth
The hollowness of rank on earth."
The agent answered, "Very true—
But I should not, if I were you."

The Reverend Simon Magus

"Who sells this rich advowson, pray?"
The agent winked—it was his way—
"His name is HART; 'twixt me and you,
He is, I'm griev'd to say, a Jew!"

"A Jew?" said SIMON, "happy find!
I purchase this advowson, mind.
My life shall be devoted to
Converting that unhappy Jew!"

HE AND SHE

HE.   I KNOW a youth who loves a little maid—
      (Hey, but his face is a sight for to see !)
  Silent is he, for he's modest and afraid—
      (Hey, but he's timid as a youth can be !)

SHE.   I know a maid who loves a gallant youth—
      (Hey, but she sickens as the days go by !)
  She cannot tell him all the sad, sad truth—
      (Hey, but I think that little maid will die !)

BOTH.   Now tell me pray, and tell me true,
        What in the world should the poor soul do ?

HE.   He cannot eat and he cannot sleep—
      (Hey, but his face is a sight for to see !)
  Daily he goes for to wail—for to weep—
      (Hey, but he's wretched as a youth can be !)

361   N 2

He and She

SHE.   She's very thin and she's very pale—
        (Hey, but she sickens as the days go by !)
    Daily she goes for to weep—for to wail—
        (Hey, but I think that little maid will die !)

BOTH.   Now tell me pray, and tell me true,
          What in the world should the poor soul do ?

SHE.   If I were the youth I should offer her my name—
        (Hey, but her face is a sight for to see !)

HE.   If I were the maid I should fan his honest flame—
        (Hey, but he's bashful as a youth can be !)

SHE.   If I were the youth I should speak to her to-day—
        (Hey, but she sickens as the days go by !)

HE.   If I were the maid I should meet the lad half way—
        (For I really do believe that timid youth will die !)

BOTH.   I thank you much for your counsel true ;
        I've learnt what that poor soul ought to do !

DAMON *v.* PYTHIAS

Two better friends you wouldn't pass
    Throughout a summer's day,
Than DAMON and his PYTHIAS,—
    Two merchant princes they.

At school together they contrived
    All sorts of boyish larks;
And, later on, together thrived
    As merry merchants' clerks.

And then, when many years had flown,
    They rose together till
They bought a business of their own—
    And they conduct it still.

They loved each other all their lives,
    Dissent they never knew,
And, stranger still, their very wives
    Were rather friendly too.

Damon *v.* Pythias

Perhaps you think, to serve my ends,
    These statements I refute,
When I admit that these dear friends
    Were parties to a suit?

But 'twas a friendly action, for
    Good PYTHIAS, as you see,
Fought merely as executor,
    And DAMON as trustee.

They laughed to think, as through the throng
    Of suitors sad they passed,
That they, who'd lived and loved so long,
    Should go to law at last.

The junior briefs they kindly let
    Two sucking counsel hold;
These learned persons never yet
    Had fingered suitors' gold.

But though the happy suitors two
    Were friendly as could be,

Damon *v.* Pythias

Not so the junior counsel who
    Were earning maiden fee.

They too, till then, were friends.   At school
    They'd done each other's sums,
And under Oxford's gentle rule
    Had been the closest chums.

But now they met with scowl and grin
    In every public place,
And often snapped their fingers in
    Each other's learned face.

It almost ended in a fight
    When they on path or stair
Met face to face.   They made it quite
    A personal affair.

And when at length the case was called
    (It came on rather late),
Spectators really were appalled
    To see their deadly hate.

One junior rose—with eyeballs tense,
    And swollen frontal veins:
To all his powers of eloquence
    He gave the fullest reins.

His argument was novel—for
    A verdict he relied
On blackening the junior
    Upon the other side.

"Oh," said the Judge, in robe and fur,
    "The matter in dispute
To arbitration pray refer—
    This is a friendly suit."

Damon *v.* Pythias

And PYTHIAS, in merry mood,
　Digged DAMON in the side;
And DAMON, tickled with the feud,
　With other digs replied.

But oh! those deadly counsel twain,
　Who were such friends before,
Were never reconciled again—
　They quarrelled more and more.

At length it happened that they met
　On Alpine heights one day,
And thus they paid each one his debt,
　Their fury had its way—

They seized each other in a trice,
　With scorn and hatred filled,
And, falling from a precipice,
　They, both of them, were killed.

THE MIGHTY MUST

COME mighty Must !
  Inevitable Shall !
In thee I trust.
  Time weaves my coronal !
Go mocking Is !
  Go disappointing Was !
That I am this
  Ye are the cursed cause !
Yet humble Second shall be First,
          I ween ;
And dead and buried be the curst
          Has Been !

Oh weak Might Be !
  Oh May, Might, Could, Would, Should !
How powerless ye
  For evil or for good !
In every sense
  Your moods I cheerless call,
Whate'er your tense
  Ye are Imperfect, all !
Ye have deceived the trust I've shown
          In ye !
Away ! The Mighty Must alone
          Shall be !

MY DREAM

THE other night, from cares exempt,
I slept—and what d'you think I dreamt?
I dreamt that somehow I had come
To dwell in Topsy-Turveydom!—

Where vice is virtue—virtue, vice:
Where nice is nasty—nasty, nice:
Where right is wrong and wrong is right—
Where white is black and black is white.

Where babies, much to their surprise,
Are born astonishingly wise;
With every Science on their lips,
And Art at all their finger-tips.

368

My Dream

For, as their nurses dandle them,
They crow binomial theorem,
With views (it seems absurd to us)
On differential calculus.

But though a babe, as I have said,
Is born with learning in his head,
He must forget it, if he can,
Before he calls himself a man.

For that which we call folly here,
Is wisdom in that favoured sphere ;
The wisdom we so highly prize
Is blatant folly in their eyes.

A boy, if he would push his way,
Must learn some nonsense every day ;
And cut, to carry out this view,
His wisdom teeth and wisdom too.

Historians burn their midnight oils,
Intent on giant-killers' toils ;
And sages close their aged eyes
To other sages' lullabies.

Our magistrates, in duty bound,
Commit all robbers who are found ;
But there the beaks (so people said)
Commit all robberies instead.

Our judges, pure and wise in tone,
Know crime from theory alone.
And glean the motives of a thief
From books and popular belief.

My Dream

But there, a judge who wants to prime
His mind with true ideas of crime,
Derives them from the common sense
Of practical experience.

Policemen march all folks away
Who practise virtue every day—
Of course, I mean to say, you know,
What we call virtue here below.

For only scoundrels dare to do
What we consider just and true,
And only good men do, in fact,
What we should think a dirty act.

But strangest of these social twirls,
The girls are boys—the boys are girls !
The men are women, too—but then
Per contra, women all are men.

My Dream

To one who to tradition clings
This seems an awkward state of things,
But if to think it out you try,
It doesn't really signify.

With them, as surely as can be,
A sailor should be sick at sea,
And not a passenger may sail
Who cannot smoke right through a gale.

A soldier (save by rarest luck)
Is always shot for showing pluck—
That is, if others can be found
With pluck enough to fire a round.

"How strange," I said to one I saw.
"You quite upset our every law.
However can you get along
So systematically wrong?"

My Dream

"Dear me," my mad informant said,
"Have you no eyes within your head?
You sneer when you your hat should doff:
Why, we begin where you leave off!

"Your wisest men are very far
Less learned than our babies are!"
I mused awhile—and then, oh me!
I framed this brilliant repartee:

"Although your babes are wiser far
Than our most valued sages are,
Your sages, with their toys and cots,
Are duller than our idiots!"

My Dream

But this remark, I grieve to state,
Came just a little bit too late;
For as I framed it in my head,
I woke and found myself in bed.

Still I could wish that, 'stead of here,
My lot were in that favoured sphere!—
Where greatest fools bear off the bell
I ought to do extremely well.

A MIRAGE

WERE I thy bride,
Then the whole world beside
Were not too wide
　　To hold my wealth of love—
Were I thy bride!
Upon thy breast
My loving head would rest,
As on her nest
　　The tender turtle-dove—
Were I thy bride!

This heart of mine
Would be one heart with thine,
And in that shrine
　　Our happiness would dwell—
Were I thy bride!

A Mirage

And all day long
Our lives should be a song:
No grief, no wrong
Should make my heart rebel—
Were I thy bride!

The silvery flute,
The melancholy lute,
Were night-owl's hoot
To my low-whispered coo—
Were I thy bride!
The skylark's trill
Were but discordance shrill
To the soft thrill
Of wooing as I'd woo—
Were I thy bride!

The rose's sigh
Were as a carrion's cry
To lullaby
Such as I'd sing to thee—
Were I thy bride!
A feather's press
Were leaden heaviness
To my caress.
But then, unhappily,
I'm not thy bride!

THE BISHOP OF RUM-TI-FOO AGAIN

I OFTEN wonder whether you
Think sometimes of that Bishop, who
From black but balmy Rum-ti-foo
    Last summer twelvemonth came.
Unto your mind I p'raps may bring
Remembrance of the man I sing
To-day, by simply mentioning
    That PETER was his name.

Remember how that holy man
Came with the great Colonial clan
To Synod, called Pan-Anglican ;
    And kindly recollect

The Bishop of Rum-ti-foo Again

How, having crossed the ocean wide,
To please his flock all means he tried
Consistent with a proper pride
     And manly self-respect.

He only, of the reverend pack
Who minister to Christians black,
Brought any useful knowledge back
     To his Colonial fold.
In consequence a place I claim
For "PETER" on the scroll of Fame
(For PETER was that Bishop's name,
     As I've already told).

He carried Art, he often said,
To places where that timid maid
(Save by Colonial Bishops' aid)
     Could never hope to roam.
The Payne-cum-Lauri feat he taught
As he had learnt it ; for he thought
The choicest fruits of Progress ought
     To bless the Negro's home.

And he had other work to do,
For, while he tossed upon the blue,
The islanders of Rum-ti-foo
     Forgot their kindly friend.
Their decent clothes they learnt to tear—
They learnt to say, " I do not care,"
Though they, of course, were well aware
     How folks, who say so, end.

Some sailors whom he did not know,
Had landed there not long ago,
And taught them "Bother !" also "Blow !"
     (Of wickedness the germs.)

The Bishop of Rum-ti-foo Again

No need to use a casuist's pen
To prove that they were merchantmen;
No sailor of the Royal N.
    Would use such awful terms.

And so, when Bishop PETER came
(That was the kindly Bishop's name),
He heard these dreadful oaths with shame,
    And chid their want of dress.
(Except a shell—a bangle rare—
A feather here—a feather there—
The South Pacific negroes wear
    Their native nothingness.)

He taught them that a Bishop loathes
To listen to unseemly oaths,
He gave them all his left-off clothes—
    They bent them to his will.

The Bishop of Rum-ti-foo Again

The Bishop's gift spreads quickly round;
In PETER's left-off clothes they bound
(His three-and-twenty suits they found
    In fair condition still).

The Bishop's eyes with water fill,
Quite overjoyed to find them still
Obedient to his sovereign will,
    And said, "Good Rum-ti-foo!
Half-way to meet you I'll prepare:
I'll dress myself in cowries rare,
And fasten feathers in my hair,
    And dance the 'Cutch-chi-boo'!"

And to conciliate his see
He married PICCADILLILLEE,
The youngest of his twenty-three,
    Tall—neither fat nor thin.
(And though the dress he made her don
Looks awkwardly a girl upon,
It was a great improvement on
    The one he found her in.)

The Bishop of Rum-ti-foo Again

The Bishop in his gay canoe
(His wife, of course, went with him too),
To some adjacent island flew,
    To spend his honeymoon.
Some day in sunny Rum-ti-foo
A little PETER 'll be on view;
And that (if people tell me true)
    Is like to happen soon.

THE GHOSTS' HIGH NOON

WHEN the night wind howls in the chimney cowls, and the
    bat in the moonlight flies,
And inky clouds, like funeral shrouds, sail over the
    midnight skies—
When the footpads quail at the night-bird's wail, and black
    dogs bay the moon,
Then is the spectres' holiday—then is the ghosts' high
    noon !

As the sob of the breeze sweeps over the trees, and the
    mists lie low on the fen,
From grey tombstones are gathered the bones that once
    were women and men,
And away they go, with a mop and a mow, to the revel
    that ends too soon,
For cockcrow limits our holiday—the dead of the night's
    high noon !

The Ghosts' High Noon

And then each ghost with his ladye-toast to their churchyard
    beds take flight,
With a kiss, perhaps, on her lantern chaps, and a grisly
    grim "good night";
Till the welcome knell of the midnight bell rings forth its
    jolliest tune,
And ushers our next high holiday—the dead of the night's
    high noon!

A WORM WILL TURN

I LOVE a man who'll smile and joke
    When with misfortune crowned;
Who'll pun beneath a pauper's yoke,
And as he breaks his daily toke,
    Conundrums gay propound.

Just such a man was BERNARD JUPP,
    He scoffed at Fortune's frown;
He gaily drained his bitter cup—
Though Fortune often threw him up,
    It never cast him down.

Though years their share of sorrow bring,
    We know that far above
All other griefs, are griefs that spring
From some misfortune happening
    To those we really love.

A Worm will Turn

E'en sorrow for another's woe
    Our BERNARD failed to quell;
Though by this special form of blow
No person ever suffered so,
    Or bore his grief so well.

His father, wealthy and well clad,
    And owning house and park,
Lost every halfpenny he had,
And then became (extremely sad!)
    A poor attorney's clerk.

All sons it surely would appal,
    Except the passing meek,
To see a father lose his all,
And from an independence fall
    To one pound ten a week!

But JUPP shook off this sorrow's weight,
    And, like a Christian son,
Proved Poverty a happy fate—
Proved Wealth to be a devil's bait,
    To lure poor sinners on.

With other sorrows BERNARD coped,
    For sorrows came in packs;
His cousins with their housemaids sloped—
His uncles forged—his aunts eloped—
    His sisters married blacks.

A Worm will Turn

But BERNARD, far from murmuring
    (Exemplar, friends, to us),
Determined to his faith to cling,—
He made the best of everything,
    And argued softly thus:

"'Twere harsh my uncles' forging knack
    Too rudely to condemn—
My aunts, repentant, may come back,
And blacks are nothing like as black
    As people colour them!"

Still Fate, with many a sorrow rife,
    Maintained relentless fight:
His grandmamma next lost her life,
Then died the mother of his wife,
    But still he seemed all right.

o

A Worm will Turn

His brother fond (the only link
    To life that bound him now)
One morning, overcome by drink,
He broke his leg (the right, I think)
    In some disgraceful row.

But did my BERNARD swear and curse ?
    Oh no—to murmur loth,
He only said, "Go, get a nurse :
Be thankful that it isn't worse ;
    You might have broken both ! "

But worms who watch without concern
    The cockchafer on thorns,
Or beetles smashed, themselves will turn
If, walking through the slippery fern,
    You tread upon their corns.

One night as BERNARD made his track
    Through Brompton home to bed,
A footpad, with a vizor black,
Took watch and purse, and dealt a crack
    On BERNARD's saint-like head.

It was too much—his spirit rose,
    He looked extremely cross.
Men thought him steeled to mortal foes,
But no—he bowed to countless blows,
    But kicked against this loss.

A Worm will Turn

He finally made up his mind
    Upon his friends to call;
Subscription lists were largely signed,
For men were really glad to find
    Him mortal, after all!

THE HUMANE MIKADO

A MORE humane Mikado never
   Did in Japan exist;
     To nobody second,
     I'm certainly reckoned
A true philanthropist.
It is my very humane endeavour
   To make, to some extent,
     Each evil liver
     A running river
Of harmless merriment.

     My object all sublime
     I shall achieve in time—
   To let the punishment fit the crime—
      The punishment fit the crime;

The Humane Mikado

And make each prisoner pent
Unwillingly represent
A source of innocent merriment—
Of innocent merriment!

All prosy dull society sinners,
Who chatter and bleat and bore,
Are sent to hear sermons
From mystical Germans
Who preach from ten to four:
The amateur tenor, whose vocal villainies
All desire to shirk,
Shall, during off-hours,
Exhibit his powers
To Madame Tussaud's waxwork:
The lady who dyes a chemical yellow,
Or stains her grey hair puce,
Or pinches her figger,
Is blacked like a nigger
With permanent walnut juice:
The idiot who, in railway carriages,
Scribbles on window panes,
We only suffer
To ride on a buffer
In Parliamentary trains.

My object all sublime
I shall achieve in time—
To let the punishment fit the crime—
The punishment fit the crime;
And make each prisoner pent
Unwillingly represent
A source of innocent merriment—
Of innocent merriment!

The Humane Mikado

The advertising quack who wearies
    With tales of countless cures,
      His teeth, I've enacted,
      Shall all be extracted
By terrified amateurs :
The music-hall singer attends a series
    Of masses and fugues and " ops "
      By Bach, interwoven
      With Spohr and Beethoven,
At classical Monday Pops :
The billiard sharp whom any one catches
    His doom's extremely hard—
      He's made to dwell
      In a dungeon cell
On a spot that's always barred ;
And there he plays extravagant matches
    In fitless finger-stalls,
      On a cloth untrue
      With a twisted cue,
And elliptical billiard balls !

      My object all sublime
      I shall achieve in time—
    To let the punishment fit the crime—
        The punishment fit the crime ;
      And make each prisoner pent
      Unwillingly represent
    A source of innocent merriment,
        Of innocent merriment !

THE HAUGHTY ACTOR

An actor—Gibbs, of Drury Lane—
    Of very decent station,
Once happened in a part to gain
    Excessive approbation;
It sometimes turns a fellow's brain
And makes him singularly vain
When he believes that he receives
    Tremendous approbation.

His great success half drove him mad,
    But no one seemed to mind him;
Well, in another piece he had
    Another part assigned him.

391

The Haughty Actor

This part was smaller, by a bit,
Than that in which he made a hit.
So, much ill-used, he straight refused
To play the part assigned him.

    *   *   *   *   *

That night that actor slept, and I'll attempt
To tell you of the vivid dream he dreamt:

THE DREAM

In fighting with a robber band
   (A thing he loved sincerely)
A sword struck GIBBS upon the hand
   And wounded it severely.
At first he didn't heed it much,
He thought it was a simple touch,
But soon he found the weapon's bound
   Had wounded him severely.

To Surgeon COBB he made a trip,
   Who'd just effected featly
An amputation at the hip
   Particularly neatly.
A rising man was Surgeon COBB,
But this extremely ticklish job
He had achieved (as he believed)
   Particularly neatly.

The actor rang the surgeon's bell.
   "Observe my wounded finger;
Be good enough to strap it well,
   And prithee do not linger,
That I, dear sir, may fill again
The Theatre Royal, Drury Lane:
This very night I have to fight—
   So prithee do not linger."

392

The Haughty Actor

"I don't strap fingers up for doles,"
    Replied the haughty surgeon ;
"To use your cant, I don't play *rôles*
    'Utility' that verge on.
'First amputation'—nothing less—
That is my line of business :
We surgeon nobs despise all jobs
    Utility that verge on.

"When in your hip there lurks disease"
    (So dreamt this lively dreamer),
"Or devastating *caries*
    In *humerus* or *femur,*
If you can pay a handsome fee,
Oh, then you may remember me,
With joy elate I'll amputate
    Your *humerus* or *femur.*"

The disconcerted actor ceased
    The haughty leech to pester,
But when the wound in size increased,
    And then began to fester,
He sought a learned Counsel's lair,
And told that Counsel, then and there,
How COBB's neglect of his defect
    Had made his finger fester.

"Oh, bring my action, if you please,
    The case I pray you urge on,
And win me thumping damages
    From COBB, that haughty surgeon.
He culpably neglected me
Although I proffered him his fee,
So pray come down, in wig and gown,
    On COBB, that haughty surgeon !"

The Haughty Actor

That Counsel, learned in the laws,
　　With passion almost trembled,
He just had gained a mighty cause
　　Before the Peers assembled!
Said he, "How dare you have the face
To come with Common Jury case
To one who wings rhetoric flings
　　Before the Peers assembled?"

Dispirited became our friend—
　　Depressed his moral pecker—
"But stay! a thought! I'll gain my end,
　　And save my poor exchequer.
I won't be placed upon the shelf,
I'll take it into Court myself,
And legal lore display before
　　The Court of the Exchequer."

The Haughty Actor

He found a Baron—one of those
    Who with our laws supply us—
In wig and silken gown and hose,
    As if at *Nisi Prius*.
But he'd just given, off the reel,
    A famous judgment on Appeal:
It scarce became his heightened fame
    To sit at *Nisi Prius*.

Our friend began, with easy wit,
    That half concealed his terror:
"Pooh!" said the Judge, "I only sit
    In *Banco* or in Error.
Can you suppose, my man, that I'd
O'er *Nisi Prius* Courts preside,
Or condescend my time to spend
    On anything but Error?"

The Haughty Actor

"Too bad," said Gibbs, "my case to shirk!
    You must be bad innately,
To save your skill for mighty work
    Because it's valued greatly!"
But here he woke, with sudden start.

*   *   *   *   *

He wrote to say he'd play the part.
I've but to tell he played it well—
    The author's words—his native wit
    Combined, achieved a perfect "hit"—
    The papers praised him greatly.

WILLOW WALY!

HE. PRITHEE, pretty maiden—prithee, tell me true
    (Hey, but I'm doleful, willow, willow waly!)
Have you e'er a lover a-dangling after you?
      Hey, willow waly O!
        I would fain discover
        If you have a lover?
      Hey, willow waly O!

SHE. Gentle sir, my heart is frolicsome and free—
    (Hey, but he's doleful, willow, willow waly!)
Nobody I care for comes a-courting me—
      Hey, willow waly O!
        Nobody I care for
        Comes a-courting—therefore,
      Hey, willow waly O!

Willow Waly !

HE.   Prithee, pretty maiden, will you marry me?
       (Hey, but I'm hopeful, willow, willow waly!)
I may say, at once, I'm a man of propertee—
       Hey, willow waly O!
        Money, I despise it,
        But many people prize it,
       Hey, willow waly O!

SHE.   Gentle sir, although to marry I design—
       (Hey, but he's hopeful, willow, willow waly!)
As yet I do not know you, and so I must decline.
       Hey, willow waly O!
        To other maidens go you—
        As yet I do not know you,
       Hey, willow waly O!

THE TWO MAJORS

An excellent soldier who's worthy the name,
  Loves officers dashing and strict:
When good, he's content with escaping all blame,
  When naughty, he likes to be licked.

He likes for a fault to be bullied and stormed,
  Or imprisoned for several days;
And hates, for a duty correctly performed,
  To be slavered with sickening praise.

No officer sickened with praises his *corps*
  So little as Major La Guerre—
No officers swore at his warriors more
  Than Major Makredi Prepere.

Their soldiers adored them, and every grade
  Delighted to hear them abuse;
Though whenever these officers came on parade,
  They shivered and shook in their shoes.

The Two Majors

"No doubt we deserve it—no mercy we crave—
    Go on—you're conferring a boon;
We would rather be slanged by a warrior brave
    Than praised by a wretched poltroon!"

MAKREDI would say that in battle's fierce rage
    True happiness only was met:
Poor MAJOR MAKREDI, though fifty his age,
    Had never known happiness yet!

LA GUERRE would declare, "With the blood of a foe
    No tipple is worthy to clink."
Poor fellow! he hadn't, though sixty or so,
    Yet tasted his favourite drink!

They agreed at their mess—they agreed in the glass—
    They agreed in the choice of their "set,"
And they also agreed in adoring, alas!
    The Vivandière, pretty FILLETTE.

Agreement, we know, may be carried too far,
    And after agreeing all round
For years—in this soldierly "maid of the bar,"
    A bone of contention they found.

"On the day that you marry her," muttered PREPERE
    (With a pistol he quietly played),
"I'll scatter the brains in your noddle, I swear,
    All over the stony parade!"

"I cannot do *that* to you," answered LA GUERRE,
    "Whatever events may befall;
But this *I can* do—if you wed her, *mon cher!*
    I'll eat you, moustachios and all!

The Two Majors

The rivals, although they would never engage,
    Yet quarrelled whenever they met;
They met in a fury and left in a rage,
    But neither took pretty FILLETTE.

"I am not afraid," thought MAKREDI PREPERE:
    "For my country I'm ready to fall;
But nobody wants, for a mere Vivandière,
    To be eaten, moustachios and all!

"Besides, though LA GUERRE has his faults, I'll allow
    He's one of the bravest of men:
My goodness! if I disagree with him now,
    I might disagree with him then!"

"No coward am I," said LA GUERRE, "as you guess—
    I sneer at an enemy's blade;
But I don't want PREPERE to get into a mess
    For splashing the stony parade!"

The Two Majors

One day on parade to Prepere and La Guerre
    Came Corporal Jacot Debette,
And, trembling all over, he prayed of them there
    To give him the pretty Fillette.

"You see, I am willing to marry my bride
    Until you've arranged this affair;
I will blow out my brains when your honours decide
    Which marries the sweet Vivandière!"

"Well, take her," said both of them in a duet
    (A favourite form of reply),
"But when I am ready to marry Fillette,
    Remember you've promised to die!"

He married her then: from the flowery plains
    Of existence the roses they cull:
He lived and he died with his wife; and his brains
    Are reposing in peace in his skull.

LIFE IS LOVELY ALL THE YEAR

WHEN the buds are blossoming,
Smiling welcome to the spring,
Lovers choose a wedding day——
Life is love in merry May!

Spring is green—Fal lal la!
   Summer's rose—Fal lal la!
It is sad when Summer goes,
   Fal la!
Autumn's gold—Fal lal la!
   Winter's grey—Fal lal la!
Winter still is far away—
   Fal la!
Leaves in Autumn fade and fall;
Winter is the end of all.
Spring and summer teem with glee:
Spring and summer, then, for me!
   Fal la!

Life is Lovely all the Year

In the Spring-time seed is sown :
In the Summer grass is mown :
In the Autumn you may reap :
Winter is the time for sleep.

Spring is hope—Fal lal la !
    Summer's joy—Fal lal la !
Spring and Summer never cloy,
    Fal la !
Autumn, toil—Fal lal la !
    Winter, rest—Fal lal la !
Winter, after all, is best—
    Fal la !
Spring and summer pleasure you,
Autumn, ay, and winter, too—
Every season has its cheer ;
Life is lovely all the year !
    Fal la !

Bab

EMILY, JOHN, JAMES, AND I

A DERBY LEGEND

EMILY JANE was a nursery maid—
    JAMES was a bold Life Guard,
And JOHN was a constable, poorly paid
    (And I am a doggerel bard).

A very good girl was EMILY JANE,
    JIMMY was good and true,
And JOHN was a very good man in the main
    (And I am a good man, too).

405

Emily, John, James, and I

Rivals for EMMIE were JOHNNY and JAMES,
    Though EMILY liked them both ;
She couldn't tell which had the strongest claims
    (And *I* couldn't take my oath).

But sooner or later you're certain to find
    Your sentiments can't lie hid—
JANE thought it was time that she made up her mind
    (And I think it was time she did).

Said JANE, with a smirk, and a blush on her face,
    "I'll promise to wed the boy
Who takes me to-morrow to Epsom Race !"
    (Which *I* would have done, with joy.)

From JOHNNY escaped an expression of pain,
    But JIMMY said, "Done with you !
I'll take you with pleasure, my EMILY JANE"
    (And I would have said so too).

Emily, John, James, and I

JOHN lay on the ground, and he roared like mad
    (For JOHNNY was sore perplexed),
And he kicked very hard at a very small lad
    (Which *I* often do, when vexed).

For JOHN was on duty next day with the Force,
    To punish all Epsom crimes ;
Some people *will* cross, when they're clearing the course
    (I do it myself, sometimes).

    *   *   *   *   *

The Derby Day sun glittered gaily on cads,
    On maidens with gamboge hair,
On sharpers and pickpockets, swindlers and pads
    (For *I*, with my harp, was there).

And JIMMY went down with his JANE that day,
    And JOHN by the collar or nape
Seized everybody who came in his way
    (And *I* had a narrow escape).

Emily, John, James, and I

He noticed his EMILY JANE with JIM,
　　And envied the well-made elf;
And people remarked that he muttered "Oh, dim!"
　　(I often say "dim!" myself.)

JOHN dogged them all day, without asking their leaves:
　　For his sergeant he told, aside,
That JIMMY and JANE were notorious thieves
　　(And I think he was justified).

But JAMES wouldn't dream of abstracting a fork,
　　And JENNY would blush with shame
At stealing so much as a bottle or cork
　　(A bottle I think fair game).

But, ah! there's another more serious crime!
　　They wickedly strayed upon
The course, at a critical moment of time
　　(I pointed them out to JOHN).

Emily, John, James, and I

The crusher came down on the pair in a crack—
  And then, with a demon smile,
Let JENNY cross over, but sent JIMMY back
  (I played on my harp the while).

Stern JOHNNY their agony loud derides
  With a very triumphant sneer—
They weep and they wail from the opposite sides
  (And *I* shed a silent tear).

And JENNY is crying away like mad,
  And JIMMY is swearing hard;
And JOHNNY is looking uncommonly glad
  (And I am a doggerel bard).

But JIMMY he ventured on crossing again
  The scenes of our Isthmian Games—
JOHN caught him, and collared him, giving him pain
  (I felt very much for JAMES).

Emily, John, James, and I

John led him away with a victor's hand,
    And Jimmy was shortly seen
In the station-house under the grand Grand Stand
    (As many a time *I've* been).

And Jimmy, bad boy, was imprisoned for life,
    Though Emily pleaded hard ;
And Johnny had Emily Jane to wife
    (And I am a doggerel bard).

THE USHER'S CHARGE

Now, Jurymen, hear my advice—
All kinds of vulgar prejudice
    I pray you set aside:
With stern judicial frame of mind—
From bias free of every kind,
    This trial must be tried!

Oh, listen to the plaintiff's case:
Observe the features of her face—
    The broken-hearted bride!
Condole with her distress of mind—
From bias free of every kind,
    This trial must be tried!

The Usher's Charge

And when amid the plaintiff's shrieks,
The ruffianly defendant speaks—
    Upon the other side;
What *he* may say you need not mind—
From bias free of every kind,
    This trial must be tried!

THE PERILS OF INVISIBILITY

Old Peter led a wretched life——
Old Peter had a furious wife;
Old Peter, too, was truly stout,
He measured several yards about.

The little fairy Picklekin
One summer afternoon looked in,
And said, "Old Peter, how-de-do?
Can I do anything for you?

"I have three gifts——the first will give
Unbounded riches while you live;
The second, health where'er you be;
The third, invisibility."

413

The Perils of Invisibility

"O, little fairy PICKLEKIN,"
Old PETER answered, with a grin,
"To hesitate would be absurd,—
Undoubtedly I choose the third."

"'Tis yours," the fairy said ; "be quite
Invisible to mortal sight
Whene'er you please.   Remember me
Most kindly, pray, to MRS. P."

Old MRS. PETER overheard
Wee PICKLEKIN's concluding word,
And, jealous of her girlhood's choice,
Said, "That was some young woman's voice !"

Old PETER let her scold and swear—
Old PETER, bless him, didn't care.
"My dear, your rage is wasted quite—
Observe, I disappear from sight !"

A well-bred fairy (so I've heard)
Is always faithful to her word :
Old PETER vanished like a shot,
But then—*his suit of clothes did not.*

For when conferred the fairy slim
Invisibility on him,
She popped away on fairy wings,
Without referring to his "things."

So there remained a coat of blue,
A vest and double eyeglass too,
His tail, his shoes, his socks as well,
His pair of—no, I must not tell.

The Perils of Invisibility

Old MRS. PETER soon began
To see the failure of his plan,
And then resolved (I quote the bard)
To "hoist him with his own petard."

Old PETER woke next day and dressed,
Put on his coat and shoes and vest,
His shirt and stock—*but could not find
His only pair of*—never mind!

Old PETER was a decent man,
And though he twigged his lady's plan,
Yet, hearing her approaching, he
Resumed invisibility.

"Dear MRS. P., my only joy,"
Exclaimed the horrified old boy;
"Now give them up, I beg of you—
You know what I'm referring to!"

The Perils of Invisibility

But no ; the cross old lady swore
She'd keep his—what I said before—
To make him publicly absurd ;
And Mrs. PETER kept her word.

The poor old fellow had no rest ;
His coat, his stock, his shoes, his vest,
Were all that now met mortal eye—
The rest, invisibility !

" Now, madam, give them up, I beg—
I've bad rheumatics in my leg ;
Besides, until you do, it's plain
I cannot come to sight again !

" For though some mirth it might afford
To see my clothes without their lord,
Yet there would rise indignant oaths
If he were seen without his clothes ! "

But no ; resolved to have her quiz,
The lady held her own—and his—
And PETER left his humble cot
To find a pair of—you know what.

But—here's the worst of this affair—
Whene'er he came across a pair
Already placed for him to don,
He was too stout to get them on !

So he resolved at once to train,
And walked and walked with all his main ;
For years he paced this mortal earth,
To bring himself to decent girth.

The Perils of Invisibility

At night, when all around is still,
You'll find him pounding up a hill;
And shrieking peasants whom he meets,
Fall down in terror on the peats!

Old PETER walks through wind and rain,
Resolved to train, and train, and train,
Until he weighs twelve stone or so—
And when he does, I'll let you know.

THE GREAT OAK TREE

THERE grew a little flower
        'Neath a great oak tree:
When the tempest 'gan to lower
        Little heeded she:
No need had she to cower,
For she dreaded not its power—
She was happy in the bower
        Of her great oak tree!
        Sing hey,
        Lackaday!
        Let the tears fall free
For the pretty little flower and the great oak tree!

When she found that he was fickle,
        Was that great oak tree,
She was in a pretty pickle,
        As she well might be—

The Great Oak Tree

But his gallantries were mickle,
For Death followed with his sickle,
And her tears began to trickle
                    For her great oak tree!
                    Sing hey,
                    Lackaday!
                Let the tears fall free
For the pretty little flower and the great oak tree!

Said she, " He loved me never,
                    Did that great oak tree,
But I'm neither rich nor clever,
                    And so why should he?
But though fate our fortunes sever,
To be constant I'll endeavour,
Ay, for ever and for ever,
                    To my great oak tree!"
                    Sing hey,
                    Lackaday!
                Let the tears fall free
For the pretty little flower and the great oak tree!

OLD PAUL AND OLD TIM

WHEN rival adorers come courting a maid,
There's something or other may often be said,
Why *he* should be pitched upon rather than *him*.
This wasn't the case with Old PAUL and Old TIM.

No soul could discover a reason at all
For marrying TIMOTHY rather than PAUL;
Though all could have offered good reasons, on oath,
Against marrying either—or marrying both.

They were equally wealthy and equally old,
They were equally timid and equally bold;
They were equally tall as they stood in their shoes—
Between them, in fact, there was nothing to choose.

Had I been young EMILY, I should have said,
"You're both much too old for a pretty young maid,
Threescore at the least you are verging upon";
But I wasn't young EMILY.   Let us get on.

Old Paul and Old Tim

No coward's blood ran in young EMILY's veins,
Her martial old father loved bloody campaigns;
At the rumours of battles all over the globe
He pricked up his ears like the war-horse in " Job."

He chuckled to hear of a sudden surprise—
Of soldiers, compelled, through an enemy's spies,
Without any knapsacks or shakos to flee—
For an eminent army-contractor was he.

So when her two lovers, whose patience was tried,
Implored her between them at once to decide,
She told them she'd marry whichever might bring
Good proofs of his doing the pluckiest thing.

They both went away with a qualified joy:
That coward, Old PAUL, chose a very small boy,
And when no one was looking, in spite of his fears,
He set to work boxing that little boy's ears.

The little boy struggled and tugged at his hair,
But the lion was roused, and Old PAUL didn't care;
He smacked him, and whacked him, and boxed him, and
    kicked
Till the poor little beggar was royally licked.

Old Paul and Old Tim

Old TIM knew a trick worth a dozen of that,
So he called for his stick and he called for his hat.
"I'll cover myself with cheap glory—I'll go
And wallop the Frenchmen who live in Soho!

"The German invader is ravaging France
With infantry rifle and cavalry lance,
And beautiful Paris is fighting her best
To shake herself free from her terrible guest.

"The Frenchmen in London, in craven alarms,
Have all run away from the summons to arms;
They haven't the pluck of a pigeon—I'll go
And wallop the Frenchmen who skulk in Soho!"

Old TIMOTHY tried it and found it succeed:
That day he caused many French noses to bleed;
Through foggy Soho he spread fear and dismay,
And Frenchmen all round him in agony lay.

He took care to abstain from employing his fist
On the old and the crippled, for they might resist;
A crippled old man may have pluck in his breast,
But the young and the strong ones are cowards confest

Old Paul and Old Tim

Old TIM and Old PAUL, with the list of their foes,
Prostrated themselves at their EMILY'S toes:
"Oh, which of us two is the pluckier blade?"
And EMILY answered and EMILY said:

"Old TIM has thrashed runaway Frenchmen in scores,
Who ought to be guarding their cities and shores;
Old PAUL has made little chaps' noses to bleed—
Old PAUL has accomplished the pluckier deed!"

KING GOODHEART

THERE lived a King, as I've been told
In the wonder-working days of old,
When hearts were twice as good as gold,
 And twenty times as mellow.
Good temper triumphed in his face,
And in his heart he found a place
For all the erring human race
 And every wretched fellow.
When he had Rhenish wine to drink
It made him very sad to think
That some, at junket or at jink,
 Must be content with toddy:
He wished all men as rich as he
(And he was rich as rich could be),
So to the top of every tree
 Promoted everybody.

King Goodheart

Ambassadors cropped up like hay,
Prime Ministers and such as they
Grew like asparagus in May,
    And Dukes were three a penny:
Lord Chancellors were cheap as sprats,
And Bishops in their shovel hats
Were plentiful as tabby cats—
    If possible, too many.
On every side Field-Marshals gleamed,
Small beer were Lords-Lieutenants deemed,
With Admirals the ocean teemed,
    All round his wide dominions;
And Party Leaders you might meet
In twos and threes in every street
Maintaining, with no little heat,
    Their various opinions.

That King, although no one denies,
His heart was of abnormal size,
Yet he'd have acted otherwise
    If he had been acuter.
The end is easily foretold,
When every blessed thing you hold
Is made of silver, or of gold,
    You long for simple pewter.
When you have nothing else to wear
But cloth of gold and satins rare,
For cloth of gold you cease to care—
    Up goes the price of shoddy:
In short, whoever you may be,
To this conclusion you'll agree,
When every one is somebody,
    Then no one's anybody!

THE MYSTIC SELVAGEE

PERHAPS already you may know
SIR BLENNERHASSET PORTICO?
A Captain in the Navy, he—
A Baronet and K.C.B.

         You do?   I thought so!
It was that captain's favourite whim
(A notion not confined to him)
That RODNEY was the greatest tar
Who ever wielded capstan-bar.

         He had been taught so.

"BENBOW? CORNWALLIS? HOOD?—Belay!
Compared with RODNEY"—he would say—
"No other tar is worth a rap;
The great LORD RODNEY was the chap

         The French to polish!

426

The Mystic Selvagee

"Though, mind you, I respect LORD HOOD;
CORNWALLIS, too, was rather good;
BENBOW could enemies repel;
LORD NELSON, too, was pretty well—
        That is, tol-lol-ish!"

SIR BLENNERHASSET spent his days
In learning RODNEY's little ways,
And closely imitated, too,
His mode of talking to his crew—
        His port and paces.
An ancient tar he tried to catch
Who'd served in RODNEY's famous batch;
But since his time long years have fled,
And RODNEY's tars are mostly dead:
        Eheu fugaces!

But after searching near and far,
At last he found an ancient tar
Who served with RODNEY and his crew
Against the French in 'eighty-two
        (That gained the peerage).
He gave him fifty pounds a year,
His rum, his baccy, and his beer;
And had a comfortable den
Rigged up in what, by merchantmen,
        Is called the steerage.

"Now, JASPER"—'twas that sailor's name—
"Don't fear that you'll incur my blame
By saying, when it seems to you,
That there is anything I do
        That RODNEY wouldn't."

The Mystic Selvagee

The ancient sailor turned his quid,
Prepared to do as he was bid:
"Ay, ay, yer honour; to begin,
You've done away with 'swifting in'—
         Well, sir, you shouldn't!

"Upon your spars I see you've clapped
Peak-halliard blocks, all iron-capped;
I would not christen that a crime,
But 'twas not done in RODNEY's time.
         It looks half-witted!
Upon your maintop-stay, I see,
You always clap a selvagee;
Your stays, I see, are equalised—
No vessel, such as RODNEY prized,
         Would thus be fitted.

"And RODNEY, honoured sir, would grin
To see you turning deadeyes in,
Not *up*, as in the ancient way,
But downwards, like a cutter's stay—
         You didn't oughter!
Besides, in seizing shrouds on board,
Breast backstays you have quite ignored;
Great RODNEY kept unto the last
Breast backstays on topgallant mast—
         They make it tauter."

SIR BLENNERHASSET "swifted in,"
Turned deadeyes up, and lent a fin
To strip (as told by JASPER KNOX)
The iron capping from his blocks,
         Where there was any.

The Mystic Selvagee

Sir Blennerhasset does away
With selvagees from maintop-stay;
And though it makes his sailors stare,
He rigs breast backstays everywhere—
        In fact, too many.

One morning, when the saucy craft
Lay calmed, old Jasper toddled aft.
"My mind misgives me, sir, that we
Were wrong about that selvagee—
        I should restore it."
"Good," said the captain, and that day
Restored it to the maintop-stay.
Well-practised sailors often make
A much more serious mistake,
        And then ignore it.

The Mystic Selvagee

Next day old JASPER came once more:
"I think, sir, I was right before."
Well, up the mast the sailors skipped,
The selvagee was soon unshipped,
      And all were merry.
Again a day, and JASPER came:
"I p'raps deserve your honour's blame,
I can't make up my mind," said he,
"About that cursed selvagee—
      It's foolish—very.

"On Monday night I could have sworn
That maintop-stay it should adorn,
On Tuesday morning I could swear
That selvagee should not be there.
      The knot's a rasper!"
"Oh, you be hanged!" said CAPTAIN P.,
"Here, go ashore at Caribbee.
Get out—good-bye—shove off—all right!"
Old JASPER soon was out of sight—
      Farewell, old JASPER!

SLEEP ON!

FEAR no unlicensed entry,
  Heed no bombastic talk,
While guards the British Sentry
  Pall Mall and Birdcage Walk.
Let European thunders
  Occasion no alarms,
Though diplomatic blunders
    May cause a cry "To arms!"
      Sleep on, ye pale civilians;
        All thunder-clouds defy:
        On Europe's countless millions
          The Sentry keeps his eye!

Should foreign-born rapscallions
  In London dare to show
Their overgrown battalions,
  Be sure I'll let you know.

431

Sleep On !

Should Russians or Norwegians
    Pollute our favoured clime
With rough barbaric legions,
    I'll mention it in time.
        So sleep in peace, civilians,
            The Continent defy ;
        While on its countless millions
            The Sentry keeps his eye !

THE CUNNING WOMAN

On all Arcadia's sunny plain,
  On all Arcadia's hill,
None were so blithe as Bill and Jane,
  So blithe as Jane and Bill.

No social earthquake e'er occurred
  To rack their common mind:
To them a Panic was a word—
  A Crisis, empty wind.

No Stock Exchange disturbed the lad
  With overwhelming shocks—
Bill ploughed with all the shares he had,
  Jane planted all her stocks.

The Cunning Woman

And learn in what a simple way
  Their pleasures they enhanced—
JANE danced like any lamb all day,
  BILL piped as well as danced.

Surrounded by a twittling crew,
  Of linnet, lark, and thrush,
BILL treated his young lady to
  This sentimental gush:

"Oh, JANE, how true I am to you!
  How true you are to me!
And how we woo, and how we coo!
  So fond a pair are we!

"To think, dear JANE, that anyways.
  Your chiefest end and aim
Is, one of these fine summer days,
  To bear my humble name!"

Quoth JANE, "Well, as you put the case,
  I'm true enough, no doubt,
But then, you see, in this here place
  There's none to cut you out.

"But, oh! if anybody came—
  A Lord or any such—
I do not think your humble name
  Would fascinate me much.

"For though your mates, you often boast,
  You distance out-and-out;
Still, in the abstract, you're a most
  Uncompromising lout!"

The Cunning Woman

Poor BILL, he gave a heavy sigh,
    He tried in vain to speak—
A fat tear started to each eye
    And coursed adown each cheek.

For, oh! right well in truth he knew
    That very self-same day,
The LORD DE JACOB PILLALOO
    Was coming there to stay!

The LORD DE JACOB PILLALOO
    All proper maidens shun—
He loves all women, it is true,
    But never marries one.

Now JANE, with all her mad self-will,
    Was no coquette—oh no!
She really loved her faithful BILL,
    And thus she tuned her woe:

435

The Cunning Woman

"Oh, willow, willow, o'er the lea!
    And willow once again!
The Peer will fall in love with me!
    Why wasn't I made plain?"

   *   *   *   *   *

A cunning woman lived hard by,
    A sorceressing dame,
MacCatacomb de Salmon-Eye
    Was her uncommon name.

To her good Jane, with kindly yearn
    For Bill's increasing pain,
Repaired in secrecy to learn
    How best to make her plain.

"Oh, Jane," the worthy woman said,
    "This mystic phial keep,
And rub its liquor in your head
    Before you go to sleep.

436

The Cunning Woman

"When you awake next day, I trow,
   You'll look in form and hue
To others just as you do now—
   But not to PILLALOO!

"When you approach him, you will find
   He'll think you coarse—unkempt—
And rudely bid you get behind,
   With undisguised contempt."

The LORD DE PILLALOO arrived
   With his expensive train,
And when in state serenely hived,
   He sent for BILL and JANE.

"Oh, spare her, LORD OF PILLALOO!
   (Said BILL) if wed you be,
There's anything *I'd* rather do
   Than flirt with LADY P."

The Lord he gazed in Jenny's eyes,
   He looked her through and through:
The cunning woman's prophecies
   Were clearly coming true.

LORD PILLALOO, the Rustic's Bane
   (Bad person he, and proud),
He laughed Ha! ha! at pretty JANE,
   And sneered at her aloud!

The Cunning Woman

He bade her get behind him then,
    And seek her mother's stye—
Yet to her native countrymen
    She was as fair as aye!

MacCatacomb, continue green!
    Grow, Salmon-Eye, in might,
Except for you, there might have been
    The deuce's own delight!

THE LOVE-SICK BOY

WHEN first my old, old love I knew,
 My bosom welled with joy;
My riches at her feet I threw;
 I was a love-sick boy!
No terms seemed too extravagant
 Upon her to employ—
I used to mope, and sigh, and pant,
 Just like a love-sick boy!

But joy incessant palls the sense;
 And love unchanged will cloy,
And she became a bore intense
 Unto her love-sick boy?
With fitful glimmer burnt my flame,
 And I grew cold and coy,
At last, one morning, I became
 Another's love-sick boy!

PHRENOLOGY

"COME, collar this bad man—
    Around the throat he knotted me
Till I to choke began—
    In point of fact, garrotted me!"

So spake SIR HERBERT WHITE
    To JAMES, Policeman Thirty-two—
All ruffled with his fight
    SIR HERBERT was, and dirty too.

Policeman nothing said
    (Though he had much to say on it),
But from the bad man's head
    He took the cap that lay on it.

Phrenology

"No, great SIR HERBERT WHITE—
    Impossible to take him up.
This man is honest quite—
    Wherever did you rake him up?

"For Burglars, Thieves, and Co.,
    Indeed I'm no apologist;
But I, some years ago,
    Assisted a Phrenologist.

"Observe his various bumps,
    His head as I uncover it;
His morals lie in lumps
    All round about and over it."

"Now take him," said SIR WHITE,
    "Or you will soon be rueing it;
Bless me! I must be right,—
    I caught the fellow doing it!"

Policeman calmly smiled,
    "Indeed you are mistaken, sir,
You're agitated—riled—
    And very badly shaken, sir.

"Sit down, and I'll explain
    My system of Phrenology,
A second, please, remain"—
    (A second is horology).

Policeman left his beat—
    (The Bart., no longer furious,
Sat down upon a seat,
    Observing, "This is curious!")

Phrenology

"Oh, surely here are signs
    Should soften your rigidity,
This gentleman combines
    Politeness with timidity.

"Of Shyness here's a lump—
    A hole for Animosity—
And like my fist his bump
    Of Generenerosity.

"Just here the bump appears
    Of Innocent Hilarity,
And just behind his ear
    Are Faith, and Hope, and Charity.

"He of true Christian ways
    As bright example sent us is—
This maxim he obeys,
    'Sorte tuâ contentus sis.'

Phrenology

" There, let him go his ways,
    He needs no stern admonishing."
The Bart., in blank amaze,
    Exclaimed, " This is astonishing !

" I *must* have made a mull,
    This matter I've been blind in it :
Examine, please, *my* skull,
    And tell me what you find in it."

Policeman looked, and said,
    With unimpaired urbanity,
" SIR HERBERT, you've a head
    That teems with inhumanity.

" Here's Murder, Envy, Strife
    (Propensity to kill any),
And Lies as large as life,
    And heaps of Social Villainy :

" Here's Love of Bran New Clothes,
    Embezzling—Arson—Deism—
A taste for Slang and Oaths,
    And Fraudulent Trusteeism.

" Here's Love of Groundless Charge—
    Here's Malice, too, and Trickery,
Unusually large
    Your bump of Pocket-Pickery——"

" Stop ! " said the Bart., " my cup
    Is full—I'm worse than him in all—
Policeman, take me up—
    No doubt I am some criminal ! "

Phrenology

That Policeman's scorn grew large
    (Phrenology had nettled it),
He took that Bart. in charge—
    I don't know how they settled it.

POETRY EVERYWHERE

WHAT time the poet hath hymned
The writhing maid, lithe-limbed,
  Quivering on amaranthine asphodel,
How can he paint her woes,
Knowing, as well he knows,
  That all can be set right with calomel?

When from the poet's plinth
The amorous colocynth
  Yearns for the aloe, faint with rapturous thrills,
How can he hymn their throes
Knowing, as well he knows,
  That they are only uncompounded pills?

Is it, and can it be,
Nature hath this decree,
  Nothing poetic in the world shall dwell?
Or that in all her works
Something poetic lurks,
  Even in colocynth and calomel?

THE FAIRY CURATE

ONCE a fairy
Light and airy
Married with a mortal;
Men, however,
Never, never
Pass the fairy portal.
Slyly stealing,
She to Ealing
Made a daily journey;
There she found him,
Clients round him
(He was an attorney).

Long they tarried,
Then they married.
When the ceremony
Once was ended,
Off they wended
On their moon of honey.

The Fairy Curate

Twelvemonth, maybe,
Saw a baby
(Friends performed an orgie)
Much they prized him,
And baptized him
By the name of GEORGIE.

GEORGIE grew up;
Then he flew up
To his fairy mother.
Happy meeting
Pleasant greeting—
Kissing one another.
"Choose a calling
Most enthralling,
I sincerely urge ye."
"Mother," said he
(Rev'rence made he),
"I would join the clergy.

"Give permission
In addition—
Pa will let me do it:
There's a living
In his giving,
He'll appoint me to it.
Dreams of coff'ring
Easter off'ring,
Tithe and rent and pew-rate,
So inflame me
(Do not blame me),
That I'll be a curate."

She, with pleasure,
Said, "My treasure,
'Tis my wish precisely.

The Fairy Curate

            Do your duty,
            There's a beauty ;
You have chosen wisely.
            Tell your father
            I would rather
As a churchman rank you.

            You, in clover,
            I'll watch over."
GEORGIE said, "Oh, thank you !"

The Fairy Curate

GEORGIE scudded,
Went and studied,
Made all preparations,
And with credit
(Though he said it)
Passed examinations.
·(Do not quarrel
With him, moral,
Scrupulous digestions—
But his mother,
And no other,
Answered all the questions.)

Time proceeded;
Little needed
GEORGIE admonition:
He, elated,
Vindicated
Clergyman's position.
People round him
Always found him
Plain and unpretending;
Kindly teaching,
Plainly preaching—
All his money lending.

So the fairy,
Wise and wary,
Felt no sorrow rising—
No occasion
For persuasion,
Warning, or advising.
He, resuming
Fairy pluming
(That's not English, is it?)

The Fairy Curate

Oft would fly up,
To the sky up,
Pay mamma a visit.

*   *   *   *

Time progressing,
GEORGIE's blessing
Grew more Ritualistic—
Popish scandals,
Tonsures—sandals—
Genuflections mystic;
Gushing meetings—
Bosom-beatings—
Heavenly ecstatics—
Broidered spencers—
Copes and censers—
Rochets and dalmatics.

This quandary
Vexed the fairy—
Flew she down to Ealing.
"GEORGIE, stop it!
Pray you, drop it;
Hark to my appealing:
To this foolish
Papal rule-ish
Twaddle put an ending;
This a swerve is
From our Service
Plain and unpretending."

He, replying,
Answered, sighing,
Hawing, hemming, humming,

The Fairy Curate

"It's a pity—
They're so pritty;
Yet in mode becoming,
Mother tender,
I'll surrender—
I'll be unaffected—"
Then his Bishop
Into *his* shop
Entered unexpected:

"Who is this, sir,—
Ballet miss, sir?"
Said the Bishop coldly.
"'Tis my mother,
And no other,"
GEORGIE answered boldly.

The Fairy Curate

" Go along, sir !
You are wrong, sir,
You have years in plenty ;
While this hussy
(Gracious mussy !)
Isn't two-and-twenty ! "

(Fairies clever
Never, never
Grow in visage older ;
And the fairy,
All unwary,
Leant upon his shoulder !)
Bishop grieved him,
Disbelieved him,
GEORGE the point grew warm on ;
Changed religion,
Like a pigeon,[1]
And became a Mormon.

[1] " Like a bird."

HE LOVES!

HE loves!   If in the bygone years
  Thine eyes have ever shed
Tears—bitter, unavailing tears,
  For one untimely dead—
If in the eventide of life
  Sad thoughts of her arise,
Then let the memory of thy wife
  Plead for my boy—he dies!

He dies!   If fondly laid aside
  In some old cabinet,
Memorials of thy long-dead bride
  Lie, dearly treasured yet,
Then let her hallowed bridal dress—
  Her little dainty gloves—
Her withered flowers—her faded tress—
  Plead for my boy—he loves!

THE WAY OF WOOING

A MAIDEN sat at her window wide,
Pretty enough for a prince's bride,
   Yet nobody came to claim her.
She sat like a beautiful picture there,
With pretty bluebells and roses fair,
   And jasmine leaves to frame her.
And why she sat there nobody knows;
But thus she sang as she plucked a rose,
   The leaves around her strewing:
"I've time to lose and power to choose;
'Tis not so much the gallant who woos
   As the gallant's way of wooing!"

The Way of Wooing

A lover came riding by awhile,
A wealthy lover was he, whose smile
   Some maids would value greatly—
A formal lover, who bowed and bent,
With many a high-flown compliment,
   And cold demeanour stately.

" You've still," said she to her suitor stern,
" The 'prentice-work of your craft to learn,
   If thus you come a-cooing.
I've time to lose and power to choose ;
'Tis not so much the gallant who woos
   As the gallant's way of wooing ! "

The Way of Wooing

A second lover came ambling by—
A timid lad with a frightened eye
   And a colour mantling highly.
He muttered the errand on which he'd come,
Then only chuckled and bit his thumb,
   And simpered, simpered shyly.
" No," said the maiden, " go your way,
You dare but think what a man would say,
   Yet dare come a-suing !
I've time to lose and power to choose ;
'Tis not so much the gallant who woos
   As the gallant's way of wooing ! "

A third rode up at a startling pace—
A suitor poor, with a homely face—
   No doubts appeared to bind him.
He kissed her lips and he pressed her waist,
And off he rode with the maiden, placed
   On a pillion safe behind him.

The Way of Wooing

And she heard the suitor bold confide
This golden hint to the priest who tied
   The knot there's no undoing:
"With pretty young maidens who can choose,
'Tis not so much the gallant who woos
   As the gallant's way of wooing!"

TRUE DIFFIDENCE

My boy, you may take it from me,
    That of all the afflictions accurst
        With which a man's saddled
        And hampered and addled,
    A diffident nature's the worst.
Though clever as clever can be—
    A Crichton of early romance—
        You must stir it and stump it,
        And blow your own trumpet,
    Or, trust me, you haven't a chance.

Now take, for example, *my* case :
    I've a bright intellectual brain—
        In all London city
        There's no one so witty—
    I've thought so again and again.

True Diffidence

I've a highly intelligent face—
    My features cannot be denied—
        But, whatever I try, sir,
        I fail in—and why, sir?
I'm modesty personified!

As a poet, I'm tender and quaint—
    I've passion and fervour and grace—
        From Ovid and Horace
        To Swinburne and Morris,
They all of them take a back place.
Then I sing and I play and I paint;
    Though none are accomplished as I,
        To say so were treason:
        You ask me the reason?
I'm diffident, modest, and shy!

HONGREE AND MAHRY

A RICHARDSONIAN MELODRAMA

THE sun was setting in its wonted west,
When HONGREE, Sub-Lieutenant of Chassoores,
Met MAHRY DAUBIGNY, the Village Rose,
Under the Wizard's Oak—old trysting-place
Of those who loved in rosy Aquitaine.

They thought themselves unwatched, but they were not,
For HONGREE, Sub-Lieutenant of Chassoores,
Found in LIEUTENANT-COLONEL JOOLES DUBOSC
A rival, envious and unscrupulous,
Who thought it not foul scorn to dog his steps,
And listen, unperceived, to all that passed
Between the simple little Village Rose
And HONGREE, Sub-Lieutenant of Chassoores.

460

Hongree and Mahry

A clumsy barrack-bully was DUBOSC,
Quite unfamiliar with the well-bred tact
That actuates a proper gentleman
In dealing with a girl of humble rank.
You'll understand his coarseness when I say
He would have married MAHRY DAUBIGNY,
And dragged the unsophisticated girl
Into the whirl of fashionable life,
For which her singularly rustic ways,
Her breeding (moral, but extremely rude),
Her language (chaste, but ungrammatical),
Would absolutely have unfitted her.
No such intention lurked within the breast
Of HONGREE, Sub-Lieutenant of Chassoores!

Contemporary with the incident
Related in our opening paragraph,
Was that sad war 'twixt Gallia and ourselves
That followed on the treaty signed at Troyes;
And so LIEUTENANT-COLONEL JOOLES DUBOSC
(Brave soldier, he, with all his faults of style)
And HONGREE, Sub-Lieutenant of Chassoores,
Were sent by CHARLES of France against the lines
Of our Sixth HENRY (Fourteen twenty-nine),
To drive his legions out of Aquitaine.

When HONGREE, Sub-Lieutenant of Chassoores,
Returned (suspecting nothing) to his camp,
After his meeting with the Village Rose,
He found inside his barrack letter-box
A note from the commanding-officer,
Requiring his attendance at headquarters.

He went, and found LIEUTENANT-COLONEL JOOLES
"Young HONGREE, Sub-Lieutenant of Chassoores,
This night we shall attack the English camp:
Be the 'forlorn hope' yours—you'll lead it, sir,

Hongree and Mahry

And lead it too with credit, I've no doubt"
(These last words with a cruelly obvious sneer).
"As every soul must certainly be killed
(For you are twenty 'gainst two thousand men),
It is not likely that you will return;
But what of that? you'll have the benefit
Of knowing that you die a soldier's death."

Obedience was young HONGREE's strongest point,
But he imagined that he only owed
Allegiance to his MAHRY and his King.
"If MAHRY bade me lead these fated men,
I'd lead them—but I do not think she would.
If CHARLES, my King, said, 'Go, my son, and die,'
I'd go, of course—my duty would be clear.
But MAHRY is in bed asleep (I hope),
And CHARLES, my King, a hundred leagues from this.
As for LIEUTENANT-COLONEL JOOLES DUBOSC,

Hongree and Mahry

How know I that our monarch would approve
The order he has given me to-night?
My King I've sworn in all things to obey—
I'll only take my orders from my King!"
Thus HONGREE, Sub-Lieutenant of Chassoores
Interpreted the terms of his commission.

And HONGREE, who was wise as he was good,
Disguised himself that night in ample cloak,

Round flapping hat, and visor mask of black,
And made, unnoticed, for the English camp.
He passed the unsuspecting sentinels
(Who little thought a man in this disguise
Could be a proper object of suspicion),
And ere the curfew-bell had boomed "lights out,"
He found in audience Bedford's haughty Duke.

Hongree and Mahry

"Your Grace," he said, "start not—be not alarmed,
Although a Frenchman stands before your eyes.
I'm HONGREE, Sub-Lieutenant of Chassoores.
My colonel will attack your camp to-night,

And orders me to lead the hope forlorn.
Now I am sure our excellent KING CHARLES
Would not approve of this; but he's away
A hundred leagues, and rather more than that.
So, utterly devoted to my King,
Blinded by my attachment to the throne,
And having but its interest at heart,
I feel it is my duty to disclose
All schemes that emanate from COLONEL JOOLES,
If I believe that they are not the kind
Of schemes that our good monarch could approve.'
"But how," said Bedford's Duke, "do you propose

Hongree and Mahry

That we should overthrow your colonel's scheme?"
And HONGREE, Sub-Lieutenant of Chassoores,
Replied at once with never-failing tact:
"Oh, sir, I know this cursed country well.
Entrust yourself and all your host to me;
I'll lead you safely by a secret path
Into the heart of COLONEL JOOLES' array,
And you can then attack them unprepared,
And slay my fellow-countrymen unarmed."

The thing was done.   The DUKE OF BEDFORD gave
The order, and two thousand fighting-men
Crept silently into the Gallic camp,
And killed the Frenchmen as they lay asleep;
And Bedford's haughty Duke slew COLONEL JOOLES,
And married MAHRY, pride of Aquitaine,
To HONGREE, Sub-Lieutenant of Chassoores.

THE TANGLED SKEIN

TRY we life-long, we can never
    Straighten out life's tangled skein,
Why should we, in vain endeavour,
    Guess and guess and guess again?
        Life's a pudding full of plums
        Care's a canker that benumbs.
Wherefore waste our elocution
On impossible solution?
Life's a pleasant institution,
    Let us take it as it comes!

Set aside the dull enigma,
    We shall guess it all too soon;
Failure brings no kind of stigma—
    Dance we to another tune!
        String the lyre and fill the cup,
        Lest on sorrow we should sup;
Hop and skip to Fancy's fiddle,
Hands across and down the middle—
Life's perhaps the only riddle
    That we shrink from giving up!

THE REVEREND MICAH SOWLS

THE REVEREND MICAH SOWLS,
He shouts and yells and howls,
He screams, he mouths, he bumps,
He foams, he rants, he thumps.

His armour he has buckled on, to wage
The regulation war against the Stage;
And warns his congregation all to shun
"The Presence-Chamber of the Evil One."

The subject's sad enough
To make him rant and puff,
And fortunately, too,
His Bishop's in a pew.

So REVEREND MICAH claps on extra steam,
His eyes are flashing with superior gleam,
He is as energetic as can be,
For there are fatter livings in that see.

The Reverend Micah Sowls

The Bishop, when it's o'er,
Goes through the vestry door,
Where MICAH, very red,
Is mopping of his head.

"Pardon, my Lord, your SOWLS' excessive zeal,
It is a theme on which I strongly feel."
(The sermon somebody had sent him down
From London, at a charge of half-a-crown.)

The Bishop bowed his head,
And, acquiescing, said,
"I've heard your well-meant rage
Against the Modern Stage.

"A modern Theatre, as I heard you say,
Sows seeds of evil broadcast—well it may;
But let me ask you, my respected son,
Pray, have you ever ventured into one?"

The Reverend Micah Sowls

"My Lord," said MICAH, "no!
I never, never go!
What! Go and see a play?
My goodness gracious, nay!"

The worthy Bishop said, "My friend, no doubt
The Stage may be the place you make it out;
But if, my REVEREND SOWLS, you never go,
I don't quite understand how you're to know."

"Well, really," MICAH said,
"I've often heard and read,
But never go—do you?"
The Bishop said, "I do."

"That proves me wrong," said MICAH, in a trice!
"I thought it all frivolity and vice."
The Bishop handed him a printed card;
"Go to a theatre where they play our Bard."

The Bishop took his leave,
Rejoicing in his sleeve.
The next ensuing day
SOWLS went and heard a play.

He saw a dreary person on the stage,
Who mouthed and mugged in simulated rage,
Who growled and spluttered in a mode absurd,
And spoke an English SOWLS had never heard.

For "gaunt" was spoken "garnt,"
And "haunt" transformed to "harnt,"
And "wrath" pronounced as "rath,"
And "death" was changed to "dath."

The Reverend Micah Sowls

For hours and hours that dismal actor walked,
And talked, and talked, and talked, and talked,
Till lethargy upon the parson crept,
And sleepy MICAH SOWLS serenely slept.

He slept away until
The farce that closed the bill
Had warned him not to stay,
And then he went away.

"I thought *my* gait ridiculous," said he—
"*My* elocution faulty as could be;
I thought *I* mumbled on a matchless plan—
I had not seen our great Tragedian!

"Forgive me, if you can,
O great Tragedian!
I own it with a sigh—
You're drearier than I!"

MY LADY

BEDECKED in fashion trim,
　　With every curl a-quiver;
Or leaping, light of limb,
　　O'er rivulet and river;
Or skipping o'er the lea
　　On daffodil and daisy;
Or stretched beneath a tree,
　　All languishing and lazy;
　　　　Whatever be her mood—
　　　　Be she demurely prude
　　　　　Or languishingly lazy—
　　　　　My lady drives me crazy!
　　　In vain her heart is wooed,
　　　Whatever be her mood!

471

My Lady

What profit should I gain
    Suppose she loved me dearly?
Her coldness turns my brain
    To *verge* of madness merely.
Her kiss—though, Heaven knows,
    To dream of it were treason—
Would tend, as I suppose,
    To utter loss of reason!
        My state is not amiss;
        I would not have a kiss
            Which, in or out of season,
            Might tend to loss of reason:
        What profit in such bliss?
        A fig for such a kiss!

ONE AGAINST THE WORLD

It's my opinion—though I own
In thinking so I'm quite alone—
  In some respects I'm but a fright.
You like my features, I suppose?
I'm disappointed with my nose:
  Some rave about it—perhaps they're right.
My figure just sets off a fit;
But when they say it's exquisite
  (And they *do* say so), that's too strong.
I hope I'm not what people call
Opinionated! After all,
  I'm but a goose, and may be wrong!

When charms enthral
  There's some excuse
   For measures strong;
And after all
  I'm but a goose,
   And may be wrong!

One Against the World

My teeth are very neat, no doubt;
But after all they *may* fall out:
   I think they will—some think they won't.
My hands are small, as you may see,
But not as small as they might be,
   At least, *I* think so—others don't.
But there, a girl may preach and prate
From morning six to evening eight,
   And never stop to dine,
When all the world, although misled,
Is quite agreed on any head—
   And it is quite agreed on mine!

   All said and done,
     It's little I
       Against a throng.
I'm only one,
     And possibly
       I may be wrong!

THE FORCE OF ARGUMENT

LORD B. was a nobleman bold
   Who came of illustrious stocks,
He was thirty or forty years old,
   And several feet in his socks.

To Turniptopville-by-the-Sea
   This elegant nobleman went,
For that was a borough that he
   Was anxious to rep-per-re-sent.

At local assemblies he danced
   Until he felt thoroughly ill;
He waltzed, and he galoped, and lanced,
   And threaded the mazy quadrille.

The Force of Argument

The maidens of Turniptopville
    Were simple—ingenuous—pure—
And they all worked away with a will
    The nobleman's heart to secure.

Two maidens all others beyond
    Endeavoured his cares to dispel—
The one was the lively ANN POND,
    The other sad MARY MORELL.

ANN POND had determined to try
    And carry the Earl with a rush;
Her principal feature was eye,
    Her greatest accomplishment—gush.

And MARY chose this for her play:
    Whenever he looked in her eye
She'd blush and turn quickly away,
    And flitter, and flutter, and sigh.

It was noticed he constantly sighed
    As she worked out the scheme she had planned,
A fact he endeavoured to hide
    With his aristocratical hand.

Old POND was a farmer, they say,
    And so was old TOMMY MORELL.
In a humble and pottering way
    They were doing exceedingly well.

They both of them carried by vote
    The Earl was a dangerous man;
So nervously clearing his throat,
    One morning old TOMMY began:

The Force of Argument

"My darter's no pratty young doll—
  I'm a plain-spoken Zommerzet man—
Now what do 'ee mean by my POLL,
  And what do 'ee mean by his ANN?"

Said B., "I will give you my bond
  I mean them uncommonly well,
Believe me, my excellent POND,
  And credit me, worthy MORELL.

"It's quite indisputable, for
  I'll prove it with singular ease,—
You shall have it in 'Barbara' or
  'Celarent'—whichever you please.

The Force of Argument

'You see, when an anchorite bows
　　To the yoke of intentional sin,
If the state of the country allows,
　　Homogeny always steps in——

"It's a highly æsthetical bond,
　　As any mere ploughboy can tell——"
"Of course," replied puzzled old POND.
　　"I see," said old TOMMY MORELL.

"Very good, then," continued the lord;
　　"When it's fooled to the top of its bent,
With a sweep of a Damocles sword
　　The web of intention is rent.

"That's patent to all of us here,
　　As any mere schoolboy can tell."
POND answered, "Of course it's quite clear";
　　And so did that humbug MORELL.

"Its tone's esoteric in force——
　　I trust that I make myself clear?"
MORELL only answered, "Of course,"
　　While POND slowly muttered, "Hear, hear."

"Volition——celestial prize,
　　Pellucid as porphyry cell——
Is based on a principle wise."
　　"Quite so," exclaimed POND and MORELL.

"From what I have said you will see
　　That I couldn't wed either——in fine,
By Nature's unchanging decree
　　Your daughters could never be *mine*.

The Force of Argument

"Go home to your pigs and your ricks,
   My hands of the matter I've rinsed."
So they take up their hats and their sticks,
   And *exeunt ambo*, convinced.

PUT A PENNY IN THE SLOT

IF my action's stiff and crude,
Do not laugh, because it's rude.
If my gestures promise larks,
Do not make unkind remarks.
Clockwork figures may be found
Everywhere and all around.
Ten to one, if I but knew,
You are clockwork figures too.
And the motto of the lot,
"Put a penny in the slot!"

Put a Penny in the Slot

Usurer, for money lent,
Making out his cent per cent—
Widow plump or maiden rare,
Deaf and dumb to suitor's prayer—
Tax collectors, whom in vain
You implore to " call again "—
Cautious voter, whom you find
Slow in making up his mind—
If you'd move them on the spot,
Put a penny in the slot !

Bland reporters in the courts,
Who suppress police reports—
Sheriff's yeoman, pen in fist,
Making out a jury list—
Stern policemen, tall and spare,
Acting all " upon the square "—
(Which in words that plainer fall,
Means that you can square them all)—
If you want to move the lot,
Put a penny in the slot !

GOOD LITTLE GIRLS

ALTHOUGH of native maids the cream,
We're brought up on the English scheme—
    The best of all
    For great and small
        Who modesty adore.
For English girls are good as gold,
Extremely modest (so we're told),
Demurely coy—divinely cold—
        And we are that—and more.
To please papa, who argues thus—
All girls should mould themselves on us,
    Because we are,
    By furlongs far,

Good Little Girls

The best of all the bunch;
We show ourselves to loud applause
From ten to four without a pause—
Which is an awkward time because
It cuts into our lunch.

Oh, maids of high and low degree,
Whose social code is rather free,
Please look at us and you will see
What good young ladies ought to be!

And as we stand, like clockwork toys,
A lecturer papa employs
To puff and praise
Our modest ways
And guileless character—
Our well-known blush—our downcast eyes—
Our famous look of mild surprise
(Which competition still defies)—
Our celebrated "Sir!!!"
Then all the crowd take down our looks
In pocket memorandum books.
To diagnose
Our modest pose
The kodaks do their best:
If evidence you would possess
Of what is maiden bashfulness,
You only need a button press—
And *we* do all the rest.

THE PHANTOM CURATE

A FABLE

A BISHOP once—I will not name his see—
 Annoyed his clergy in the mode conventional;
From pulpit shackles never set them free,
 And found a sin where sin was unintentional.
All pleasures ended in abuse auricular—
That Bishop was so terribly particular.

Though, on the whole, a wise and upright man,
 He sought to make of human pleasures clearances,
And form his priests on that much-lauded plan
 Which pays undue attention to appearances.
He couldn't do good deeds without a psalm in 'em,
Although, in truth, he bore away the palm in 'em.

484

The Phantom Curate

Enraged to find a deacon at a dance,
　　Or catch a curate at some mild frivolity,
He sought by open censure to enhance
　　Their dread of joining harmless social jollity;
Yet he enjoyed (a fact of notoriety)
The ordinary pleasures of society.

One evening, sitting at a pantomime
　　(Forbidden treat to those who stood in fear of him),
Roaring at jokes *sans* metre, sense, or rhyme,
　　He turned, and saw immediately in rear of him—
His peace of mind upsetting, and annoying it—
A curate, also heartily enjoying it.

Again, 'twas Christmas Eve, and to enhance
　　His children's pleasure in their harmless rollicking,
He, like a good old fellow, stood to dance;
　　When something checked the current of his frolicking:
That curate, with a maid he treated loverly,
Stood up and figured with him in the "Coverley"!

Once, yielding to an universal choice
　　(The company's demand was an emphatic one,
For the old Bishop had a glorious voice),
　　In a quartet he joined—an operatic one—
Harmless enough, though ne'er a word of grace in it;
When, lo! that curate came and took the bass in it!

One day, when passing through a quiet street,
　　He stopped awhile and joined a Punch's gathering,
And chuckled more than solemn folk think meet
　　To see that gentleman his Judy lathering;
And heard, as Punch was being treated penally,
That phantom curate laughing all hyænally!

The Phantom Curate

Now at a picnic, 'mid fair golden curls,
  Bright eyes, straw hats, *bottines* that fit amazingly,
A croquêt-bout is planned by all the girls,
  And he, consenting, speaks of croquêt praisingly;
But suddenly declines to play at all in it—
The curate fiend has come to take a ball in it!

Next, when at quiet seaside village, freed
  From cares episcopal and ties monarchical,
He grows his beard, and smokes his fragrant weed,
  In manner anything but hierarchical—
He sees—and fixes an unearthly stare on it—
That curate's face, with half a yard of hair on it!

At length he gave a charge, and spake this word:
  "Vicars, your curates to enjoyment urge ye may
To check their harmless pleasuring's absurd;
  What laymen do without reproach, my clergy may."
He spake, and lo! at this concluding word of him,
The curate vanished—no one since has heard of him.

LIFE

First you're born—and I'll be bound you
Find a dozen strangers round you.
" Hallo," cries the new-born baby,
" Where's my parents? which may they be?"
Awkward silence—no reply—
Puzzled baby wonders why!
Father rises, bows politely—
Mother smiles (but not too brightly)—
Doctor mumbles like a dumb thing—
Nurse is busy mixing something.—
Every symptom tends to show
You're decidedly *de trop*—
Ho! ho! ho! ho! ho! ho! ho! ho!
Time's teetotum,
If you spin it,
Give its quotum
Once a minute:
I'll go bail
You hit the nail,
And if you fail
The deuce is in it!

Life

You grow up, and you discover
What it is to be a lover.
Some young lady is selected—
Poor, perhaps, but well-connected,
    Whom you hail (for Love is blind
    As the Queen of Fairy-kind.
Though she's plain—perhaps unsightly,
Makes her face up—laces tightly,
In her form your fancy traces
All the gifts of all the graces.
    Rivals none the maiden woo,
    So you take her and she takes you!
        Ho! ho! ho! ho! ho! ho! ho! ho!
            Joke beginning,
                Never ceases,
            Till your inning
                Time releases;
            On your way
            You blindly stray,
            And day by day
                The joke increases!

Ten years later—Time progresses—
Sours your temper—thins your tresses;
Fancy, then, her chain relaxes;
Rates are facts and so are taxes.
    Fairy Queen's no longer young—
    Fairy Queen has such a tongue!
Twins have probably intruded—
Quite unbidden—just as you did;
They're a source of care and trouble—
Just as you were—only double.
    Comes at last the final stroke—
    Time has had his little joke!

Life

Ho! ho! ho! ho! ho! ho! ho! ho!
    Daily driven
       (Wife as drover)
    Ill you've thriven—
       Ne'er in clover:
    Lastly, when
    Threescore and ten
    (And not till then),
       The joke is over!
Ho! ho! ho! ho! ho! ho! ho! ho!
    Then—and then
       The joke is over!

LIMITED LIABILITY

SOME seven men form an Association
    (If possible, all Peers and Baronets),
They start off with a public declaration
    To what extent they mean to pay their debts.
That's called their Capital: if they are wary
    They will not quote it at a sum immense.
The figure's immaterial—it may vary
    From eighteen million down to eighteenpence.
        I should put it rather low;
        The good sense of doing so
    Will be evident at once to any debtor.
        When it's left to you to say
        What amount you mean to pay,
    Why, the lower you can put it at, the better.

Limited Liability

They then proceed to trade with all who'll trust 'em,
    Quite irrespective of their capital
(It's shady, but it's sanctified by custom) ;
    Bank, Railway, Loan, or Panama Canal.
You can't embark on trading too tremendous—
    It's strictly fair, and based on common sense—
If you succeed, your profits are stupendous—
    And if you fail, pop goes your eighteenpence.
        Make the money-spinner spin !
        For you only stand to win,
And you'll never with dishonesty be twitted.
        For nobody can know,
        To a million or so,
To what extent your capital's committed !

If you come to grief, and creditors are craving
    (For nothing that is planned by mortal head
Is certain in this Vale of Sorrow—saving
    That one's Liability is Limited),—
Do you suppose that signifies perdition ?
    If so you're but a monetary dunce—
You merely file a Winding-Up Petition,
    And start another Company at once !
        Though a Rothschild you may be
        In your own capacity,
As a Company you've come to utter sorrow—
        But the Liquidators say,
        " Never mind—you needn't pay,"
So you start another Company to-morrow !

THE SENSATION CAPTAIN

No nobler captain ever trod
Than CAPTAIN PARKLEBURY TODD,
   So good—so wise—so brave, he!
But still, as all his friends would own,
He had one folly—one alone—
   This Captain in the Navy.

I do not think I ever knew
A man so wholly given to
   Creating a sensation;
Or p'raps I should in justice say—
To what in an Adelphi play
   Is known as "situation."

He passed his time designing traps
To flurry unsuspicious chaps—
   The taste was his innately;
He couldn't walk into a room
Without ejaculating "Boom!"
   Which startled ladies greatly.

The Sensation Captain

He'd wear a mask and muffling cloak,
Not, you will understand, in joke,
   As some assume disguises ;
He did it, actuated by
A simple love of mystery
   And fondness for surprises.

I need not say he loved a maid—
His eloquence threw into shade
   All others who adored her.
The maid, though pleased at first, I know,
Found, after several years or so,
   Her startling lover bored her.

So, when his orders came to sail,
She did not faint or scream or wail,
   Or with her tears anoint him :
She shook his hand, and said "Good-bye,"
With laughter dancing in her eye—
   Which seemed to disappoint him.

But ere he went aboard his boat,
He placed around her little throat
   A ribbon, blue and yellow,
On which he hung a double tooth—
A simple token this, in sooth—
   'Twas all he had, poor fellow !

"I often wonder," he would say,
When very, very far away,
   "If ANGELINA wears it ?
A plan has entered in my head :
I will pretend that I am dead,
   And see how ANGY bears it."

The Sensation Captain

The news he made a messmate tell.
His ANGELINA bore it well,
   No sign gave she of crazing;
But, steady as the Inchcape Rock,
His ANGELINA stood the shock
   With fortitude amazing.

She said, "Some one I must elect
Poor ANGELINA to protect
   From all who wish to harm her.
Since worthy CAPTAIN TODD is dead
I rather feel inclined to wed
   · A comfortable farmer."

A comfortable farmer came
(BASSANIO TYLER was his name),
   Who had no end of treasure.
He said, "My noble gal, be mine!"
The noble gal did not decline,
   But simply said, "With pleasure."

The Sensation Captain

When this was told to CAPTAIN TODD,
At first he thought it rather odd,
   And felt some perturbation;
But very long he did not grieve,
He thought he could a way perceive
   To *such* a situation!

"I'll not reveal myself," said he,
"Till they are both in the Eccle-
   siastical arena;
Then suddenly I will appear,
And paralysing them with fear,
   Demand my ANGELINA!"

At length arrived the wedding day;
Accoutred in the usual way
   Appeared the bridal body;
The worthy clergyman began,
When in the gallant Captain ran
   And cried, "Behold your TODDY!"

495

The Sensation Captain

The bridegroom, p'raps, was terrified,
And also possibly the bride——
   The bridesmaids *were* affrighted;
But ANGELINA, noble soul,
Contrived her feelings to control,
   And really seemed delighted.

"My bride!" said gallant CAPTAIN TODD,
"She's mine, uninteresting clod!
   My own, my darling charmer!"
"Oh dear," said she, "you're just too late——
I'm married to, I beg to state,
   This comfortable farmer!"

"Indeed," the farmer said, "she's mine:
You've been and cut it far too fine!"
   "I see," said TODD, "I'm beaten."
And so he went to sea once more,
"Sensation" he for aye forswore,
And married on her native shore
A lady whom he'd met before——
   A lovely Otaheitan.

ANGLICISED UTOPIA

Society has quite forsaken all her wicked courses,
Which empties our police courts, and abolishes divorces.
   (Divorce is nearly obsolete in England.)
No tolerance we show to undeserving rank and splendour;
For the higher his position is, the greater the offender.
   (That's a maxim that is prevalent in England.)
No Peeress at our Drawing-Room before the Presence passes
Who wouldn't be accepted by the lower-middle classes;
Each shady dame, whatever be her rank, is bowed out neatly.
In short, this happy country has been Anglicised completely!
   It really is surprising
   What a thorough Anglicising
  We've brought about—Utopia's quite another land;
   In her enterprising movements,
   She is England—with improvements,
  Which we dutifully offer to our mother-land!

Anglicised Utopia

Our city we have beautified—we've done it willy-nilly—
And all that isn't Belgrave Square is Strand and Piccadilly.
      (They haven't any slummeries in England.)
We have solved the labour question with discrimination
    polished,
So poverty is obsolete and hunger is abolished—
      (They are going to abolish it in England.)
The Chamberlain our native stage has purged, beyond a
    question,
Of " risky " situation and indelicate suggestion ;
No piece is tolerated if it's costumed indiscreetly—
In short, this happy country has been Anglicised completely!
      It really is surprising
      What a thorough Anglicising
    We've brought about—Utopia's quite another land ;
      In her enterprising movements,
      She is England—with improvements,
    Which we dutifully offer to our mother-land !

Our Peerage we've remodelled on an intellectual basis,
Which certainly is rough on our hereditary races—
      (They are going to remodel it in England.)
The Brewers and the Cotton Lords no longer seek admission,
And Literary Merit meets with proper recognition—
      (As Literary Merit does in England !)
Who knows but we may count among our intellectual chickens
Like them an Earl of Thackeray and p'raps a Duke of
    Dickens—
Lord Fildes and Viscount Millais (when they come) we'll
    welcome sweetly—
And then, this happy country will be Anglicised completely!
      It really is surprising
      What a thorough Anglicising
    We've brought about—Utopia's quite another land ;
      In her enterprising movements,
      She is England—with improvements,
    Which we dutifully offer to our mother-land !

Bab

AN ENGLISH GIRL

A WONDERFUL joy our eyes to bless,
In her magnificent comeliness,
Is an English girl of eleven stone two,
And five foot ten in her dancing shoe !
 She follows the hounds, and on she pounds—
  The "field" tails off and the muffs diminish—
 Over the hedges and brooks she bounds—
  Straight as a crow, from find to finish.
 At cricket, her kin will lose or win—
  She and her maids, on grass and clover,
 Eleven maids out—eleven maids in—
  (And perhaps an occasional "maiden over").
Go search the world and search the sea,
Then come you home and sing with me
There's no such gold and no such pearl
As a bright and beautiful English girl !

An English Girl

With a ten-mile spin she stretches her limbs,
She golfs, she punts, she rows, she swims—
She plays, she sings, she dances, too,
From ten or eleven till all is blue!
    At ball or drum, till small hours come
        (Chaperon's fan conceals her yawning),
    She'll waltz away like a teetotum,
        And never go home till daylight's dawning.
    Lawn tennis may share her favours fair—
        Her eyes a-dance and her cheeks a-glowing—
    Down comes her hair, but what does she care?
        It's all her own and it's worth the showing!
Go search the world and search the sea,
Then come you home and sing with me
There's no such gold and no such pearl
As a bright and beautiful English girl!

Her soul is sweet as the ocean air,
For prudery knows no haven there;
To find mock-modesty, please apply
To the conscious blush and the downcast eye.
    Rich in the things contentment brings,
        In every pure enjoyment wealthy,
    Blithe as a beautiful bird she sings,
        For body and mind are hale and healthy.
    Her eyes they thrill with right goodwill—
        Her heart is light as a floating feather—
    As pure and bright as the mountain rill
        That leaps and laughs in the Highland heather!
Go search the world and search the sea,
Then come you home and sing with me
There's no such gold and no such pearl
As a bright and beautiful English girl!

TEMPORA MUTANTUR

Letters, letters, letters, letters!
   Some that please and some that bore,
Some that threaten prison fetters
(Metaphorically, fetters
Such as bind insolvent debtors)—
   Invitations by the score.

One from Cogson, Wiles, and Railer,
   My attorneys, off the Strand;
One from Copperblock, my tailor—
My unreasonable tailor—
   One in Flagg's disgusting hand.

One from Ephraim and Moses,
   Wanting coin without a doubt,
I should like to pull their noses—
Their uncompromising noses;
One from Alice with the roses—
   Ah, I know what that's about!

501

Tempora Mutantur

Time was when I waited, waited
   For the missives that she wrote,
Humble postmen execrated—
Loudly, deeply execrated—
When I heard I wasn't fated
   To be gladdened with a note!

Time was when I'd not have bartered
   Of her little pen a dip
For a peerage duly gartered—
For a peerage starred and gartered—
With a palace-office chartered,
   Or a Secretaryship.

But the time for that is over,
   And I wish we'd never met.
I'm afraid I've proved a rover—
I'm afraid a heartless rover—
Quarters in a place like Dover
   Tend to make a man forget.

Bills for carriages and horses,
   Bills for wine and light cigar,
Matters that concern the Forces—
News that may affect the Forces—
News affecting my resources,
   Much more interesting are!

And the tiny little paper,
   With the words that seem to run
From her little fingers taper
(They are very small and taper),
By the tailor and the draper
   Are in interest outdone.

Tempora Mutantur

And unopened it's remaining !
I can read her gentle hope—
Her entreaties, uncomplaining
(She was always uncomplaining),
Her devotion never waning—
Through the little envelope !

Bab

A MANAGER'S PERPLEXITIES

WERE I a king in very truth,
And had a son—a guileless youth—
 In probable succession;
To teach him patience, teach him tact,
How promptly in a fix to act,
He should adopt, in point of fact,
 A manager's profession.
To that condition he should stoop
 (Despite a too fond mother),
With eight or ten "stars" in his troupe,
 All jealous of each other!
Oh, the man who can rule a theatrical crew,
Each member a genius (and some of them two),
And manage to humour them, little and great,
Can govern a tuppenny-ha'penny State!

A Manager's Perplexities

Both A and B rehearsal slight—
They say they'll be "all right at night"
    (They've both to go to school yet);
C in each act *must* change her dress,
D *will* attempt to "square the press";
E won't play Romeo unless
    His grandmother plays Juliet;
F claims all hoydens as her rights
    (She's played them thirty seasons);
And G must show herself in tights
    For two convincing reasons—
    Two very well-shaped reasons!
Oh, the man who can drive a theatrical team,
With wheelers and leaders in order supreme,
Can govern and rule, with a wave of his fin,
All Europe and Asia—with Ireland thrown in!

OUT OF SORTS

WHEN you find you're a broken-down critter,
Who is all of a trimmle and twitter,
With your palate unpleasantly bitter,
    As if you'd just bitten a pill—
When your legs are as thin as dividers,
And you're plagued with unruly insiders,
And your spine is all creepy with spiders,
    And you're highly gamboge in the gill—
When you've got a beehive in your head,
    And a sewing machine in each ear,
And you feel that you've eaten your bed,
    And you've got a bad headache *down here*—
      When such facts are about,
        And these symptoms you find
          In your body or crown—
      Well, it's time to look out,
        You may make up your mind
          You had better lie down!

Out of Sorts

When your lips are all smeary—like tallow,
And your tongue is decidedly yallow,
With a pint of warm oil in your swallow,
  And a pound of tin-tacks in your chest—
When you're down in the mouth with the vapours,
And all over your new Morris papers
Black-beetles are cutting their capers,
  And crawly things never at rest—
When you doubt if your head is your own,
  And you jump when an open door slams—
Then you've got to a state which is known
  To the medical world as " jim-jams."
   If such symptoms you find
    In your body or head,
     They're not easy to quell—
   You may make up your mind
    You are better in bed,
     For you're not at all well !

AT A PANTOMIME

BY A BILIOUS ONE

AN actor sits in doubtful gloom,
 His stock-in-trade unfurled,
In a damp funereal dressing-room
 In the Theatre Royal, World.

He comes to town at Christmas-time
 And braves its icy breath,
To play in that favourite pantomime.
 Harlequin Life and Death.

A hoary flowing wig his weird,
 Unearthly cranium caps ;
He hangs a long benevolent beard
 On a pair of empty chaps.

At a Pantomime

To smooth his ghastly features down
    The actor's art he cribs;
A long and a flowing padded gown
    Bedecks his rattling ribs.

He cries, " Go on—begin, begin !
    Turn on the light of lime;
I'm dressed for jolly Old Christmas in
    A favourite pantomime ! "

The curtain's up—the stage all black—
    Time and the Year nigh sped—
(Time as an advertising quack)
    The Old Year nearly dead.

The wand of Time is waved, and lo !
    Revealed Old Christmas stands,
And little children chuckle and crow,
    And laugh and clap their hands.

The cruel old scoundrel brightens up
    At the death of the Olden Year,
And he waves a gorgeous golden cup,
    And bids the world good cheer.

The little ones hail the festive King—
    No thought can make them sad;
Their laughter comes with a sounding ring,
    They clap and crow like mad !

They only see in the humbug old
    A holiday every year,
And handsome gifts, and joys untold,
    And unaccustomed cheer.

At a Pantomime

The old ones, palsied, blear, and hoar,
    Their breasts in anguish beat—
They've seen him seventy times before,
    How well they know the cheat!

They've seen that ghastly pantomime,
    They've felt its blighting breath,
They know that rollicking Christmas-time
    Meant cold and want and death—

Starvation—Poor Law Union fare,
    And deadly cramps and chills,
And illness—illness everywhere—
    And crime, and Christmas bills.

At a Pantomime

They know Old Christmas well, I ween,
  Those men of ripened age;
They've often, often, often seen
  That actor off the stage.

They see in his gay rotundity
  A clumsy stuffed-out dress;
They see in the cup he waves on high
  A tinselled emptiness.

Those aged men so lean and wan,
  They've seen it all before;
They know they'll see the charlatan
  But twice or three times more.

And so they bear with dance and song,
  And crimson foil and green;
They wearily sit, and grimly long
  For the Transformation Scene.

HOW IT'S DONE

BOLD-faced ranger
(Perfect stranger)
Meets two well-behaved young ladies.
He's attractive,
Young and active—
Each a little bit afraid is.
Youth advances,
At his glances
To their danger they awaken;
They repel him
As they tell him
He is very much mistaken.
Though they speak to him politely,
Please observe they're sneering slightly,
Just to show he's acting vainly.
This is Virtue saying plainly,
"Go away, young bachelor,
We are not what you take us for!"

How it's Done

(When addressed impertinently,
English ladies answer gently,
    "Go away, young bachelor,
    We are not what you take us for!")

    As he gazes,
    Hat he raises,
Enters into conversation.
    Makes excuses—
    This produces
Interesting agitation.
    He, with daring,
    Undespairing,
Gives his card—his rank discloses—
    Little heeding
    This proceeding,
They turn up their little noses.
Pray observe this lesson vital—
When a man of rank and title
His position first discloses,
Always cock your little noses.
    When at home, let all the class
    Try this in the looking-glass.
(English girls of well-bred notions
Shun all unrehearsed emotions,
    English girls of highest class
    Practise them before the glass.)

    His intentions
    Then he mentions,
Something definite to go on—
    Makes recitals
    Of his titles,
Hints at settlements, and so on.
    Smiling sweetly,
    They, discreetly,

How it's Done

Ask for further evidences:
      Thus invited,
      He, delighted,
Gives the usual references.
This is business.   Each is fluttered
When the offer's fairly uttered.
"Which of them has his affection?"
He declines to make selection.
      Do they quarrel for his dross?
      Not a bit of it—they toss!
Please observe this cogent moral—
English ladies never quarrel.
      When a doubt they come across,
      English ladies always toss.

A CLASSICAL REVIVAL

At the outset I may mention it's my sovereign intention
    To revive the classic memories of Athens at its best,
For my company possesses all the necessary dresses,
    And a course of quiet cramming will supply us with the
        rest.
We've a choir hyporchematic (that is, ballet-operatic)
    Who respond to the *choreutae* of that cultivated age,
And our clever chorus-master, all but captious criticaster,
    Would accept as the *choregus* of the early Attic stage.
This return to classic ages is considered in their wages,
    Which are always calculated by the day or by the week—
And I'll pay 'em (if they'll back me) all in *oboloi* and
    drachmae,
    Which they'll get (if they prefer it) at the Kalends that
      are Greek !

        (At this juncture I may mention
           That this erudition sham
           Is but classical pretension,
           The result of steady " cram.":

A Classical Revival

Periphrastic methods spurning,
To my readers all discerning
I admit this show of learning
  Is the fruit of steady " cram." !)

In the period Socratic every dining-room was Attic
  (Which suggests an architecture of a topsy-turvy kind),
There they'd satisfy their twist on a *recherché* cold ἄριστον,
  Which is what they called their lunch—and so may you,
  if you're inclined.
As they gradually got on, they'd τρέπεσθαι πρὸς τὸν πότον
  (Which is Attic for a steady and a conscientious drink).
But they mixed their wine with water—which I'm sure they
  didn't oughter—
  And we Anglo-Saxons know a trick worth two of that, I
  think !
Then came rather risky dances (under certain circumstances)
  Which would shock that worthy gentleman, the Licenser
  of Plays,
Corybantian mani*ac* kick—Dionysiac or Bacchic—
  And the Dithyrambic revels of those indecorous days.

            (And perhaps I'd better mention
              Lest alarming you I am,
            That it isn't our intention
              To perform a Dithyramb—
            It displays a lot of stocking,
            Which is always very shocking,
            And of course I'm only mocking
              At the prevalence of " cram.")

Yes, on reconsideration, there are customs of that nation
  Which are not in strict accordance with the habits of
  our day,
And when I come to codify, their rules I mean to modify,
  Or Mrs. Grundy, p'r'aps, may have a word or two
  to say :
For they hadn't macintoshes or umbrellas or goloshes—

A Classical Revival

And a shower with their dresses must have played the
very deuce,
And it must have been unpleasing when they caught a fit
of sneezing,
For, it seems, of pocket-handkerchiefs they didn't know
the use.
They wore little underclothing — scarcely anything — or
no-thing—
And their dress of Coan silk was quite transparent in
design—
Well, in fact, in summer weather, something like the
"altogether."
And it's *there*, I rather fancy, I shall have to draw the
line !

(And again I wish to mention
That this erudition sham
Is but classical pretension,
The result of steady "cram."
Yet my classic love aggressive,
If you'll pardon the possessive,
Is exceedingly impressive
When you're passing an exam.)

THE STORY OF PRINCE AGIB

Strike the concertina's melancholy string!
Blow the spirit-stirring harp like anything!
    Let the piano's martial blast
    Rouse the echoes of the past,
For of Agib, Prince of Tartary, I sing!

Of Agib, who, amid Tartaric scenes,
Wrote a lot of ballet-music in his teens:
    His gentle spirit rolls
    In the melody of souls—
Which is pretty, but I don't know what it means.

Of Agib, who could readily, at sight,
Strum a march upon the loud Theodolite.
    He would diligently play
    On the Zoetrope all day,
And blow the gay Pantechnicon all night.

The Story of Prince Agib

One winter—I am shaky in my dates—
Came two starving Tartar minstrels to his gates;
    Oh, Allah be obeyed,
    How infernally they played!
I remember that they called themselves the "Oüaits."

Oh! that day of sorrow, misery, and rage,
I shall carry to the Catacombs of Age,
    Photographically lined
    On the tablet of my mind,
When a yesterday has faded from its page!

Alas! Prince Agib went and asked them in;
Gave them beer, and eggs, and sweets, and scent, and tin;
    And when (as snobs would say)
    They had "put it all away,"
He requested them to tune up and begin.

Though its icy horror chill you to the core,
I will tell you what I never told before—
    The consequences true
    Of that awful interview,
For I listened at the keyhole in the door!

They played him a sonata—let me see!
"*Medulla oblongata*"—key of G.
    Then they began to sing
    That extremely lovely thing,
"*Scherzando! ma non troppo, ppp.*"

He gave them money, more than they could count,
Scent from a most ingenious little fount,
    More beer in little kegs,
    Many dozen hard-boiled eggs,
And goodies to a fabulous amount.

The Story of Prince Agib

Now follows the dim horror of my tale,
And I feel I'm growing gradually pale;
    For even at this day,
    Though its sting has passed away,
When I venture to remember it, I quail!

The elder of the brothers gave a squeal,
All-overish it made me for to feel.
    "O Prince," he says, says he,
    "If a Prince indeed you be,
I've a mystery I'm going to reveal!

"Oh, listen, if you'd shun a horrid death,
To what the gent who's speaking to you saith:
    No 'Oüaits' in truth are we,
    As you fancy that we be,
For (ter-remble!) I am ALECK—this is BETH!"

The Story of Prince Agib

Said AGIB, "Oh! accursed of your kind,
I have heard that ye are men of evil mind!"
    BETH gave a dreadful shriek—
    But before he'd time to speak
I was mercilessly collared from behind.

In number ten or twelve, or even more,
They fastened me, full length, upon the floor.
    On my face extended flat,
    I was walloped with a cat,
For listening at the keyhole of a door.

Oh! the horror of that agonising thrill!
(I can feel the place in frosty weather still.)
    For a week from ten to four
    I was fastened to the floor,
While a mercenary wopped me with a will!

The Story of Prince Agib

They branded me and broke me on a wheel,
And they left me in an hospital to heal;
    And, upon my solemn word,
     I have never, never heard
What those Tartars had determined to reveal.

But that day of sorrow, misery, and rage,
I shall carry to the Catacombs of Age,
    Photographically lined
    On the tablet of my mind,
When a yesterday has faded from its page!

THE PRACTICAL JOKER

OH what a fund of joy jocund lies hid in harmless hoaxes!
    What keen enjoyment springs
    From cheap and simple things!
What deep delight from sources trite inventive humour coaxes,
    That pain and trouble brew
    For every one but you!
Gunpowder placed inside its waist improves a mild Havanah,
    Its unexpected flash
    Burns eyebrows and moustache;
When people dine no kind of wine beats ipecacuanha,
    But common sense suggests
    You keep it for your guests—
Then naught annoys the organ boys like throwing red-hot coppers,
    And much amusement bides
    In common butter-slides:
And stringy snares across the stairs cause unexpected croppers.

The Practical Joker

Coal scuttles, recollect,
Produce the same effect.
A man possessed
Of common sense
Need not invest
At great expense—
It does not call
For pocket deep,
These jokes are all
Extremely cheap.
If you commence with eighteenpence (it's all you'll have
to pay),
You may command a pleasant and a most instructive day.

A good spring gun breeds endless fun, and makes men
jump like rockets,
And turnip-heads on posts
Make very decent ghosts:
Then hornets sting like anything, when placed in waist-
coat pockets—
Burnt cork and walnut juice
Are not without their use.

The Practical Joker

No fun compares with easy chairs whose seats are stuffed
with needles—
       Live shrimps their patience tax
       When put down people's backs—
Surprising, too, what one can do with fifty fat black
beedles—
       And treacle on a chair
       Will make a Quaker swear !
         Then sharp tin tacks
           And pocket squirts—
       And cobblers' wax
         For ladies' skirts—
       And slimy slugs
         On bedroom floors—
       And water jugs
         On open doors—
Prepared with these cheap properties, amusing tricks to
play,
Upon a friend a man may spend a most delightful day !

THE NATIONAL ANTHEM

A MONARCH is pestered with cares,
    Though, no doubt, he can often trepan them;
But one comes in a shape he can never escape—
    The implacable National Anthem!
       Though for quiet and rest he may yearn,
       It pursues him at every turn—
         No chance of forsaking
         Its *rococo* numbers;
       They haunt him when waking—
         They poison his slumbers—
Like the Banbury Lady, whom every one knows,
He's cursed with its music wherever he goes!
    Though its words but imperfectly rhyme,
       And the devil himself couldn't scan them;
    With composure polite he endures day and night
      That illiterate National Anthem!

The National Anthem

It serves a good purpose, I own :
    Its strains are devout and impressive—
Its heart-stirring notes raise a lump in our throats
    As we burn with devotion excessive :
        But the King, who's been bored by that song
        From his cradle—each day—all day long—
        Who's heard it loud-shouted
          By throats operatic,
        And loyally spouted
          By courtiers emphatic—
By soldier—by sailor—by drum and by fife—
Small blame if he thinks it the plague of his life !
    While his subjects sing loudly and long,
        Their King—who would willingly ban them—
Sits, worry disguising, anathematising
        That Bogie, the National Anthem !

JOE GOLIGHTLY

OR, THE FIRST LORD'S DAUGHTER

A TAR, but poorly prized,
   Long, shambling, and unsightly,
Thrashed, bullied, and despised,
   Was wretched JOE GOLIGHTLY.

He bore a workhouse brand;
   No Pa or Ma had claimed him,
The Beadle found him, and
   The Board of Guardians named him.

P'r'aps some Princess's son—
   A beggar p'r'aps his mother.
He rather thought the one,
   I rather think the other.

Joe Golightly

He liked his ship at sea,
 He loved the salt sea-water,
He worshipped junk, and he
 Adored the First Lord's daughter.

The First Lord's daughter, proud,
 Snubbed Earls and Viscounts nightly ;
She sneered at Barts. aloud,
 And spurned poor Joe Golightly.

Whene'er he sailed afar
 Upon a Channel cruise, he
Unpacked his light guitar
 And sang this ballad (Boosey):

Ballad

The moon is on the sea,
 Willow !
The wind blows towards the lee,
 Willow !
But though I sigh and sob and cry,
No Lady Jane for me,
 Willow !

She says, " 'Twere folly quite,
 Willow !
For me to wed a wight,
 Willow !
Whose lot is cast before the mast ";
And possibly she's right,
 Willow !

His skipper (CAPTAIN JOYCE),
 He gave him many a rating,
And almost lost his voice
 From thus expostulating :

Joe Golightly

"Lay aft, you lubber, do!
  What's come to that young man, JOE?
Belay!—'vast heaving! you!
  Do kindly stop that banjo!

"I wish, I do—O lor'!—
  You'd shipped aboard a trader:
Are you a sailor or
  A negro serenader?"

But still the stricken lad,
  Aloft or on his pillow,
Howled forth in accents sad
  His aggravating "Willow!"

Stern love of duty had
  Been JOYCE's chiefest beauty;
Says he, "I love that lad,
  But duty, damme! duty!

"Twelve months' black-hole, I say,
  Where daylight never flashes;
And always twice a day
  A good six dozen lashes!"

Joe Golightly

But JOSEPH had a mate,
    A sailor stout and lusty,
A man of low estate,
    But singularly trusty.

Says he, "Cheer hup, young JOE!
    I'll tell you what I'm arter—
To that Fust Lord I'll go
    And ax him for his darter.

"To that Fust Lord I'll go
    And say you love her dearly."
And JOE said (weeping low),
    "I wish you would, sincerely!"

That sailor to that Lord
    Went, soon as he had landed,
And of his own accord
    An interview demanded.

Joe Golightly

Says he, with seaman's roll,
  "My Captain (wot's a Tartar)
Guv JOE twelve months' black-hole,
  For lovering your darter.

"He loves MISS LADY JANE
  (I own she is his betters),
But if you'll jine them twain,
  They'll free him from his fetters.

"And if so be as how
  You'll let her come aboard ship,
I'll take her with me now."
  "Get out!" remarked his Lordship.

That honest tar repaired
  To JOE upon the billow,
And told him how he'd fared.
  JOE only whispered, "Willow!"

Joe Golightly

And for that dreadful crime
   (Young sailors, learn to shun it)
He's working out his time ;
   In six months he'll have done it.

HER TERMS

My wedded life
    Must every pleasure bring
        On scale extensive!
If I'm your wife
    I must have everything
        That's most expensive—
A lady's-maid—
    (My hair alone to do
        I am not able)—
And I'm afraid
    I've been accustomed to
        A first-rate table.
These things one must consider when one marries—
And everything I wear must come from Paris!
        Oh, think of that!
        Oh, think of that!
I can't wear anything that's not from Paris!
    From top to toes
        Quite Frenchified I am,
            If you examine.
    And then—who knows?—
        Perhaps some day a fam—
            Perhaps a famine!
My argument's correct, if you examine,
What should we do, if there should come a f-famine!

Though in green pea
    Yourself you needn't stint
        In July sunny,
In Januaree
    It really costs a mint—
        A mint of money!

534

Her Terms

No lamb for us—
  House lamb at Christmas sells
    At prices handsome:
Asparagus,
  In winter, parallels
    A Monarch's ransom:
When purse to bread and butter barely reaches,
What is your wife to do for hot-house peaches?
      Ah! tell me that!
      Ah! tell me that!
What *is* your wife to do for hot-house peaches?
  Your heart and hand
    Though at my feet you lay,
      All others scorning!
  As matters stand,
    There's nothing now to say
      Except—good morning!
Though virtue be a husband's best adorning,
That won't pay rates and taxes--so, good morning!

535

THE INDEPENDENT BEE

A HIVE of bees, as I've heard say,
Said to their Queen one sultry day,
   "Please your Majesty's high position,
      The hive is full and the weather is warm,
   We rather think, with a due submission,
      The time has come when we ought to swarm."
        Buzz, buzz, buzz, buzz.
Up spake their Queen and thus spake she—
"This is a matter that rests with me,
Who dares opinions thus to form?
I'll tell you when it is time to swarm!"
    Buzz, buzz, buzz, buzz.

The Independent Bee

Her Majesty wore an angry frown,
In fact, her Majesty's foot was down—
Her Majesty sulked—declined to sup—
In short, her Majesty's back was up.
    Buzz, buzz, buzz, buzz.
Her foot was down and her back was up!

That hive contained one obstinate bee
(His name was Peter), and thus spake he—
    "Though every bee has shown white feather,
      To bow to tyranny I'm not prone—
Why should a hive swarm all together?
    Surely a bee can swarm alone?"
      Buzz, buzz, buzz, buzz.
Upside down and inside out,
Backwards, forwards, round about,
Twirling here and twisting there,
Topsy turvily everywhere—
      Buzz, buzz, buzz, buzz.
Pitiful sight it was to see
Respectable elderly high-class bee,
Who kicked the beam at sixteen stone,
Trying his best to swarm alone!
      Buzz, buzz, buzz, buzz.
Trying his best to swarm alone!

The hive were shocked to see their chum
(A strict teetotaller) teetotum—
    The Queen exclaimed, "How terrible, very!
      It's perfectly clear to all the throng
Peter's been at the old brown sherry.
    Old brown sherry is much too strong—
      Buzz, buzz, buzz, buzz.
Of all who thus themselves degrade,
A stern example must be made,

The Independent Bee

To Coventry go, you tipsy bee!"
So off to Coventry town went he.
    Buzz, buzz, buzz, buzz.
There, classed with all who misbehave,
Both plausible rogue and noisome knave,
In dismal dumps he lived to own
The folly of trying to swarm alone!
    Buzz, buzz, buzz, buzz.
All came of trying to swarm alone.

TO THE TERRESTRIAL GLOBE

BY A MISERABLE WRETCH

ROLL on, thou ball, roll on!
Through pathless realms of Space
      Roll on!
What though I'm in a sorry case?
What though I cannot meet my bills?
What though I suffer toothache's ills?
What though I swallow countless pills?
     Never *you* mind!
      Roll on!

Roll on, thou ball, roll on!
Through seas of inky air
      Roll on!
It's true I have no shirts to wear;

To the Terrestrial Globe

It's true my butcher's bill is due;
It's true my prospects all look blue—
But don't let that unsettle you:
    Never *you* mind!
    Roll on!

                        [It rolls on.

ETIQUETTE [1]

THE *Ballyshannon* foundered off the coast of Cariboo,
And down in fathoms many went the captain and the
    crew;
Down went the owners—greedy men whom hope of gain
    allured:
Oh, dry the starting tear, for they were heavily insured.

Besides the captain and the mate, the owners and the
    crew,
The passengers were also drowned excepting only two:
Young PETER GRAY, who tasted teas for BAKER, CROOP,
    AND CO.,
And SOMERS, who from Eastern shores imported indigo.

[1] Reprinted from the *Graphic*, by permission of the proprietors.

Etiquette

These passengers, by reason of their clinging to a mast,
Upon a desert island were eventually cast.
They hunted for their meals, as ALEXANDER SELKIRK used,
But they couldn't chat together—they had not been intro-
duced.

For PETER GRAY, and SOMERS too, though certainly in
trade,
Were properly particular about the friends they made ;
And somehow thus they settled it without a word of
mouth—
That GRAY should take the northern half, while SOMERS
took the south.

On PETER's portion oysters grew—a delicacy rare,
But oysters were a delicacy PETER couldn't bear.
On SOMERS' side was turtle, on the shingle lying thick,
Which SOMERS couldn't eat, because it always made him
sick.

GRAY gnashed his teeth with envy as he saw a mighty
store
Of turtle unmolested on his fellow-creature's shore :
The oysters at his feet aside impatiently he shoved,
For turtle and his mother were the only things he loved.

And SOMERS sighed in sorrow as he settled in the south,
For the thought of PETER's oysters brought the water to
his mouth.
He longed to lay him down upon the shelly bed, and stuff :
He had often eaten oysters, but had never had enough.

How they wished an introduction to each other they had
had
When on board the *Ballyshannon !* And it drove them
nearly mad
To think how very friendly with each other they might get,
If it wasn't for the arbitrary rule of etiquette !

Etiquette

One day, when out a-hunting for the *mus ridiculus*,
GRAY overheard his fellow-man soliloquising thus:
"I wonder how the playmates of my youth are getting on,
    M'CONNELL, S. B. WALTERS, PADDY BYLES, and ROBIN-
      SON?"

These simple words made PETER as delighted as could be,
Old chummies at the Charterhouse were ROBINSON and
    he!
He walked straight up to SOMERS, then he turned ex-
    tremely red,
Hesitated, hummed and hawed a bit, then cleared his
    throat, and said:

Etiquette

"I beg your pardon—pray forgive me if I seem too bold,
But you have breathed a name I knew familiarly of old.
You spoke aloud of ROBINSON—I happened to be by—
You know him?" "Yes, extremely well." "Allow me
    —so do I!"

It was enough: they felt they could more sociably get on,
For (ah, the magic of the fact!) they each knew ROBINSON!
And MR. SOMERS' turtle was at PETER'S service quite,
And MR. SOMERS punished PETER'S oyster-beds all night.

They soon became like brothers from community of
    wrongs:
They wrote each other little odes and sang each other
    songs;
They told each other anecdotes disparaging their wives;
On several occasions, too, they saved each other's lives.

They felt quite melancholy when they parted for the
    night,
And got up in the morning soon as ever it was light;
Each other's pleasant company they reckoned so upon,
And all because it happened that they both knew
    ROBINSON!

They lived for many years on that inhospitable shore,
And day by day they learned to love each other more and
    more.
At last, to their astonishment, on getting up one day,
They saw a vessel anchored in the offing of the bay!

To PETER an idea occurred. "Suppose we cross the
    main?
So good an opportunity may not occur again."
And SOMERS thought a minute, then ejaculated, "Done!
I wonder how my business in the City's getting on?"

Etiquette

"But stay," said Mr. Peter: "when in England, as you
  know,
I earned a living tasting teas for Baker, Croop, and Co.,
I may be superseded—my employers think me dead!"
"Then come with me," said Somers, "and taste indigo
  instead."

But all their plans were scattered in a moment when they
  found
The vessel was a convict ship from Portland, outward
  bound!
When a boat came off to fetch them, though they felt it
  very kind,
To go on board they firmly but respectfully declined.

As both the happy settlers roared with laughter at the joke,
They recognised an unattractive fellow pulling stroke:

Etiquette

'Twas ROBINSON—a convict, in an unbecoming frock!
Condemned to seven years for misappropriating stock!!!

They laughed no more, for SOMERS thought he had been
    rather rash
In knowing one whose friend had misappropriated cash;
And PETER thought a foolish tack he must have gone
    upon
In making the acquaintance of a friend of ROBINSON.

At first they didn't quarrel very openly, I've heard;
They nodded when they met, and now and then exchanged
    a word:
The word grew rare, and rarer still the nodding of the
    head,
And when they meet each other now, they cut each other
    dead.

To allocate the island they agreed by word of mouth,
And PETER takes the north again, and SOMERS takes the
    south;
And PETER has the oysters, which he loathes with horror
    grim,
And SOMERS has the turtle—turtle disagrees with him.

THE DISCONCERTED TENOR

A TENOR, all singers above
    (This doesn't admit of a question),
        Should keep himself quiet,
        Attend to his diet,
    And carefully nurse his digestion.
But when he is madly in love,
    It's certain to tell on his singing—
        You can't do chromatics
        With proper emphatics
    When anguish your bosom is wringing!
When distracted with worries in plenty,
And his pulse is a hundred and twenty,
And his fluttering bosom the slave of mistrust is,
    A tenor can't do himself justice.
        Now observe—(*sings a high note*)—
You see, I can't do myself justice!

The Disconcerted Tenor

I could sing, if my fervour were mock,
　　It's easy enough if you're acting;
　　　　But when one's emotion
　　　　Is born of devotion,
　　You mustn't be over-exacting.
One ought to be firm as a rock
　　To venture a shake in *vibrato;*
　　　　When fervour's expected,
　　　　Keep cool and collected,
　　Or never attempt *agitato.*
But, of course, when his tongue is of leather,
And his lips appear pasted together,
And his sensitive palate as dry as a crust is,
　　A tenor can't do himself justice.
　　　　Now observe—(*sings a cadence*)—
　　It's no use—I can't do myself justice!

BEN ALLAH ACHMET;

OR, THE FATAL TUM

I ONCE did know a Turkish man
    Whom I upon a two-pair-back met,
His name it was EFFENDI KHAN
    BACKSHEESH PASHA BEN ALLAH ACHMET.

A DOCTOR BROWN I also knew—
    I've often eaten of his bounty;
The Turk and he they lived at Hooe,
    In Sussex, that delightful county!

I knew a nice young lady there,
    Her name was EMILY MACPHERSON,
And though she wore another's hair,
    She was an interesting person.

The Turk adored the maid of Hooe
    (Although his harem would have shocked her).
But BROWN adored that maiden too:
    He was a most seductive doctor.

Ben Allah Achmet

They'd follow her where'er she'd go—
    A course of action most improper;
She neither knew by sight, and so
    For neither of them cared a copper.

BROWN did not know that Turkish male,
    He might have been his sainted mother:
The people in this simple tale
    Are total strangers to each other.

One day that Turk he sickened sore,
    And suffered agonies oppressive;
He threw himself upon the floor
    And rolled about in pain excessive.

It made him moan, it made him groan,
    And almost wore him to a mummy.
Why should I hesitate to own
    That pain was in his little tummy?

At length a doctor came, and rung
    (As ALLAH ACHMET had desired),
Who felt his pulse, looked up his tongue,
    And hemmed and hawed, and then inquired:

"Where is the pain that long has preyed
    Upon you in so sad a way, sir?"
The Turk he giggled, blushed, and said:
    "I don't exactly like to say, sir."

"Come, nonsense!" said good DOCTOR BROWN.
    "So this is Turkish coyness, is it?
You must contrive to fight it down—
    Come, come, sir, please to be explicit."

Ben Allah Achmet

The Turk he shyly bit his thumb,
    And coyly blushed like one half-witted,
"The pain is in my little tum,"
    He, whispering, at length admitted.

"Then take you this, and take you that—
    Your blood flows sluggish in its channel—
You must get rid of all this fat,
    And wear my medicated flannel.

"You'll send for me when you're in need—
    My name is BROWN—your life I've saved it."
"My rival!" shrieked the invalid,
    And drew a mighty sword and waved it:

"This to thy weazand, Christian pest!"
    Aloud the Turk in frenzy yelled it,
And drove right through the doctor's chest
    The sabre and the hand that held it.

Bab

The blow was a decisive one,
    And DOCTOR BROWN grew deadly pasty,
"Now see the mischief that you've done—
    You Turks are so extremely hasty.

Ben Allah Achmet

"There are two DOCTOR BROWNS in Hooe—
 He's short and stout, *I'm* tall and wizen;
You've been and run the wrong one through,
 That's how the error has arisen."

The accident was thus explained,
 Apologies were only heard now:
"At my mistake I'm really pained—
 I am, indeed—upon my word now.

"With me, sir, you shall be interred,
 A mausoleum grand awaits me."
"Oh, pray don't say another word,
 I'm sure that more than compensates me.

"But p'r'aps, kind Turk, you're full inside?"
 "There's room," said he, "for any number."
And so they laid them down and died.
 In proud Stamboul they sleep their slumber.

THE PLAYED-OUT HUMORIST

QUIXOTIC is his enterprise, and hopeless his adventure is,
    Who seeks for jocularities that haven't yet been said.
The world has joked incessantly for over fifty centuries,
    And every joke that's possible has long ago been made.
I started as a humorist with lots of mental fizziness,
    But humour is a drug which it's the fashion to abuse;
For my stock-in-trade, my fixtures, and the goodwill of the
        business
    No reasonable offer I am likely to refuse.
            And if anybody choose
            He may circulate the news
    That no reasonable offer I'm likely to refuse.

Oh happy was that humorist—the first that made a pun
        at all—
    Who when a joke occurred to him, however poor and
        mean,
Was absolutely certain that it never had been done at all—
    How popular at dinners must that humorist have been!

553

The Played-out Humorist

Oh the days when some stepfather for the query held a
    handle out,
  The door-mat from the scraper, is it distant very far?
And when no one knew where Moses was when Aaron
    blew the candle out,
    And no one had discovered that a door could be a-jar!
        But your modern hearers are
        In their tastes particular,
    And they sneer if you inform them that a door can be
    a-jar!

In search of quip and quiddity, I've sat all day, alone, apart—
  And all that I could hit on as a problem was—to find
Analogy between a scrag of mutton and a Bony-part,
  Which offers slight employment to the speculative mind:
For you cannot call it very good, however great your charity—
  It's not the sort of humour that is greeted with a shout—
And I've come to the conclusion that my mine of jocularity,
  In present Anno Domini, is worked completely out!
        Though the notion you may scout,
        I can prove beyond a doubt
    That my mine of jocularity is utterly worked out!

INDEX TO FIRST LINES

Index to First Lines

Index to First Lines

Index to First Lines

Index to First Lines

Index to First Lines

ALPHABETICAL INDEX TO TITLES

561

Alphabetical Index to Titles

Alphabetical Index to Titles

Alphabetical Index to Titles

THE END

Printed in Great Britain by R. & R. CLARK, LIMITED, *Edinburgh.*